PETER PANZERFAUST™

VOLUME III: CRY OF THE WOLF

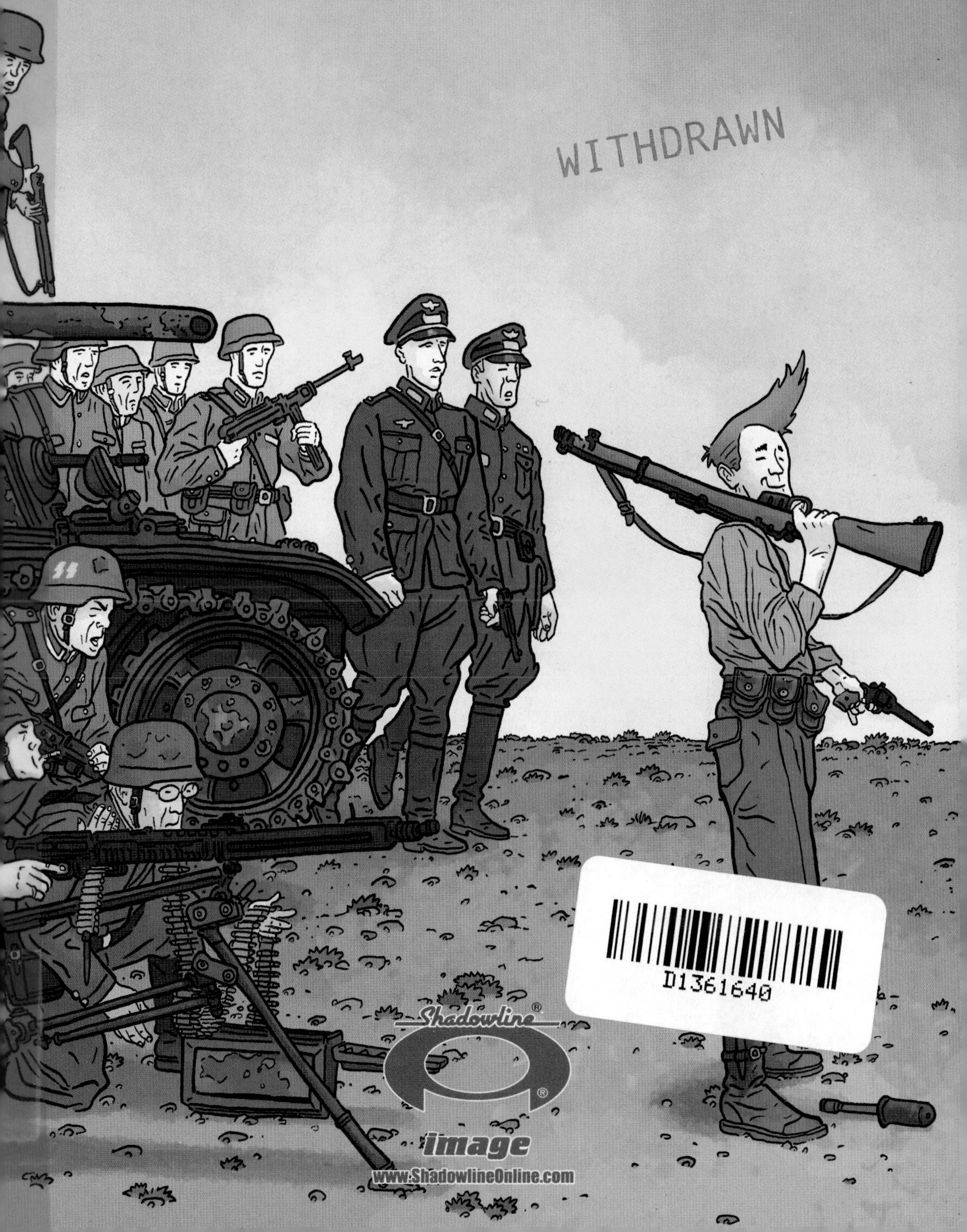
SS

Shadowline®
image®
www.ShadowlineOnline.com

PETER PANZERFAUST VOLUME THREE: CRY OF THE WOLF

First Printing February, 2014

ISBN: 978-1-60706-864-8

Published by Image Comics, Inc. Office of publication: 2001 Center Street, Sixth Floor, Berkeley, California 94704. Copyright © 2014 KURTIS J. WIEBE and TYLER JENKINS. Originally published in single magazine form as PETER PANZERFAUST #11-15. All rights reserved. PETER PANZERFAUST™ (including all prominent characters featured herein), its logo and all character likenesses are trademarks of KURTIS J. WIEBE and TYLER JENKINS, unless otherwise noted. Image Comics® and its logos are registered trademarks of Image Comics, Inc. Shadowline and its logos are registered trademarks ® of Jim Valentino. No part of this publication may be reproduced or transmitted, in any form or by any means (except for short excerpts for review purposes) without the express written permission of Mr. Wiebe and/or Jenkins. All names, characters, events and locales in this publication are entirely fictional. Any resemblance to actual persons (living or dead), events or places, without satiric intent, is coincidental. For information regarding the CPSIA on this printed material call: 203-595-3636 and provide reference # RICH – 546520. PRINTED IN USA. International Rights / Foreign Licensing -- foreignlicensing@imagecomics.com

image COMICS PRESENTS

CO-CREATORS

KURTIS J. WIEBE
WORDS

TYLER JENKINS
PICTURES

HEATHER BRECKEL
COLORS

ED BRISSON
LETTERS

LAURA TAVISHATI
EDITS

MARC LOMBARDI
COMMUNICATIONS

JIM VALENTINO
PUBLISHER/BOOK DESIGN

IMAGE COMICS, INC.
Robert Kirkman - Chief Operating Officer
Erik Larsen - Chief Financial Officer
Todd McFarlane - President
Marc Silvestri - Chief Executive Officer
Jim Valentino - Vice-President

Eric Stephenson - Publisher
Ron Richards - Director of Business Development
Jennifer de Guzman - Director of Trade Book Sales
Kat Salazar - Director of PR & Marketing
Jeremy Sullivan - Director of Digital Sales
Emilio Bautista - Sales Assistant
Branwyn Bigglestone - Senior Accounts Manager
Emily Miller - Accounts Manager
Jessica Ambriz - Administrative Assistant
Tyler Shainline - Events Coordinator
David Brothers - Content Manager
Jonathan Chan - Production Manager
Drew Gill - Art Director
Meredith Wallace - Print Manager
Monica Garcia - Senior Production Artist
Jenna Savage - Production Artist
Addison Duke - Production Artist
IMAGECOMICS.COM

A **Shadowline** PRODUCTION

www.ShadowlineOnline.com
Follow SHADOWLINECOMICS on f FACEBOOK and TWITTER

CHAPTER ELEVEN

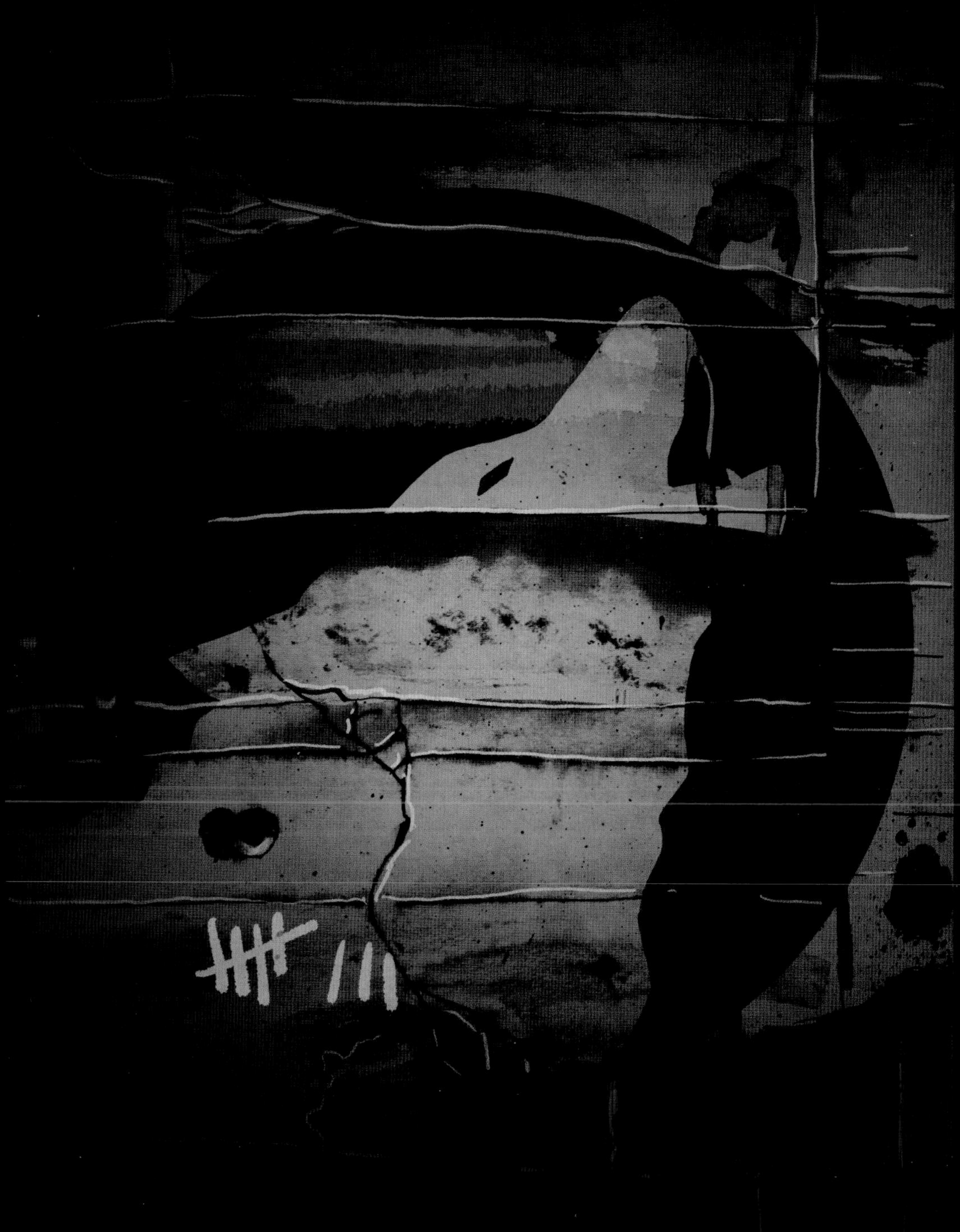

ISSUE ELEVEN COVER B

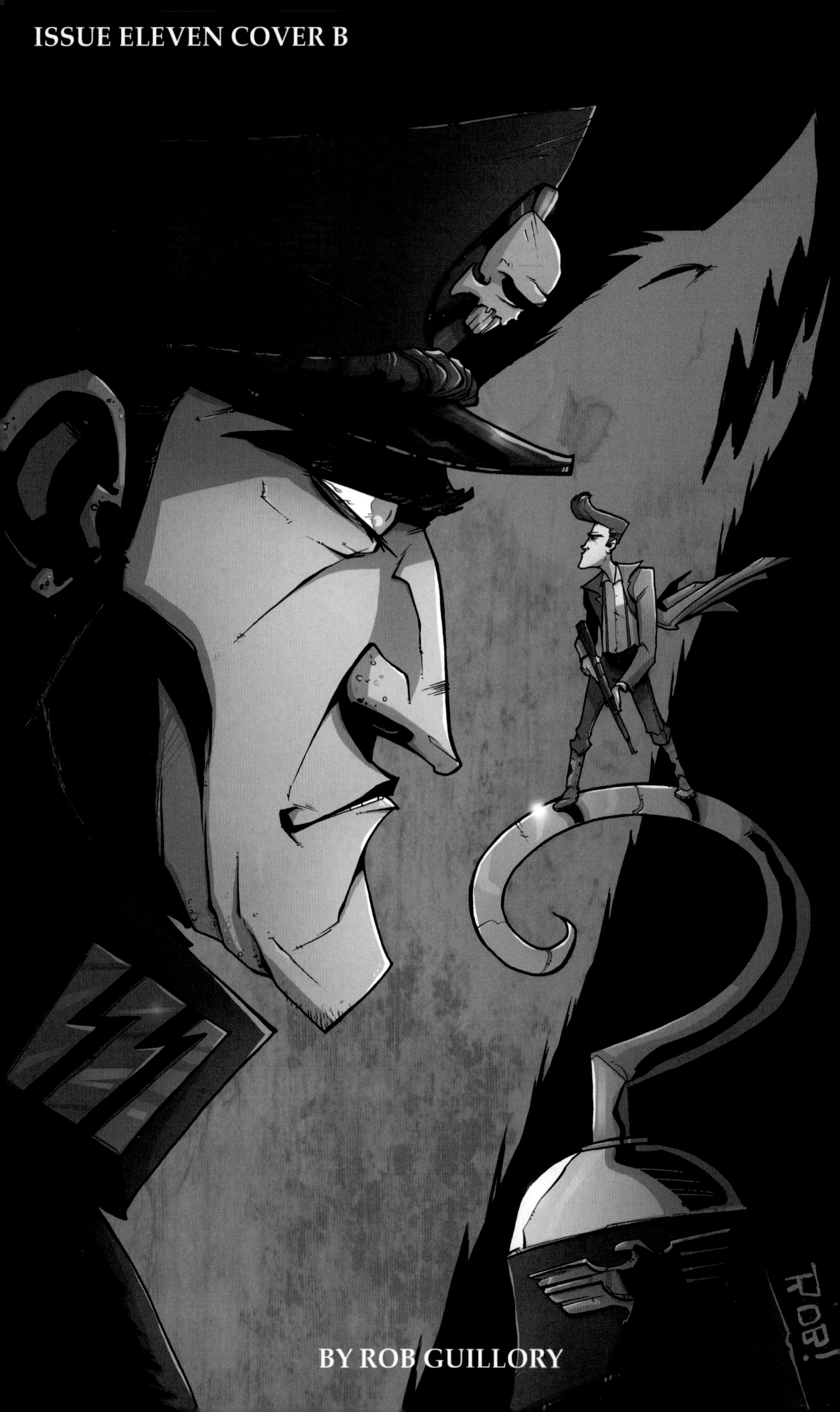
ROB!

BY ROB GUILLORY

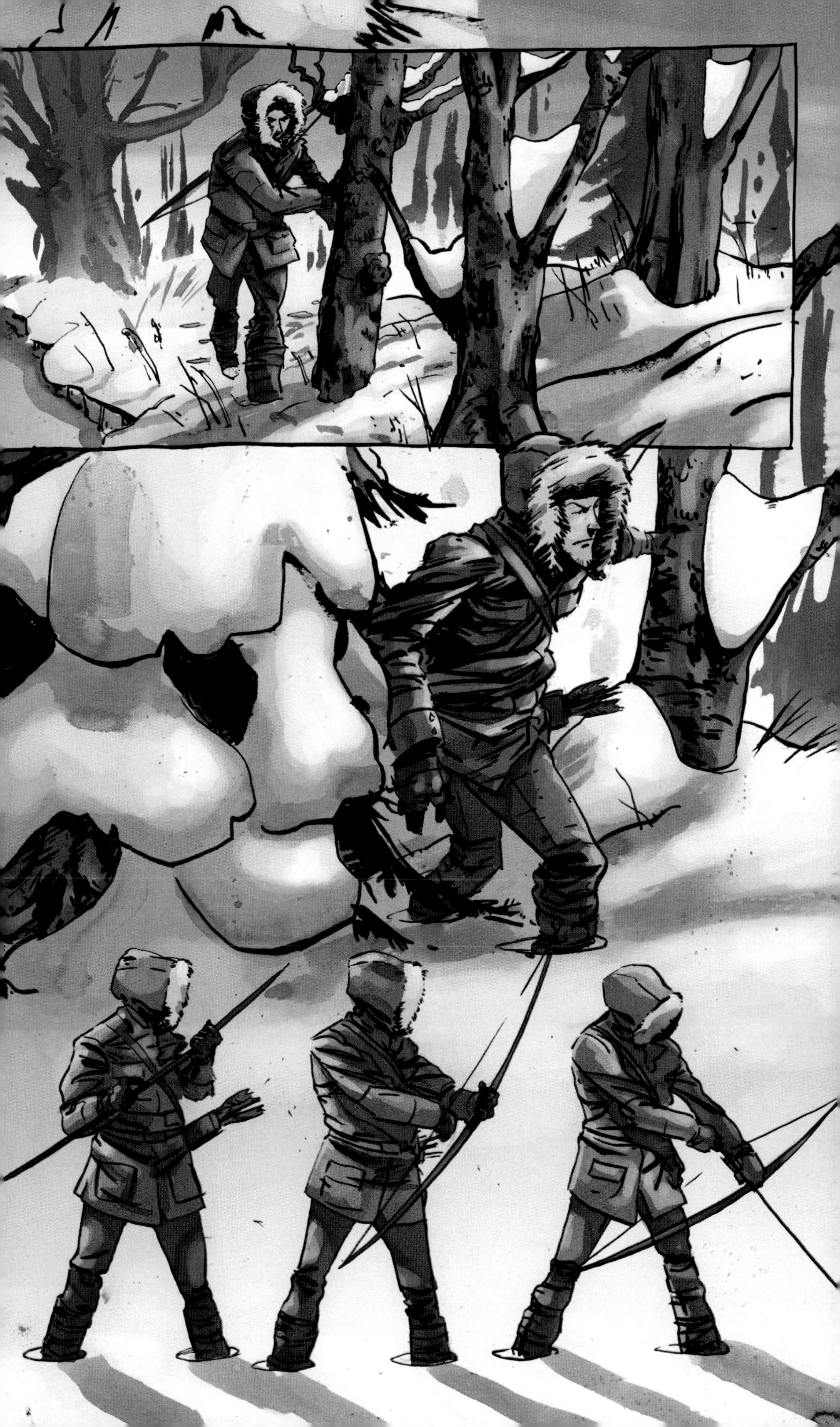

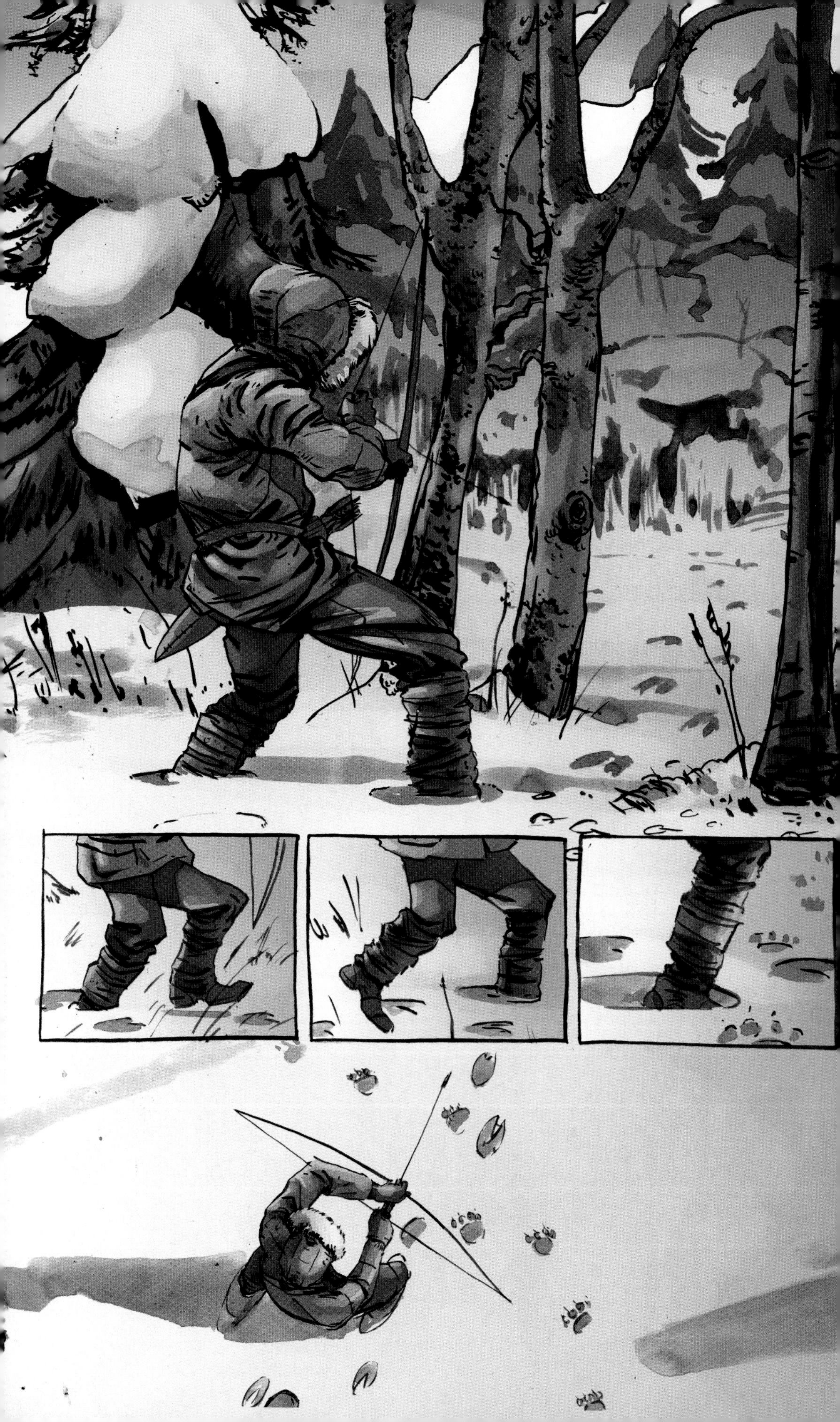

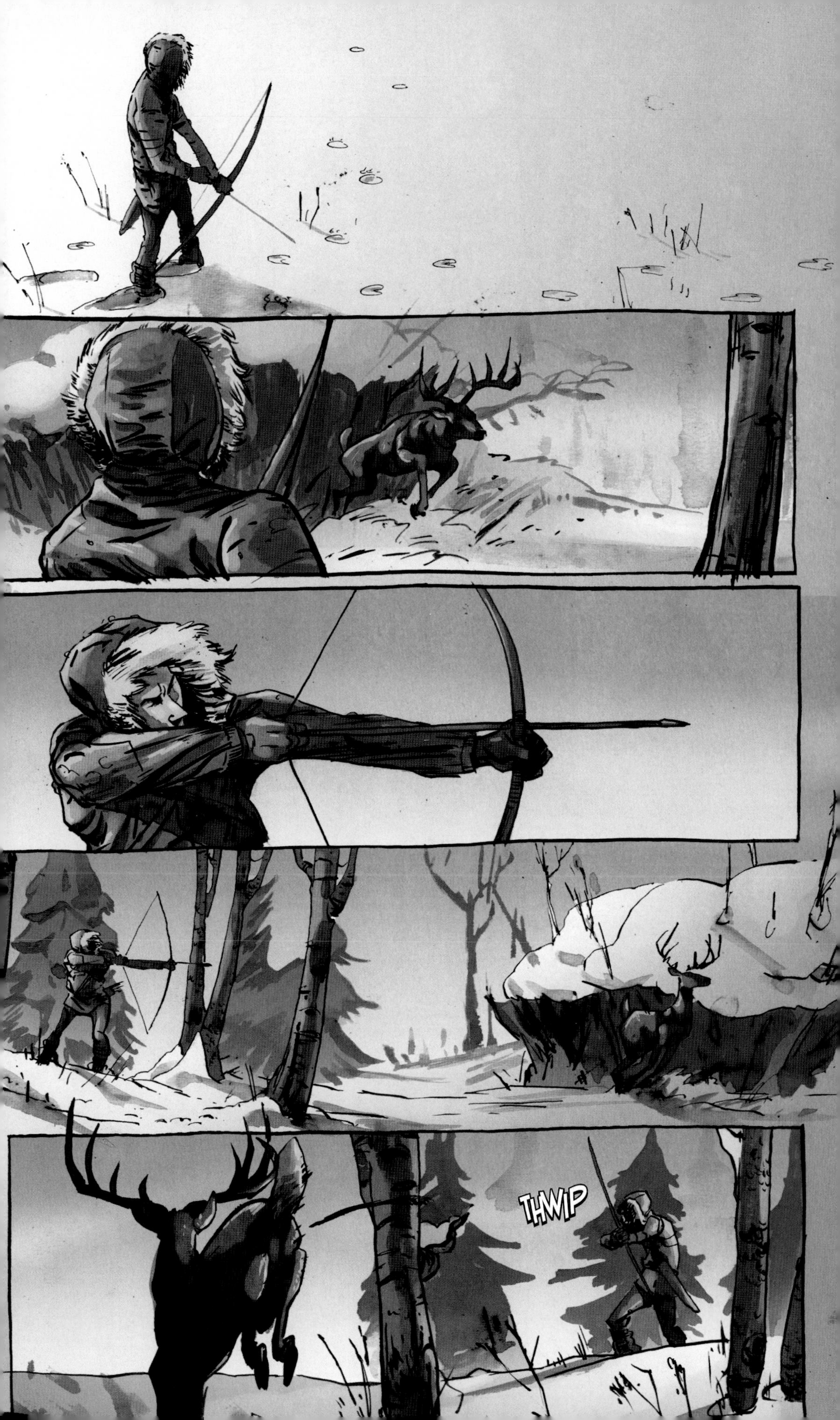
THWIP

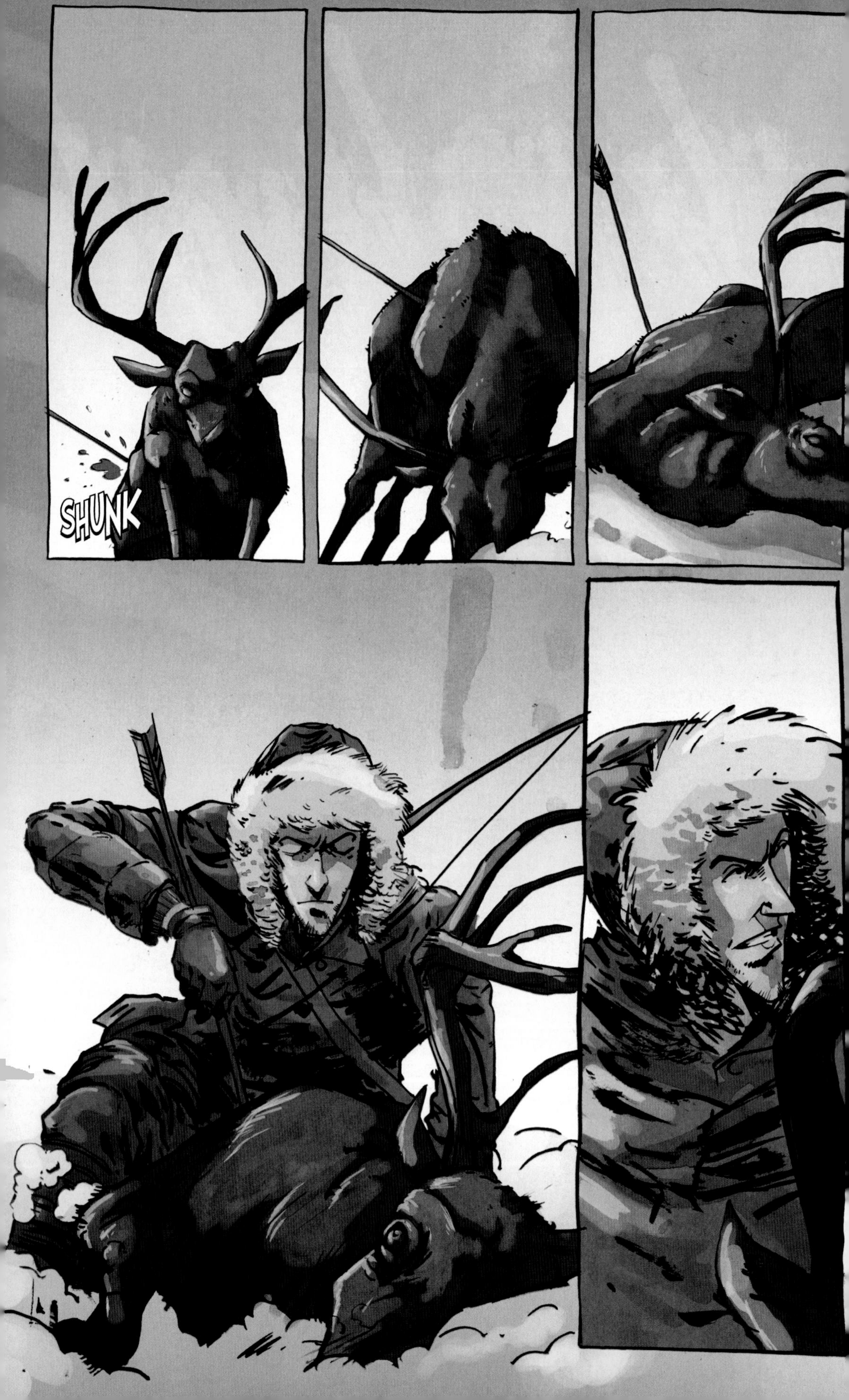
SHUNK

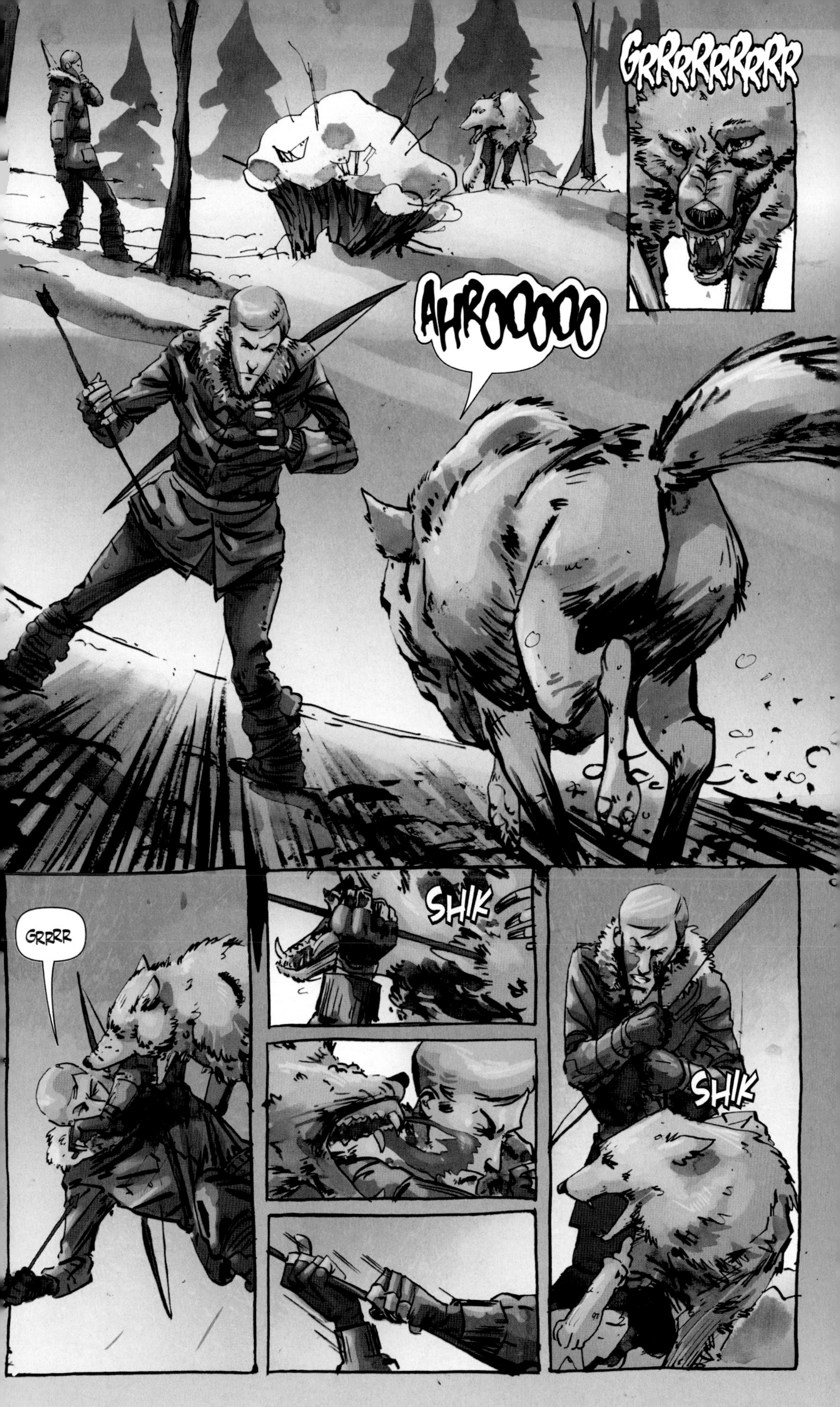
GRRRRRRRRR
AHROOOOO
GRRRR
SHIK
SHIK

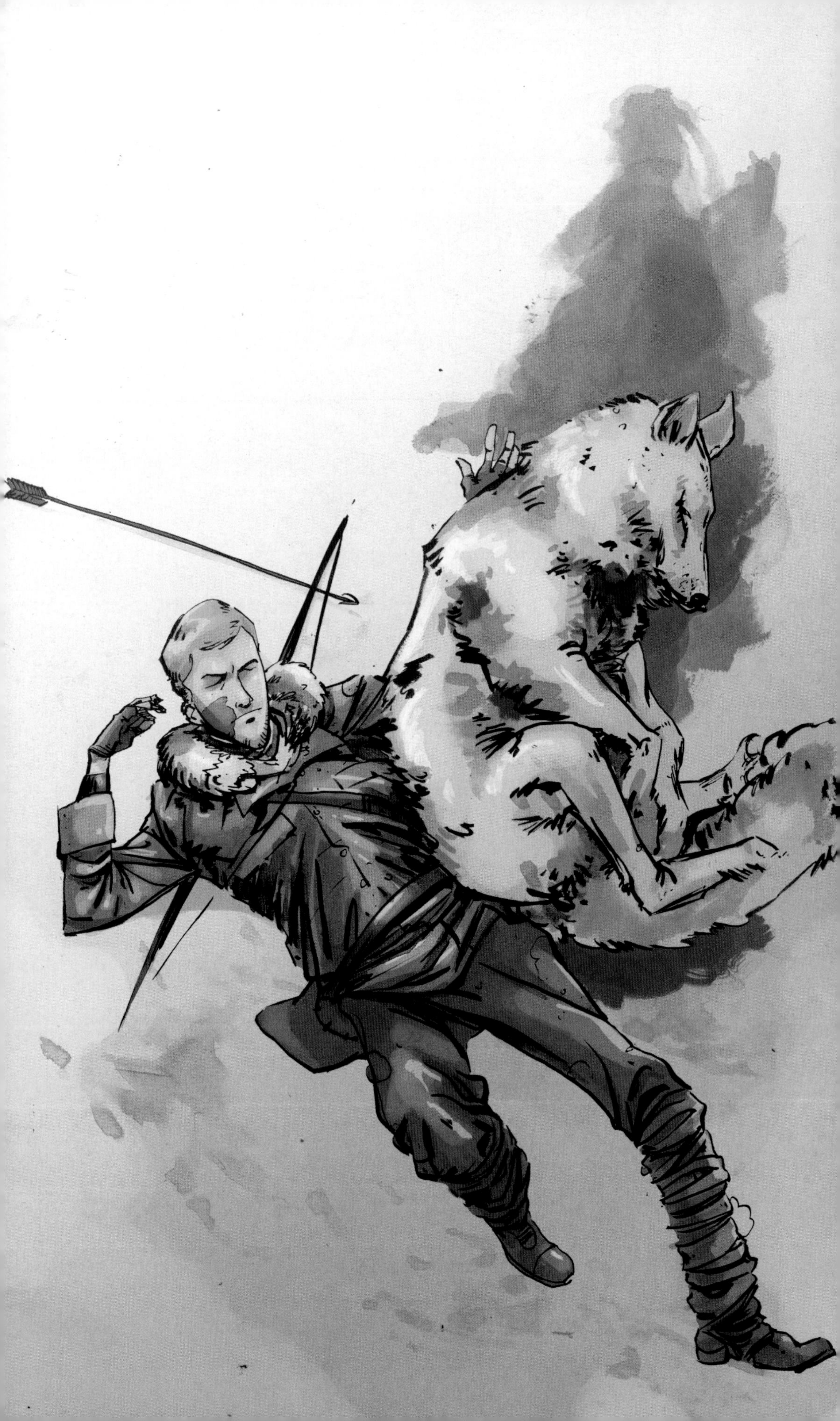

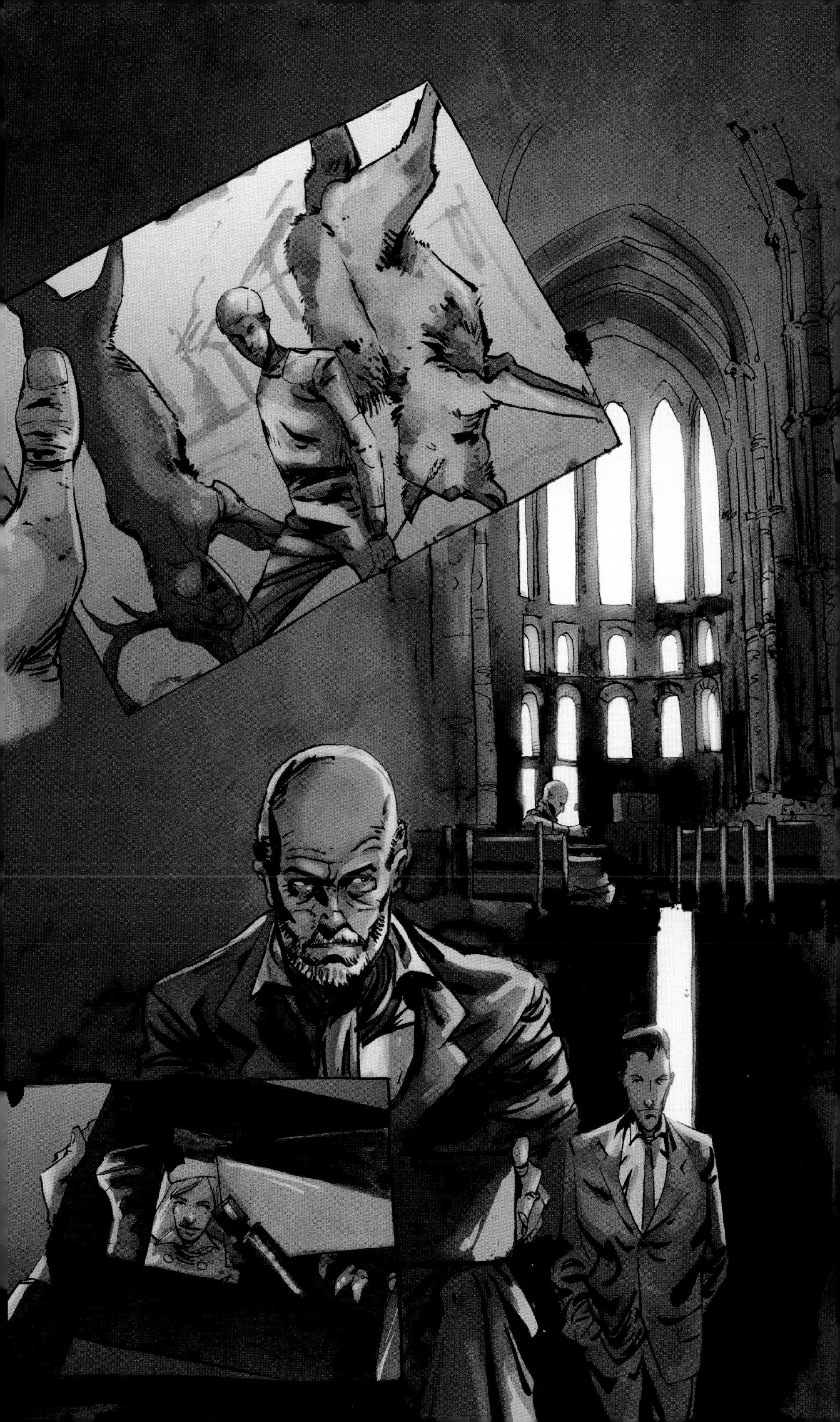

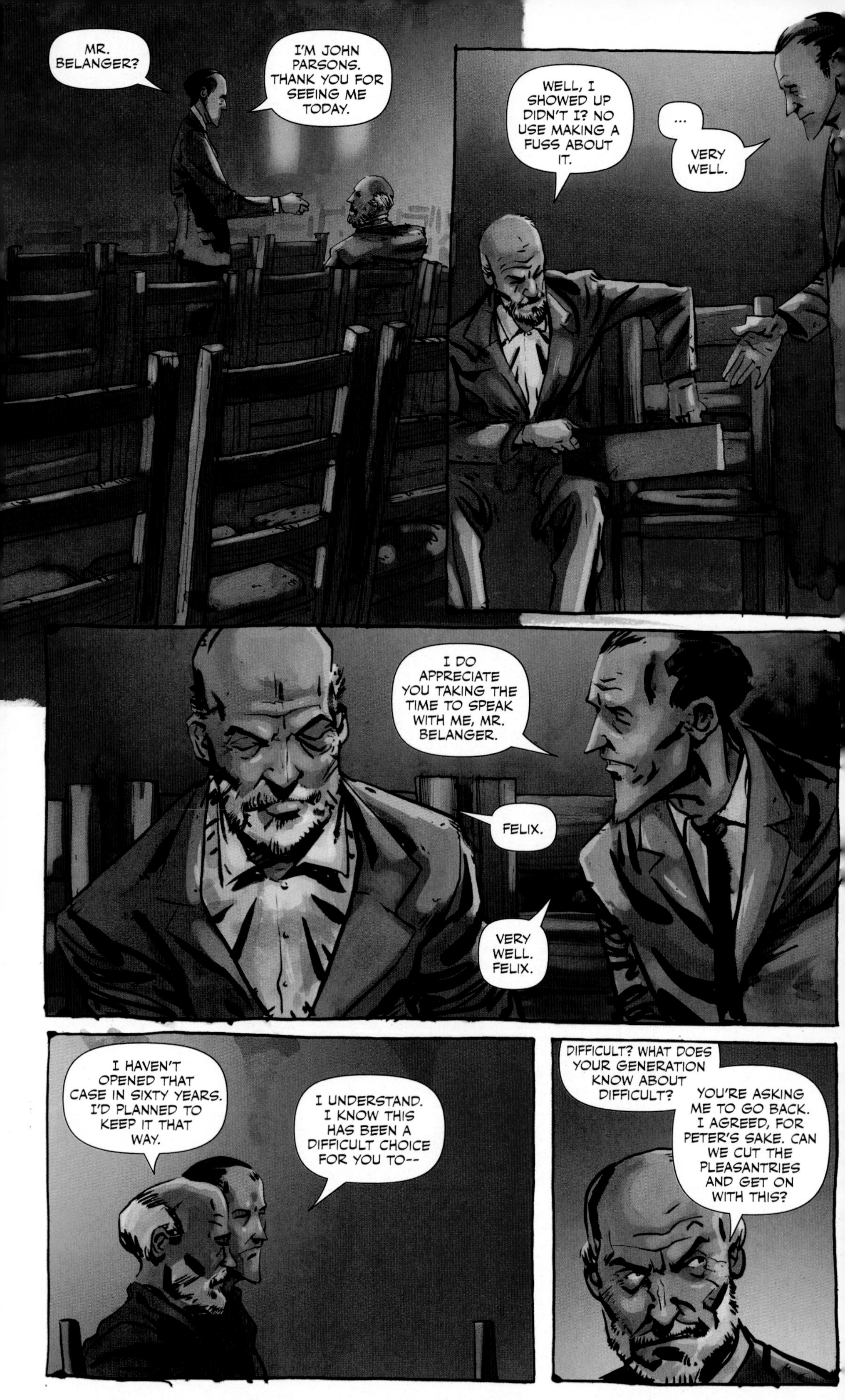
MR. BELANGER?
I'M JOHN PARSONS. THANK YOU FOR SEEING ME TODAY.
WELL, I SHOWED UP DIDN'T I? NO USE MAKING A FUSS ABOUT IT.
...
VERY WELL.
I DO APPRECIATE YOU TAKING THE TIME TO SPEAK WITH ME, MR. BELANGER.
FELIX.
VERY WELL. FELIX.
I HAVEN'T OPENED THAT CASE IN SIXTY YEARS. I'D PLANNED TO KEEP IT THAT WAY.
I UNDERSTAND. I KNOW THIS HAS BEEN A DIFFICULT CHOICE FOR YOU TO--
DIFFICULT? WHAT DOES YOUR GENERATION KNOW ABOUT DIFFICULT?
YOU'RE ASKING ME TO GO BACK. I AGREED, FOR PETER'S SAKE. CAN WE CUT THE PLEASANTRIES AND GET ON WITH THIS?

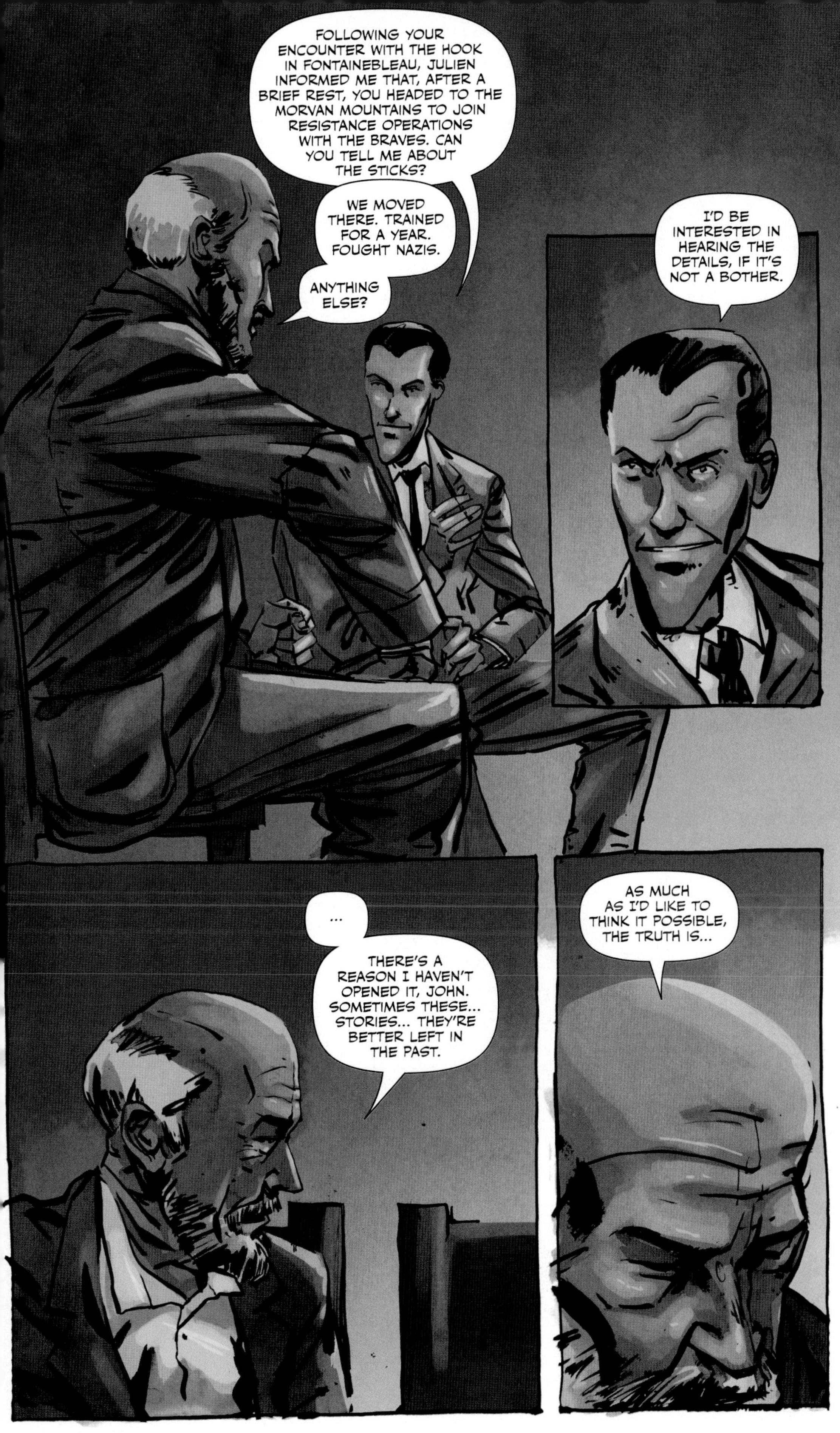
FOLLOWING YOUR ENCOUNTER WITH THE HOOK IN FONTAINEBLEAU, JULIEN INFORMED ME THAT, AFTER A BRIEF REST, YOU HEADED TO THE MORVAN MOUNTAINS TO JOIN RESISTANCE OPERATIONS WITH THE BRAVES. CAN YOU TELL ME ABOUT THE STICKS?
WE MOVED THERE. TRAINED FOR A YEAR. FOUGHT NAZIS.
ANYTHING ELSE?
I'D BE INTERESTED IN HEARING THE DETAILS, IF IT'S NOT A BOTHER.
...
THERE'S A REASON I HAVEN'T OPENED IT, JOHN. SOMETIMES THESE... STORIES... THEY'RE BETTER LEFT IN THE PAST.
AS MUCH AS I'D LIKE TO THINK IT POSSIBLE, THE TRUTH IS...

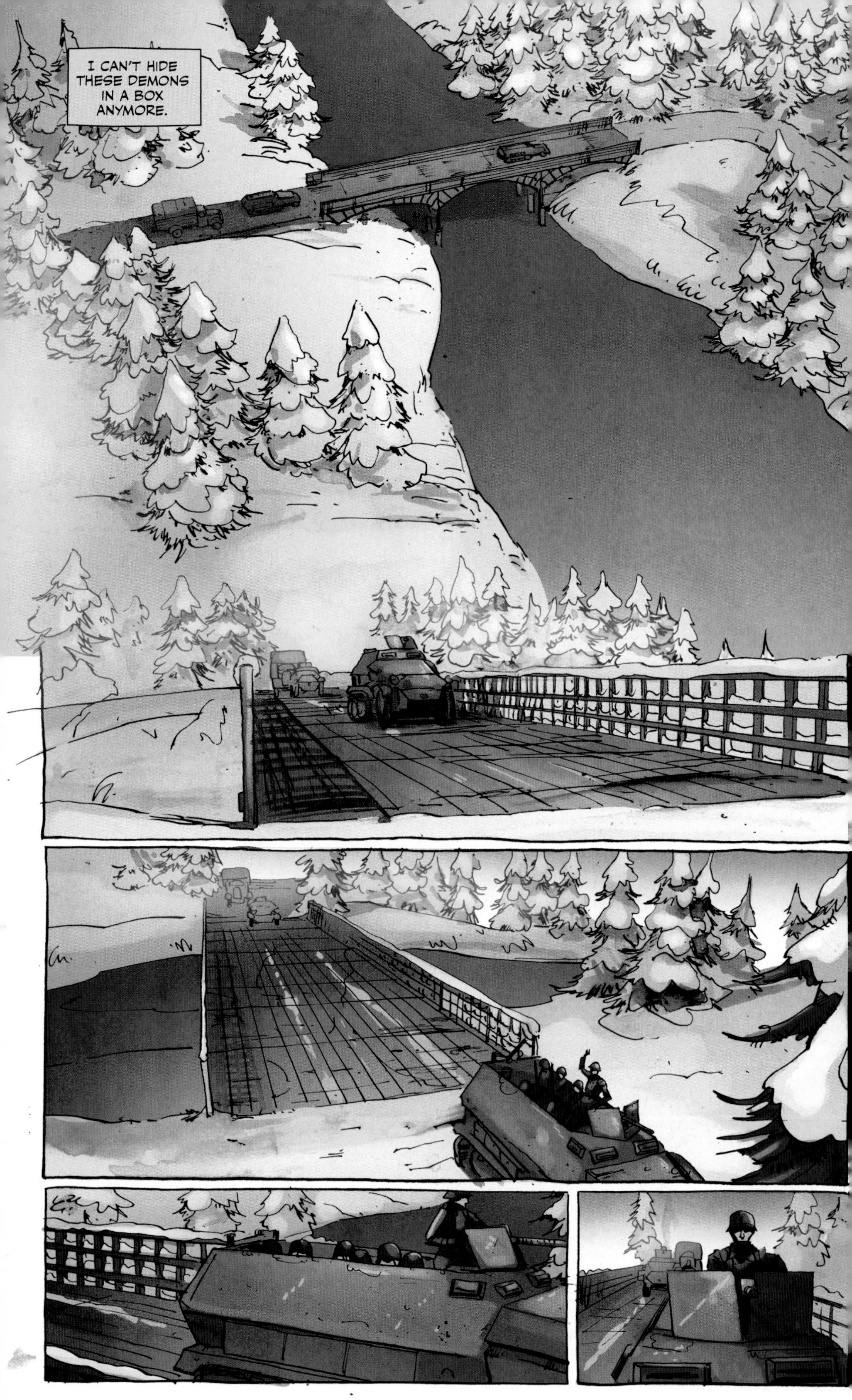
I CAN'T HIDE THESE DEMONS IN A BOX ANYMORE.

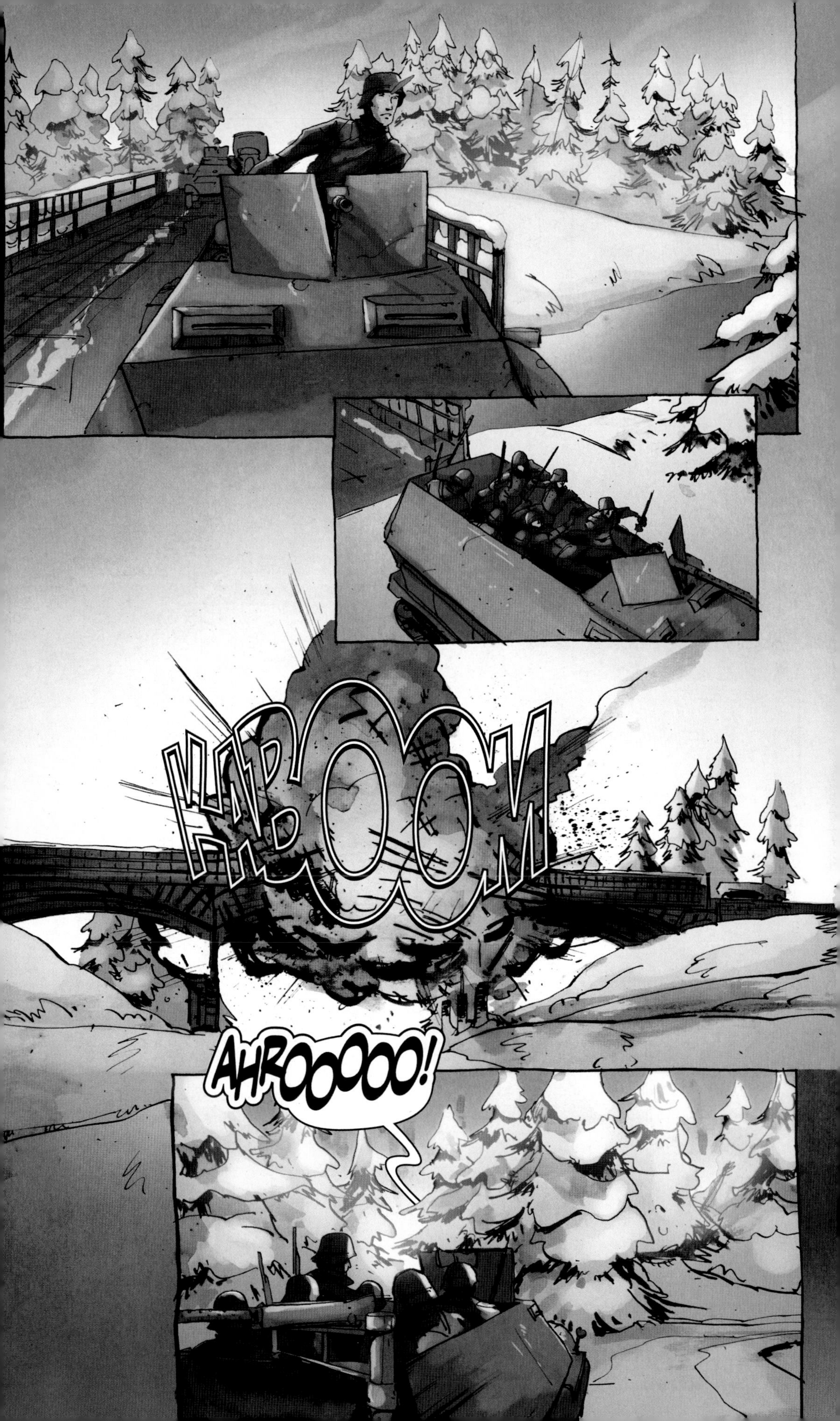
KABOOM
AHROOOOOO!

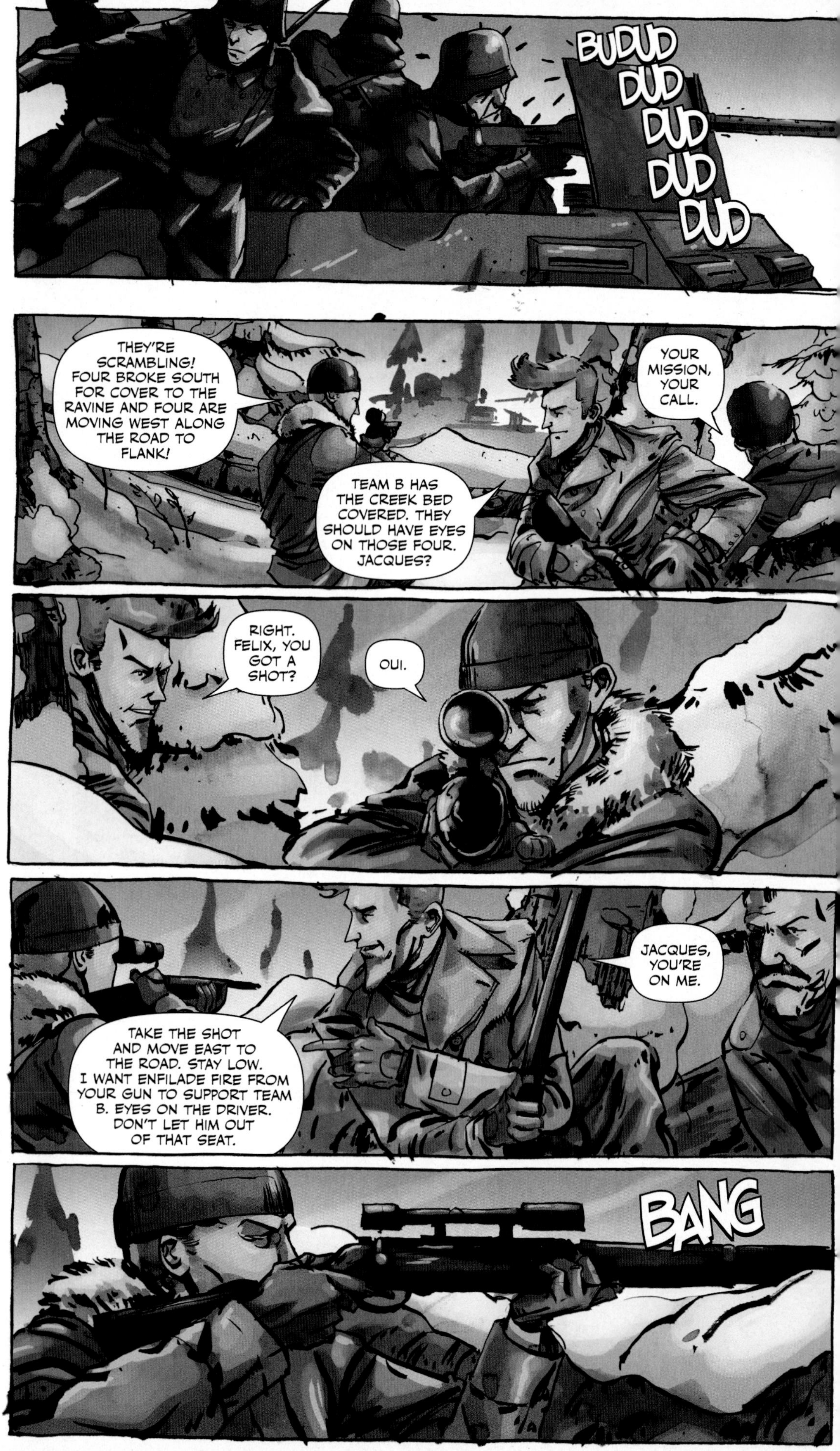
BUDUD DUD DUD DUD DUD
THEY'RE SCRAMBLING! FOUR BROKE SOUTH FOR COVER TO THE RAVINE AND FOUR ARE MOVING WEST ALONG THE ROAD TO FLANK!
YOUR MISSION, YOUR CALL.
TEAM B HAS THE CREEK BED COVERED. THEY SHOULD HAVE EYES ON THOSE FOUR. JACQUES?
RIGHT. FELIX, YOU GOT A SHOT?
OUI.
JACQUES, YOU'RE ON ME.
TAKE THE SHOT AND MOVE EAST TO THE ROAD. STAY LOW. I WANT ENFILADE FIRE FROM YOUR GUN TO SUPPORT TEAM B. EYES ON THE DRIVER. DON'T LET HIM OUT OF THAT SEAT.
BANG

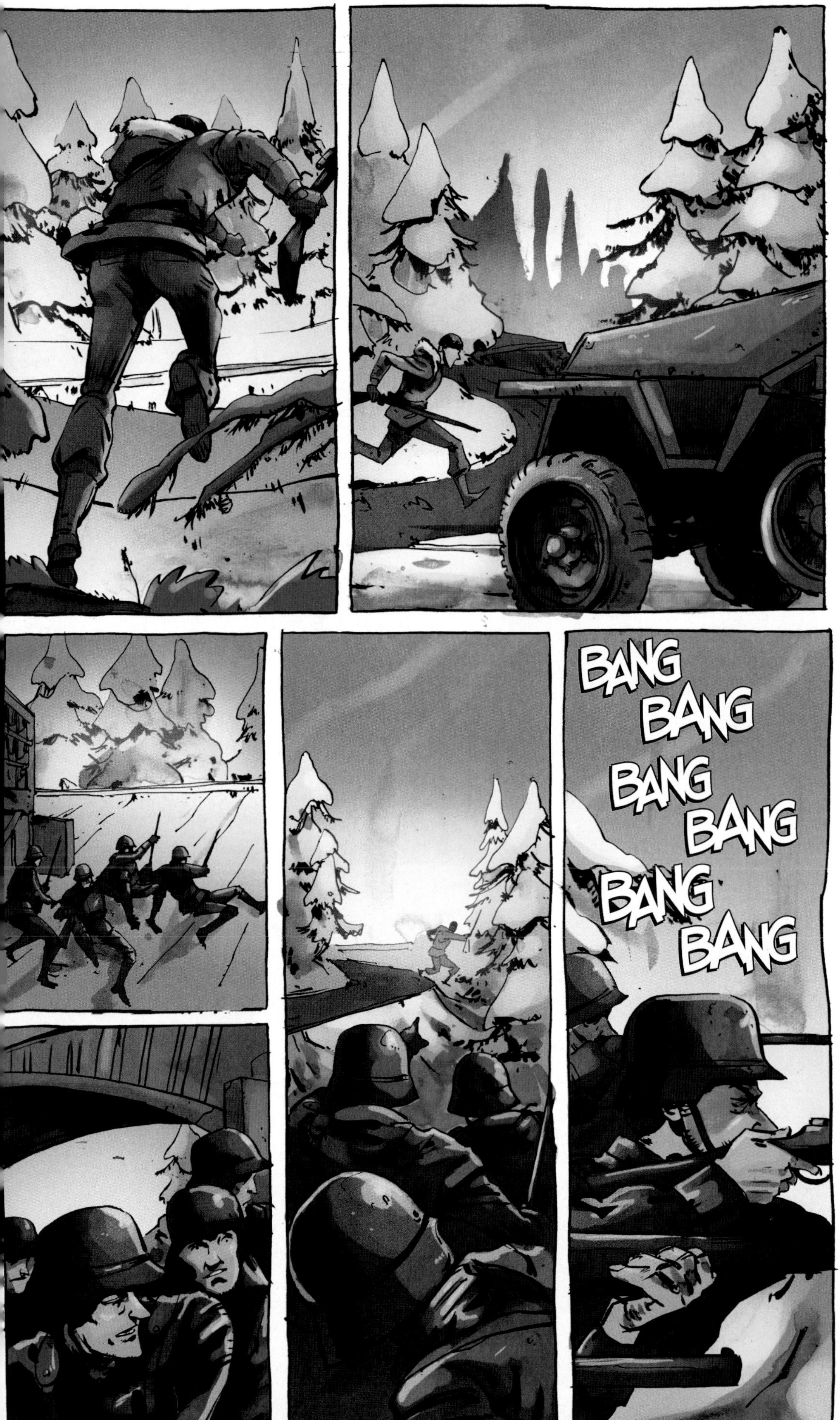
BANG
BANG
BANG
BANG
BANG
BANG

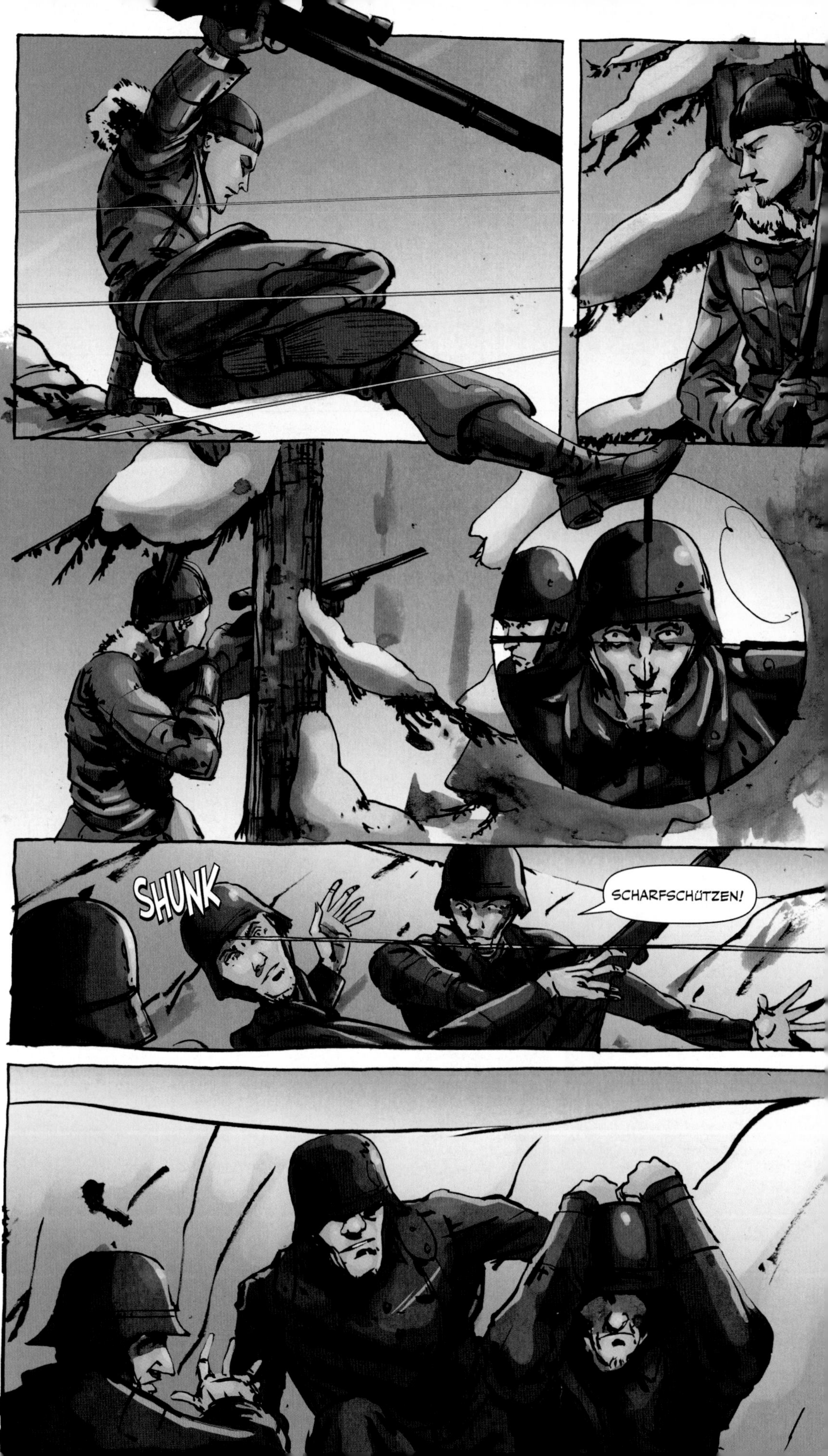
SHUNK
SCHARFSCHÜTZEN!

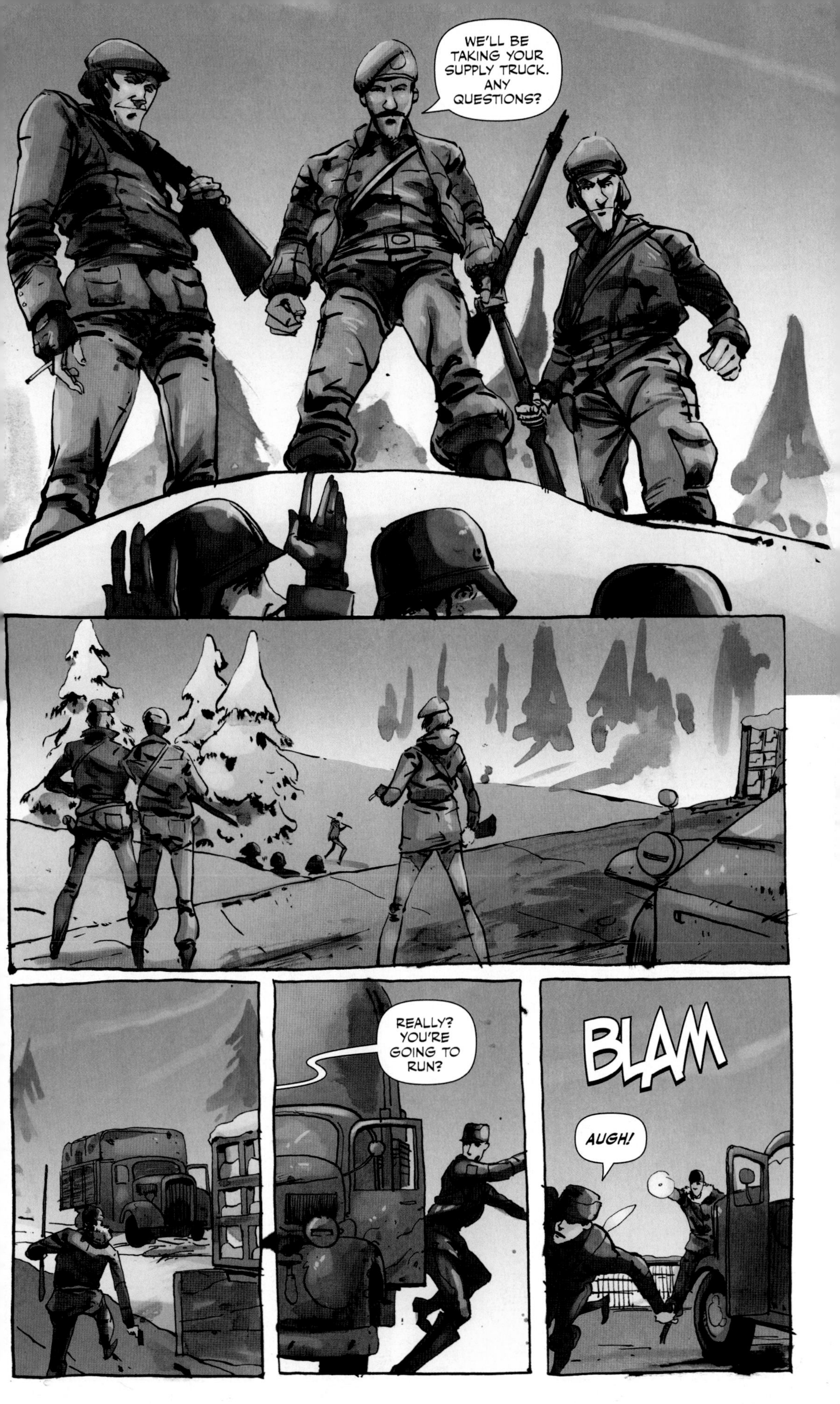
WE'LL BE TAKING YOUR SUPPLY TRUCK. ANY QUESTIONS?
REALLY? YOU'RE GOING TO RUN?
BLAM
AUGH!

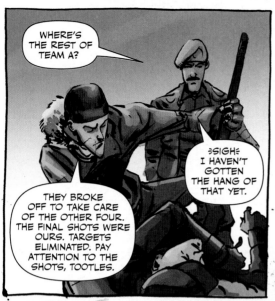

WHERE'S THE REST OF TEAM A?

THEY BROKE OFF TO TAKE CARE OF THE OTHER FOUR. THE FINAL SHOTS WERE OURS. TARGETS ELIMINATED. PAY ATTENTION TO THE SHOTS, TOOTLES.

≡SIGH≡ I HAVEN'T GOTTEN THE HANG OF THAT YET.

TEAM C CAPTURED THE SUPPLY TRUCK. WHAT DID YOU FIND, FELIX?

THE CHILDREN'S HOSPITAL APPRECIATES YOUR GENEROUS DONATION.

GENUINE GRADE A GERMAN FOODSTUFFS.

INTELLIGENCE WAS RIGHT ON THIS ONE. GOOD WORK, TEAM.

SITUATION REPORT.

SITE SECURE. TEAM C HAS CAPTURED THE TRUCK AND ALL ENEMY COMBATANTS ARE NEUTRALIZED. NO INJURIES OR FATALITIES ON OUR SIDE.

WHAT'S THIS? YOU KNOW I CAN'T READ GERMAN.

READ IT, PETE.

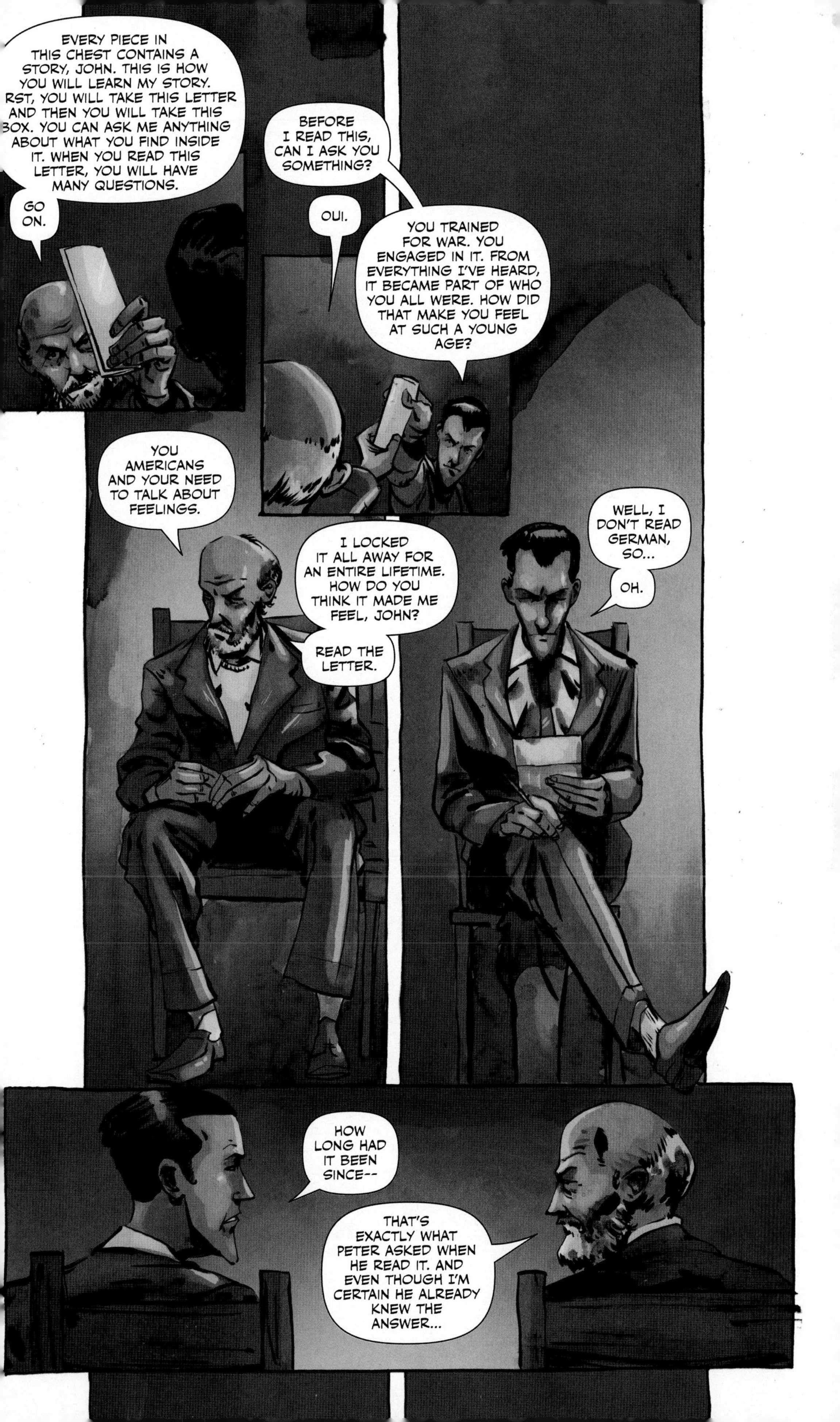
EVERY PIECE IN THIS CHEST CONTAINS A STORY, JOHN. THIS IS HOW YOU WILL LEARN MY STORY. RST, YOU WILL TAKE THIS LETTER AND THEN YOU WILL TAKE THIS BOX. YOU CAN ASK ME ANYTHING ABOUT WHAT YOU FIND INSIDE IT. WHEN YOU READ THIS LETTER, YOU WILL HAVE MANY QUESTIONS.
GO ON.
BEFORE I READ THIS, CAN I ASK YOU SOMETHING?
OUI.
YOU TRAINED FOR WAR. YOU ENGAGED IN IT. FROM EVERYTHING I'VE HEARD, IT BECAME PART OF WHO YOU ALL WERE. HOW DID THAT MAKE YOU FEEL AT SUCH A YOUNG AGE?
YOU AMERICANS AND YOUR NEED TO TALK ABOUT FEELINGS.
I LOCKED IT ALL AWAY FOR AN ENTIRE LIFETIME. HOW DO YOU THINK IT MADE ME FEEL, JOHN?
READ THE LETTER.
WELL, I DON'T READ GERMAN, SO...
OH.
HOW LONG HAD IT BEEN SINCE--
THAT'S EXACTLY WHAT PETER ASKED WHEN HE READ IT. AND EVEN THOUGH I'M CERTAIN HE ALREADY KNEW THE ANSWER...

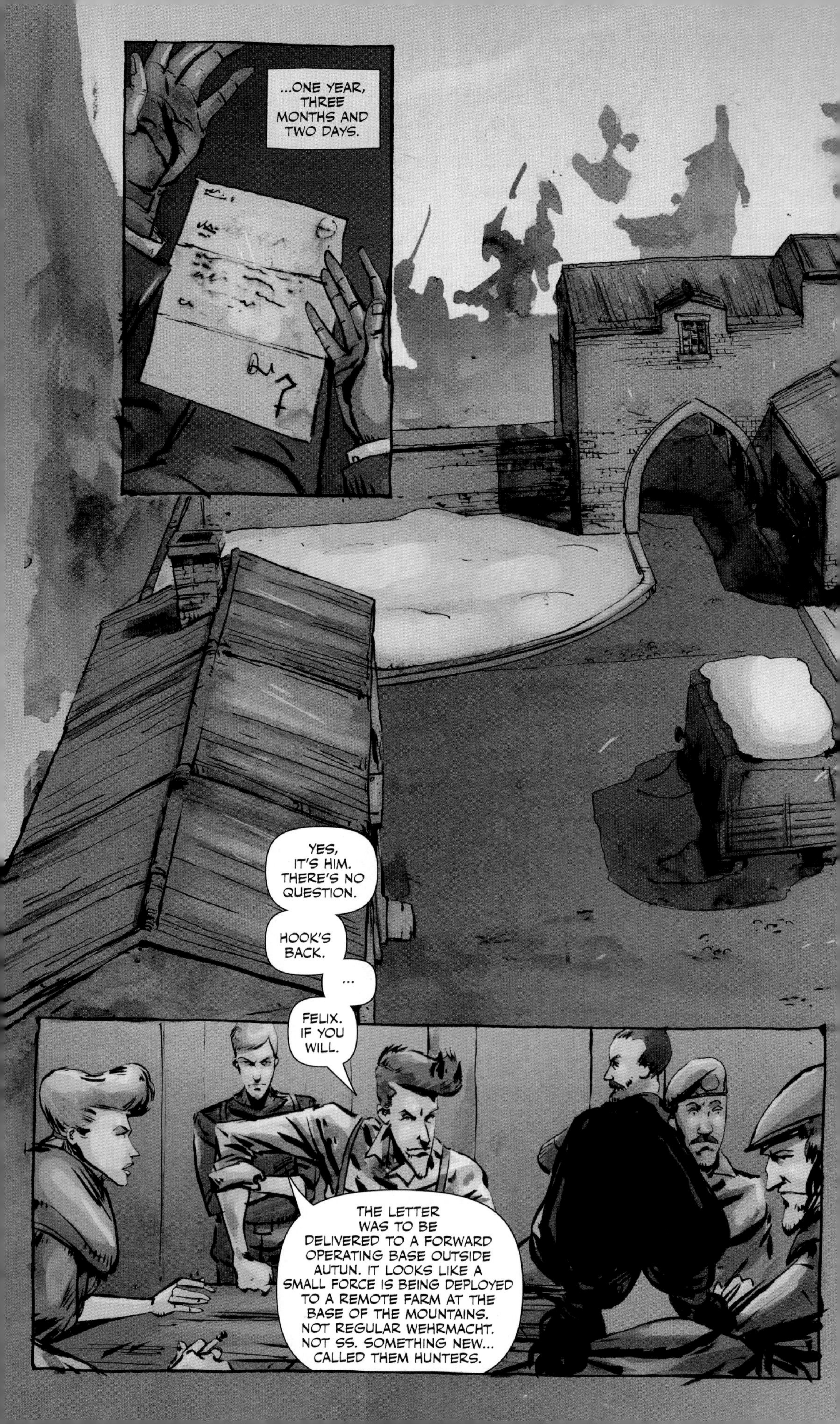
...ONE YEAR, THREE MONTHS AND TWO DAYS.
YES, IT'S HIM. THERE'S NO QUESTION.
HOOK'S BACK.
...
FELIX. IF YOU WILL.
THE LETTER WAS TO BE DELIVERED TO A FORWARD OPERATING BASE OUTSIDE AUTUN. IT LOOKS LIKE A SMALL FORCE IS BEING DEPLOYED TO A REMOTE FARM AT THE BASE OF THE MOUNTAINS. NOT REGULAR WEHRMACHT. NOT SS. SOMETHING NEW... CALLED THEM HUNTERS.

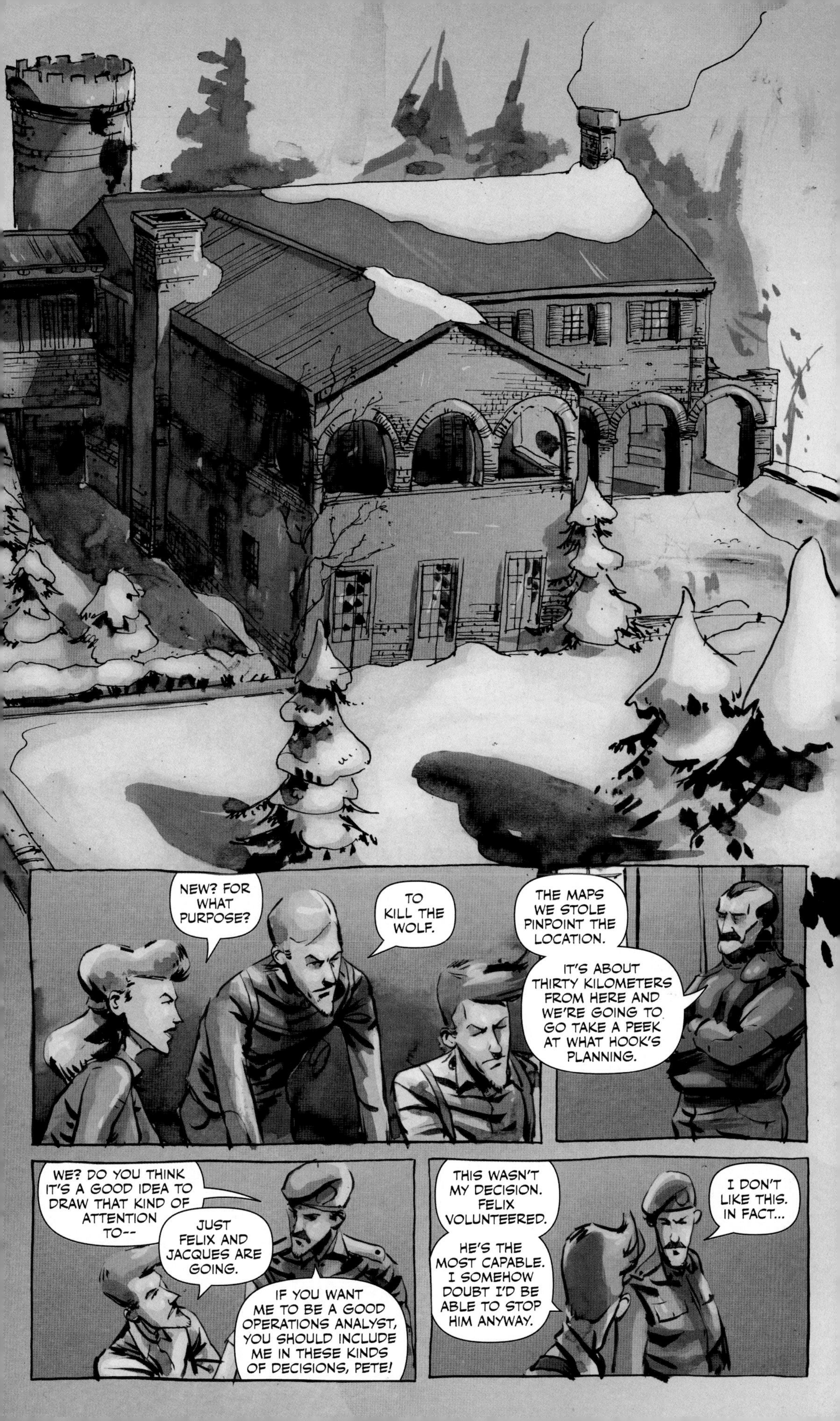
NEW? FOR WHAT PURPOSE?
TO KILL THE WOLF.
THE MAPS WE STOLE PINPOINT THE LOCATION.
IT'S ABOUT THIRTY KILOMETERS FROM HERE AND WE'RE GOING TO GO TAKE A PEEK AT WHAT HOOK'S PLANNING.
WE? DO YOU THINK IT'S A GOOD IDEA TO DRAW THAT KIND OF ATTENTION TO--
JUST FELIX AND JACQUES ARE GOING.
IF YOU WANT ME TO BE A GOOD OPERATIONS ANALYST, YOU SHOULD INCLUDE ME IN THESE KINDS OF DECISIONS, PETE!
THIS WASN'T MY DECISION. FELIX VOLUNTEERED.
HE'S THE MOST CAPABLE. I SOMEHOW DOUBT I'D BE ABLE TO STOP HIM ANYWAY.
I DON'T LIKE THIS. IN FACT...

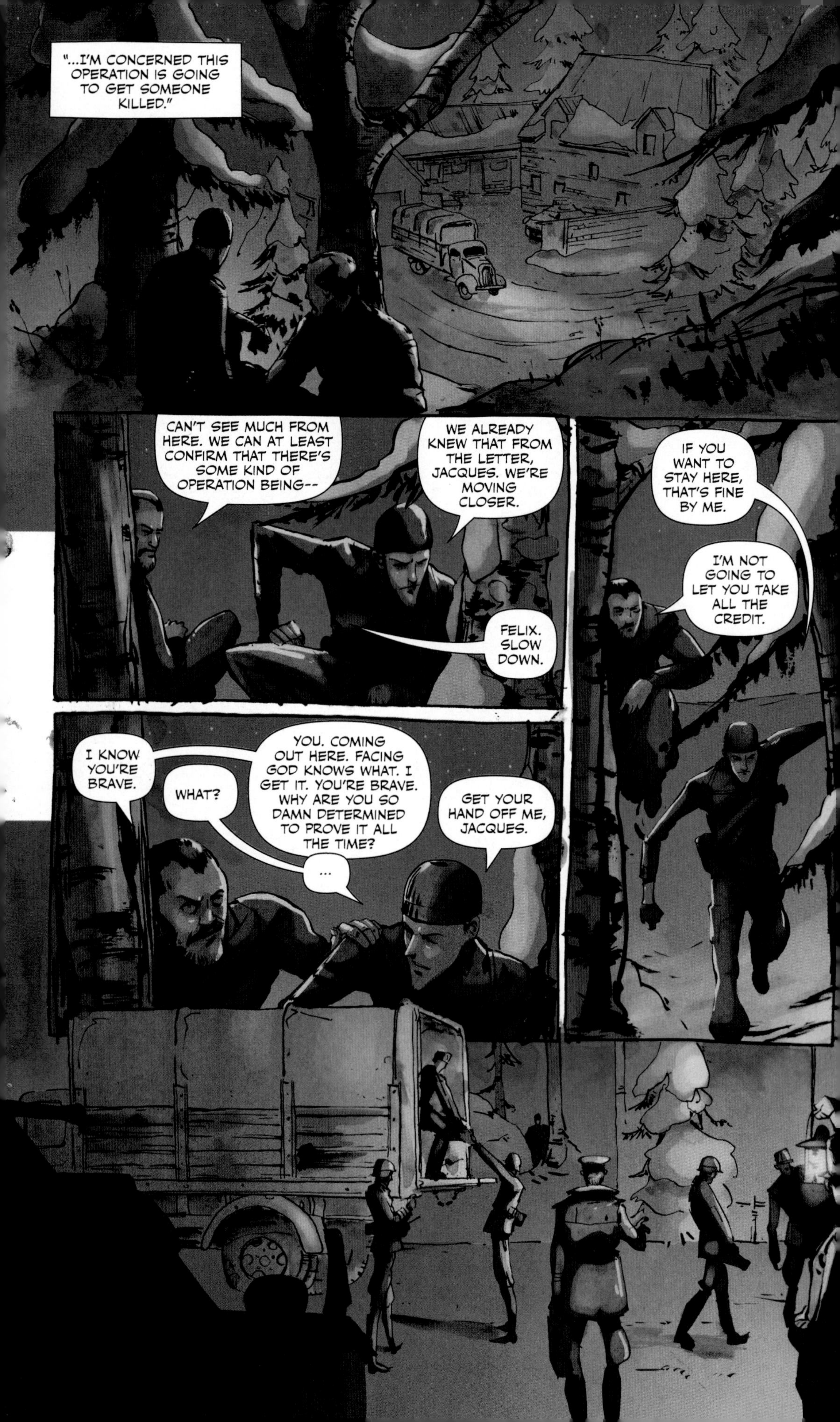
"...I'M CONCERNED THIS OPERATION IS GOING TO GET SOMEONE KILLED."
CAN'T SEE MUCH FROM HERE. WE CAN AT LEAST CONFIRM THAT THERE'S SOME KIND OF OPERATION BEING--
WE ALREADY KNEW THAT FROM THE LETTER, JACQUES. WE'RE MOVING CLOSER.
FELIX. SLOW DOWN.
IF YOU WANT TO STAY HERE, THAT'S FINE BY ME.
I'M NOT GOING TO LET YOU TAKE ALL THE CREDIT.
I KNOW YOU'RE BRAVE.
WHAT?
YOU. COMING OUT HERE. FACING GOD KNOWS WHAT. I GET IT. YOU'RE BRAVE. WHY ARE YOU SO DAMN DETERMINED TO PROVE IT ALL THE TIME?
...
GET YOUR HAND OFF ME, JACQUES.

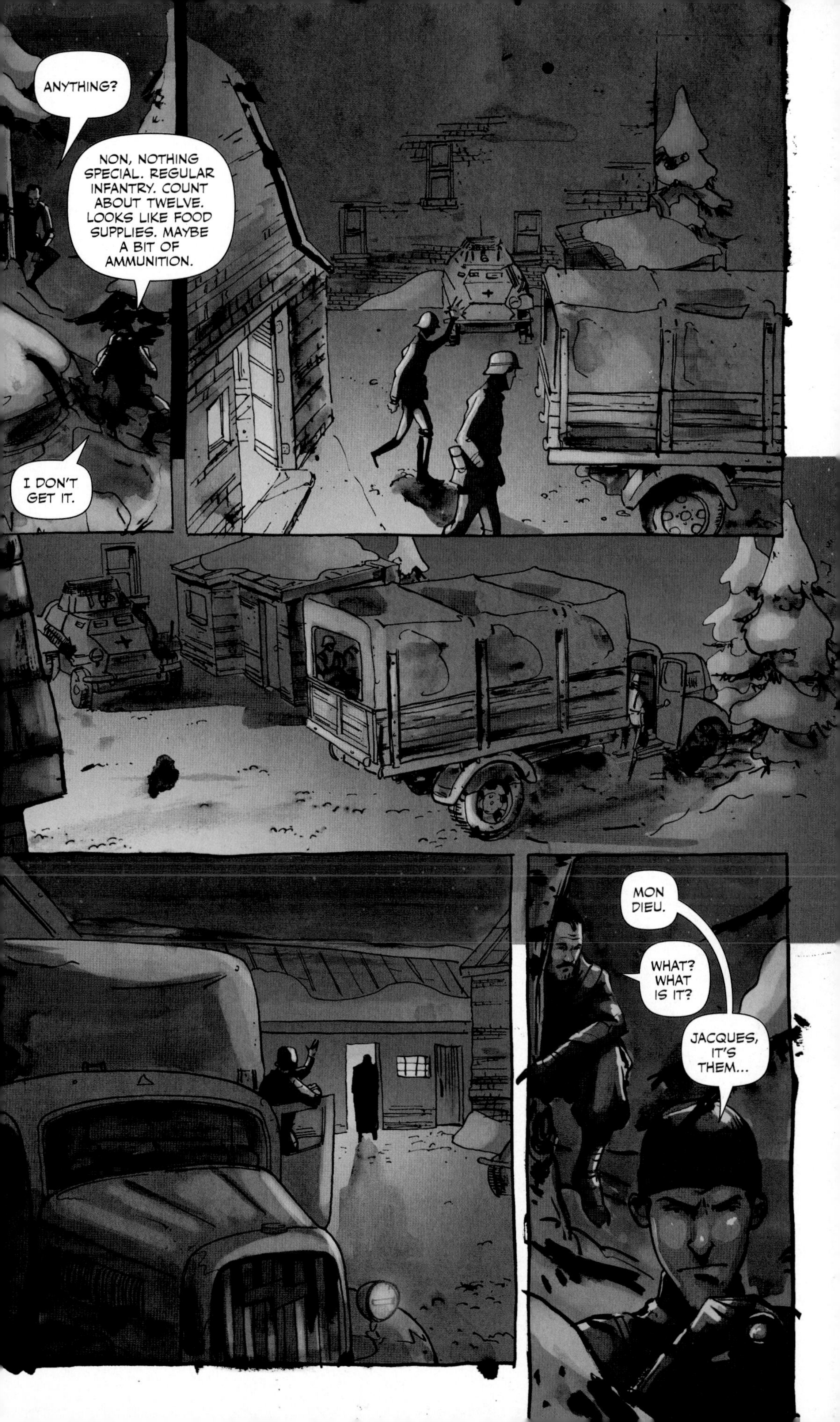
ANYTHING?
NON, NOTHING SPECIAL. REGULAR INFANTRY. COUNT ABOUT TWELVE. LOOKS LIKE FOOD SUPPLIES. MAYBE A BIT OF AMMUNITION.
I DON'T GET IT.
MON DIEU.
WHAT? WHAT IS IT?
JACQUES, IT'S THEM...

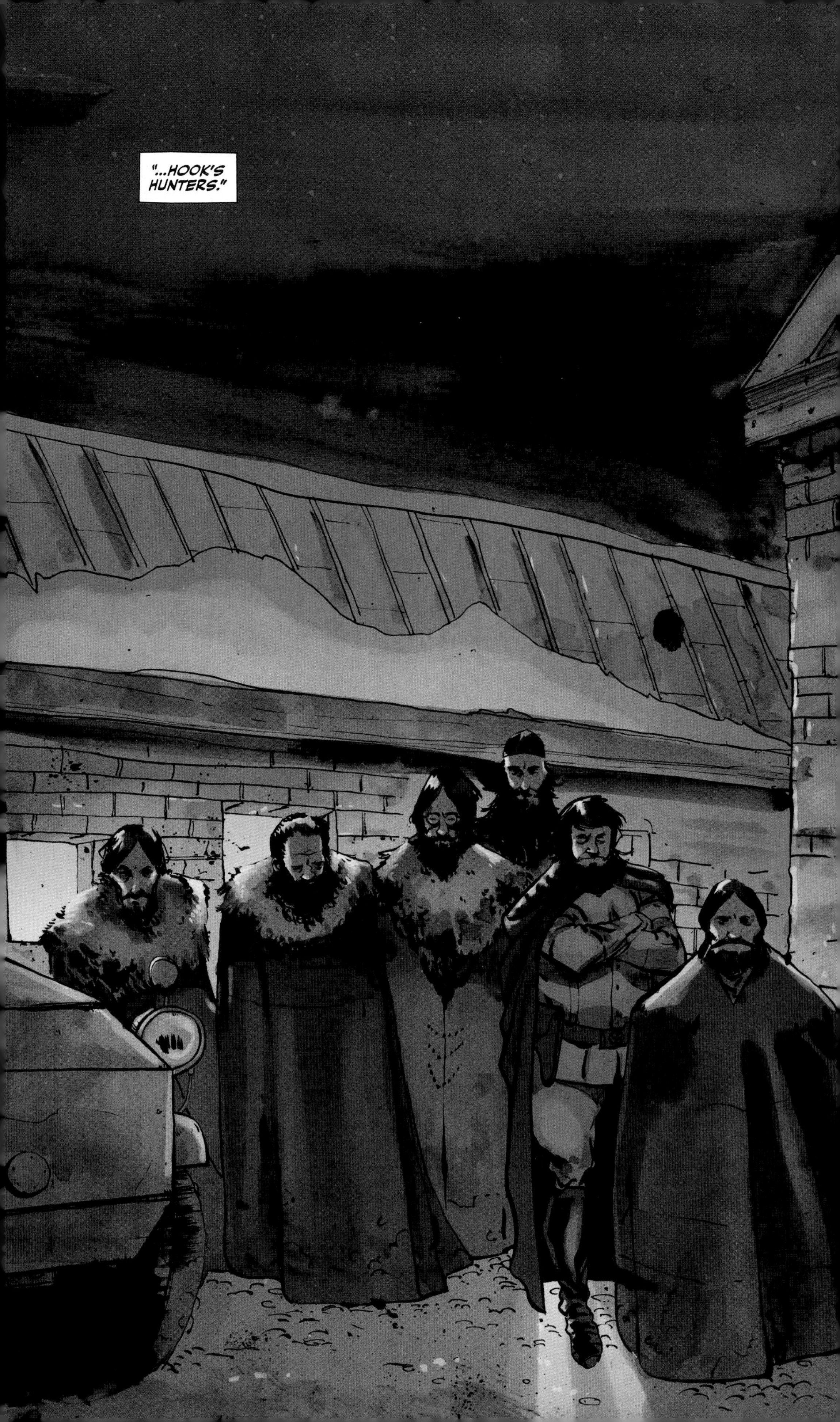
"...HOOK'S HUNTERS."

CHAPTER TWELVE

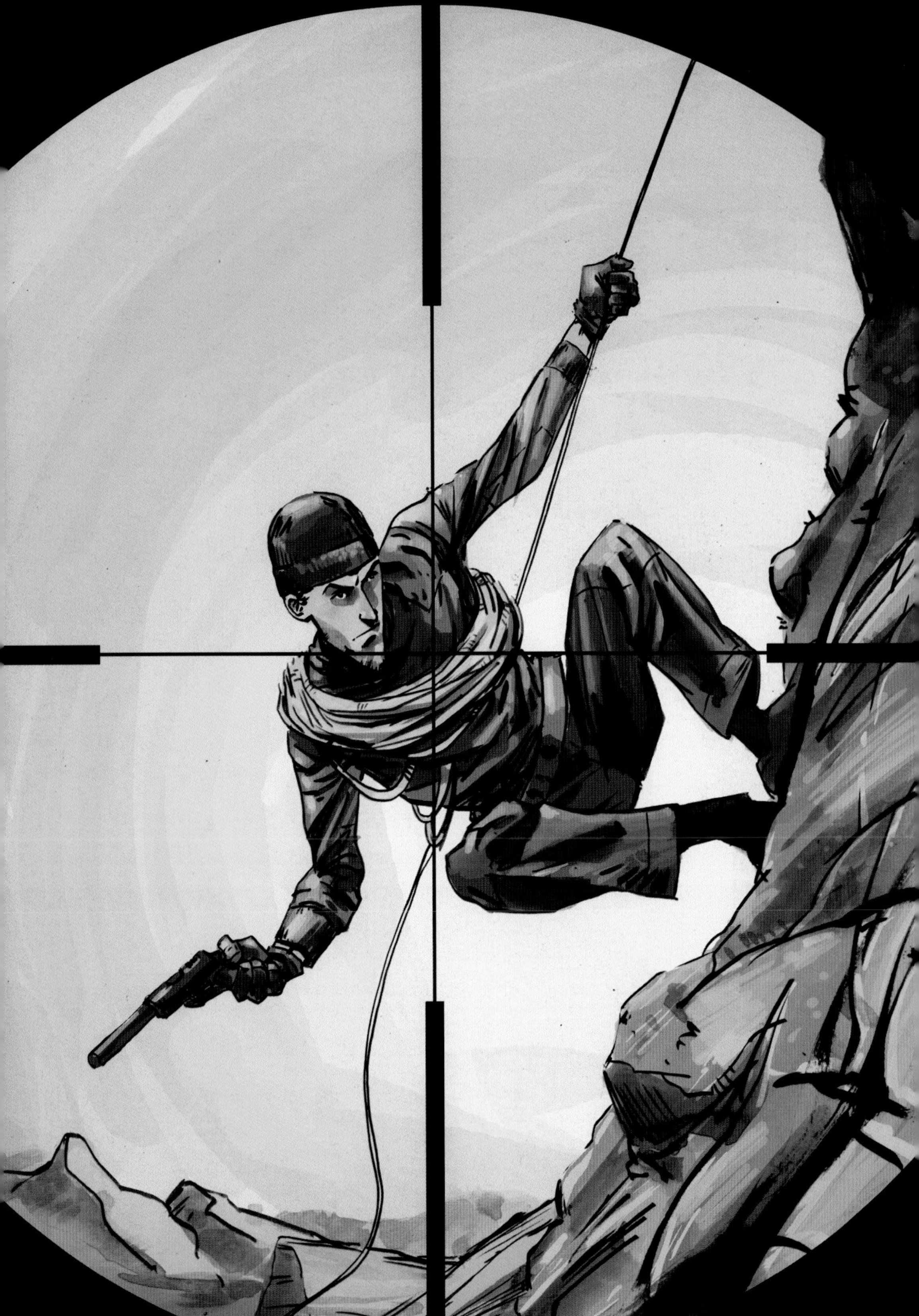

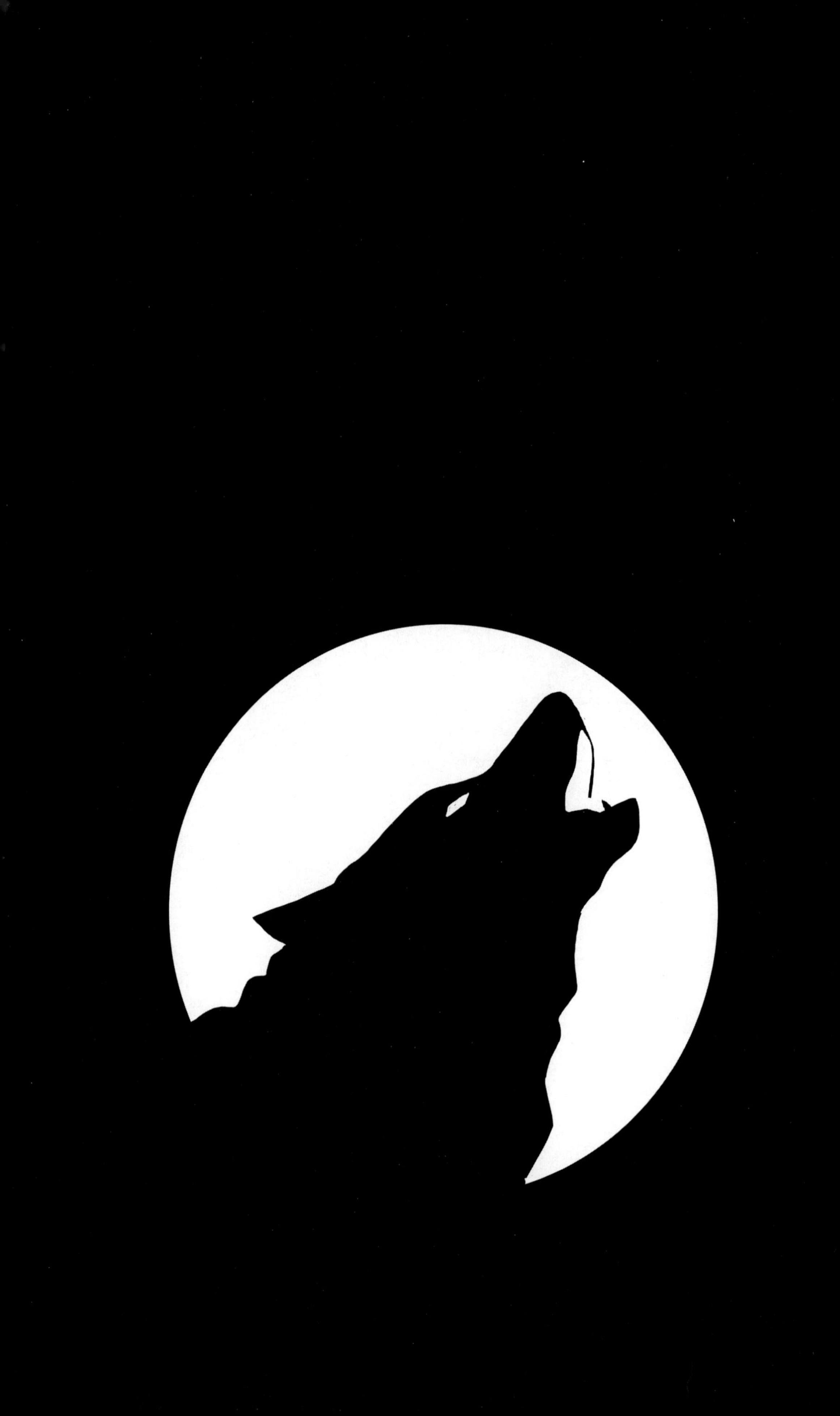

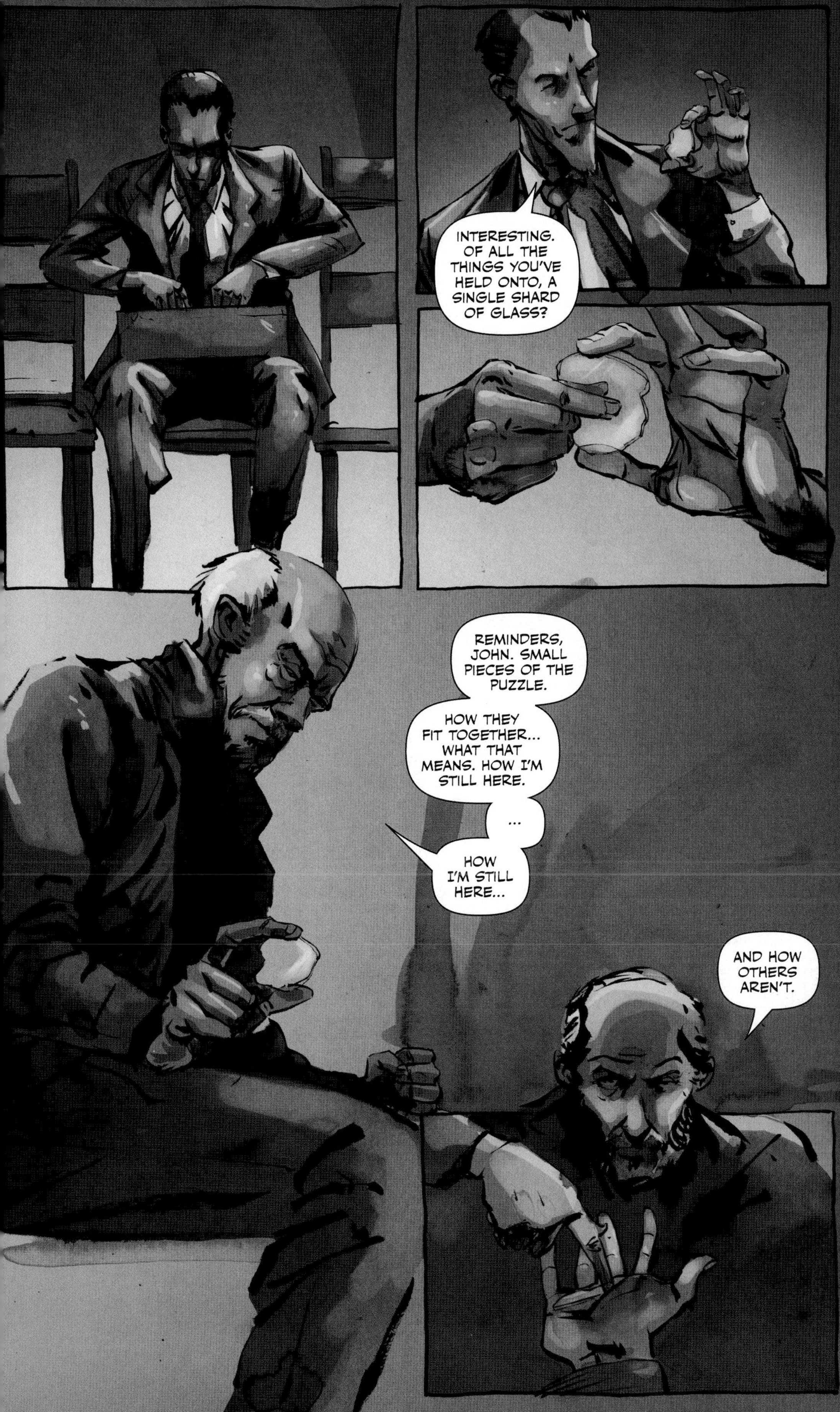
INTERESTING. OF ALL THE THINGS YOU'VE HELD ONTO, A SINGLE SHARD OF GLASS?
REMINDERS, JOHN. SMALL PIECES OF THE PUZZLE.
HOW THEY FIT TOGETHER... WHAT THAT MEANS. HOW I'M STILL HERE.
...
HOW I'M STILL HERE...
AND HOW OTHERS AREN'T.

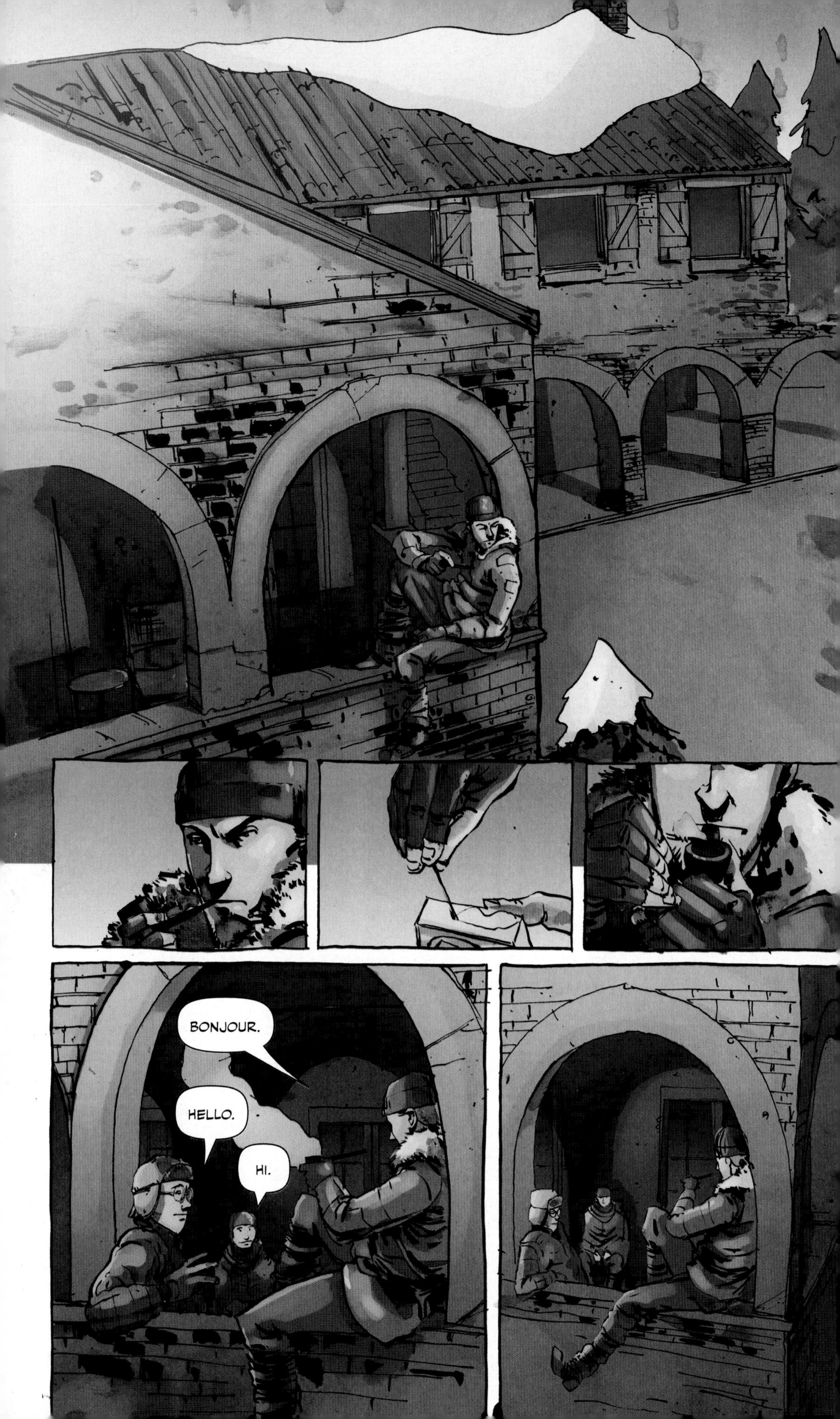
BONJOUR.
HELLO.
HI.

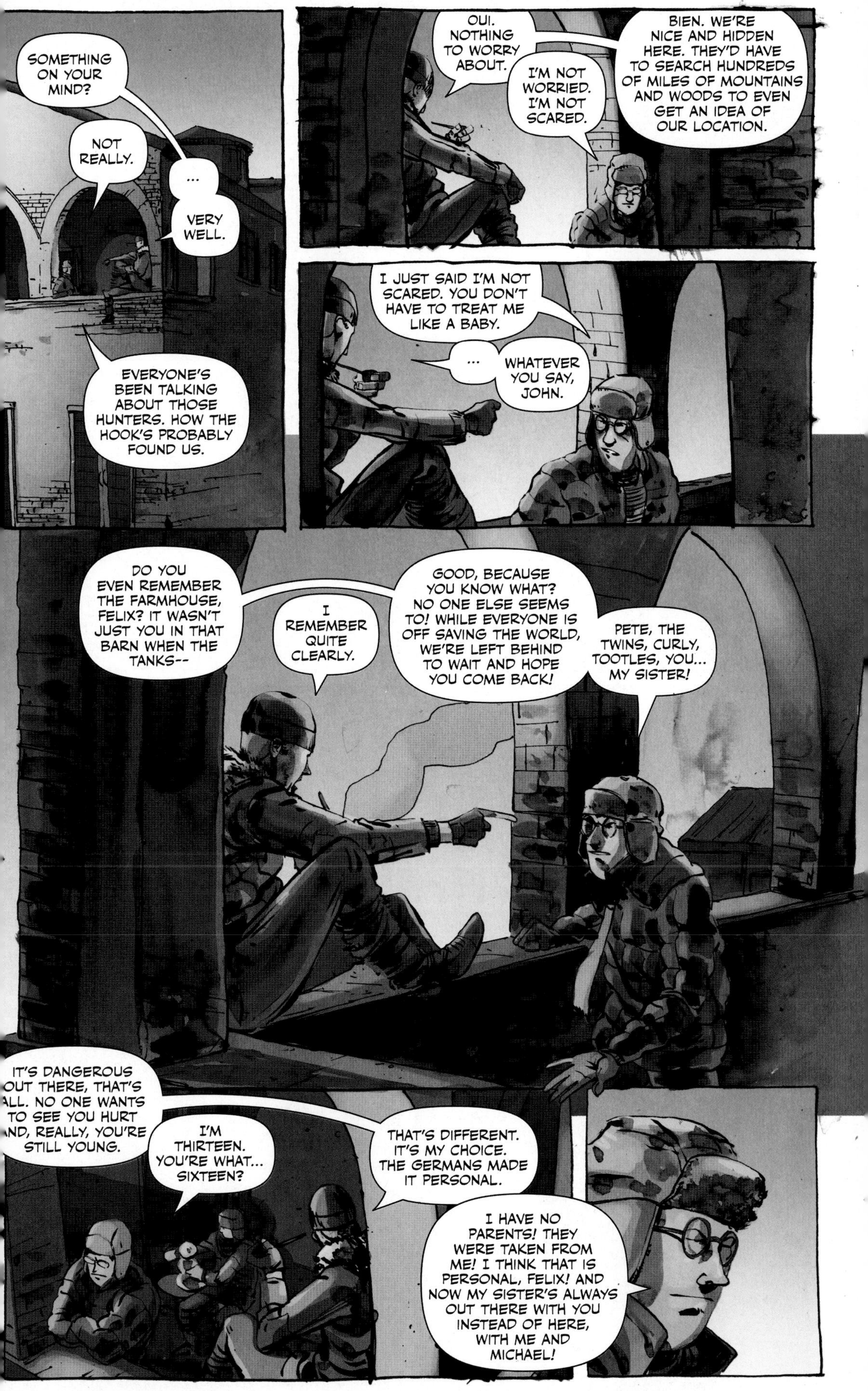
SOMETHING ON YOUR MIND?
NOT REALLY.
...
VERY WELL.
EVERYONE'S BEEN TALKING ABOUT THOSE HUNTERS. HOW THE HOOK'S PROBABLY FOUND US.
OUI. NOTHING TO WORRY ABOUT.
BIEN. WE'RE NICE AND HIDDEN HERE. THEY'D HAVE TO SEARCH HUNDREDS OF MILES OF MOUNTAINS AND WOODS TO EVEN GET AN IDEA OF OUR LOCATION.
I'M NOT WORRIED. I'M NOT SCARED.
I JUST SAID I'M NOT SCARED. YOU DON'T HAVE TO TREAT ME LIKE A BABY.
...
WHATEVER YOU SAY, JOHN.
DO YOU EVEN REMEMBER THE FARMHOUSE, FELIX? IT WASN'T JUST YOU IN THAT BARN WHEN THE TANKS--
I REMEMBER QUITE CLEARLY.
GOOD, BECAUSE YOU KNOW WHAT? NO ONE ELSE SEEMS TO! WHILE EVERYONE IS OFF SAVING THE WORLD, WE'RE LEFT BEHIND TO WAIT AND HOPE YOU COME BACK!
PETE, THE TWINS, CURLY, TOOTLES, YOU... MY SISTER!
IT'S DANGEROUS OUT THERE, THAT'S ALL. NO ONE WANTS TO SEE YOU HURT AND, REALLY, YOU'RE STILL YOUNG.
I'M THIRTEEN. YOU'RE WHAT... SIXTEEN?
THAT'S DIFFERENT. IT'S MY CHOICE. THE GERMANS MADE IT PERSONAL.
I HAVE NO PARENTS! THEY WERE TAKEN FROM ME! I THINK THAT IS PERSONAL, FELIX! AND NOW MY SISTER'S ALWAYS OUT THERE WITH YOU INSTEAD OF HERE, WITH ME AND MICHAEL!

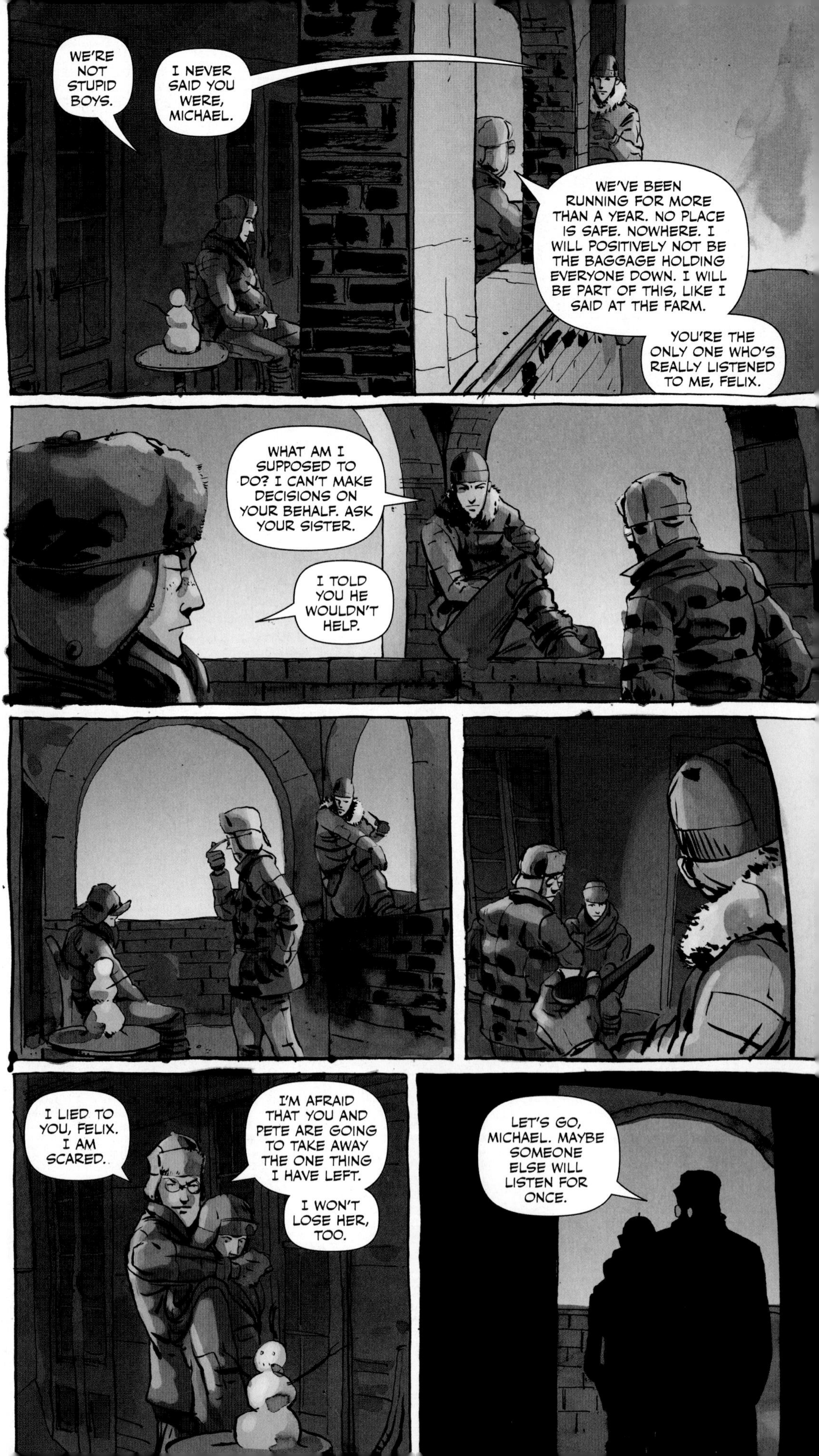
WE'RE NOT STUPID BOYS.
I NEVER SAID YOU WERE, MICHAEL.
WE'VE BEEN RUNNING FOR MORE THAN A YEAR. NO PLACE IS SAFE. NOWHERE. I WILL POSITIVELY NOT BE THE BAGGAGE HOLDING EVERYONE DOWN. I WILL BE PART OF THIS, LIKE I SAID AT THE FARM.
YOU'RE THE ONLY ONE WHO'S REALLY LISTENED TO ME, FELIX.
WHAT AM I SUPPOSED TO DO? I CAN'T MAKE DECISIONS ON YOUR BEHALF. ASK YOUR SISTER.
I TOLD YOU HE WOULDN'T HELP.
I LIED TO YOU, FELIX. I AM SCARED.
I'M AFRAID THAT YOU AND PETE ARE GOING TO TAKE AWAY THE ONE THING I HAVE LEFT.
I WON'T LOSE HER, TOO.
LET'S GO, MICHAEL. MAYBE SOMEONE ELSE WILL LISTEN FOR ONCE.

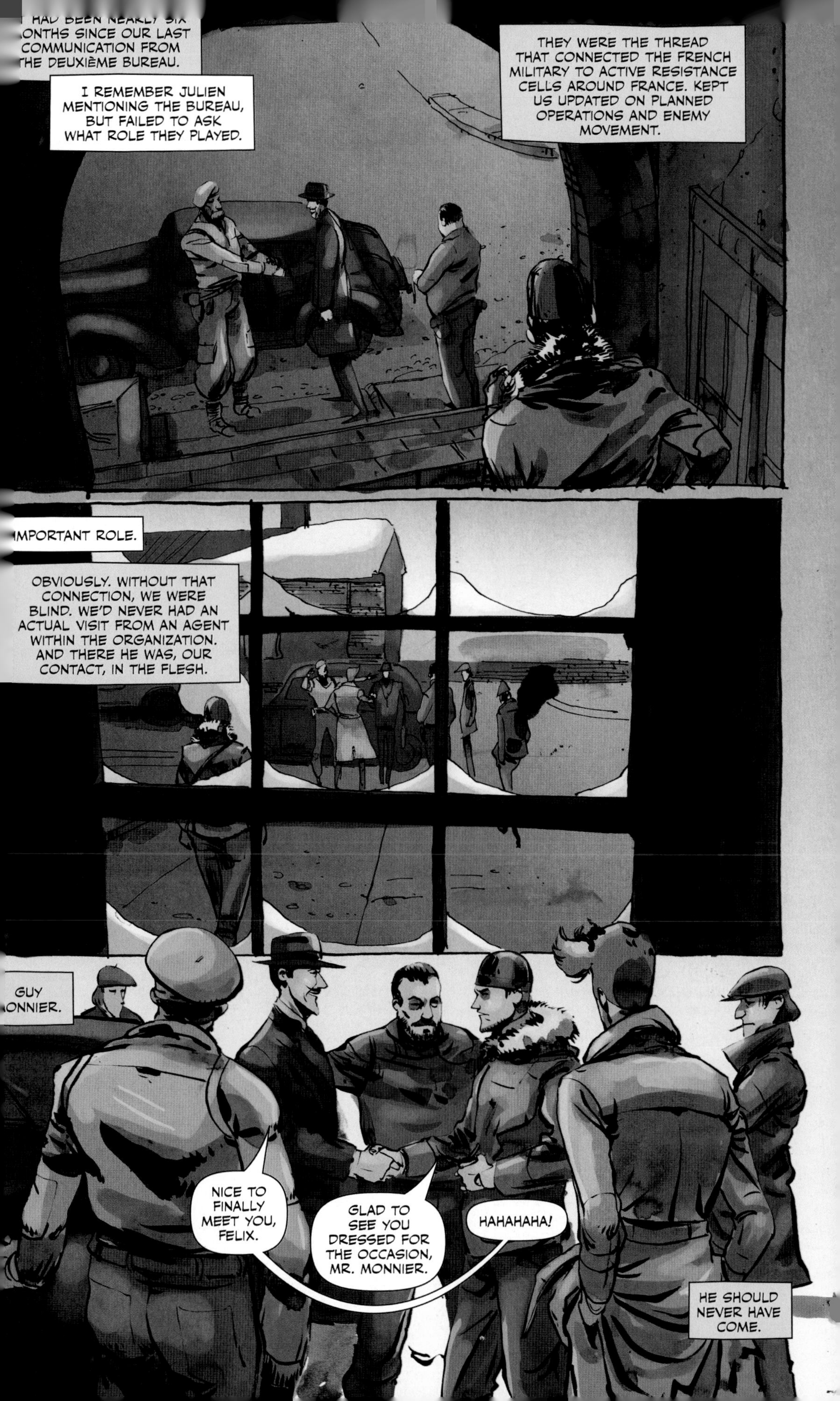

T HAD BEEN NEARLY SIX
ONTHS SINCE OUR LAST
COMMUNICATION FROM
THE DEUXIÈME BUREAU.
I REMEMBER JULIEN MENTIONING THE BUREAU, BUT FAILED TO ASK WHAT ROLE THEY PLAYED.
THEY WERE THE THREAD THAT CONNECTED THE FRENCH MILITARY TO ACTIVE RESISTANCE CELLS AROUND FRANCE. KEPT US UPDATED ON PLANNED OPERATIONS AND ENEMY MOVEMENT.
MPORTANT ROLE.
OBVIOUSLY. WITHOUT THAT CONNECTION, WE WERE BLIND. WE'D NEVER HAD AN ACTUAL VISIT FROM AN AGENT WITHIN THE ORGANIZATION. AND THERE HE WAS, OUR CONTACT, IN THE FLESH.
GUY
ONNIER.
NICE TO FINALLY MEET YOU, FELIX.
GLAD TO SEE YOU DRESSED FOR THE OCCASION, MR. MONNIER.
HAHAHAHA!
HE SHOULD NEVER HAVE COME.

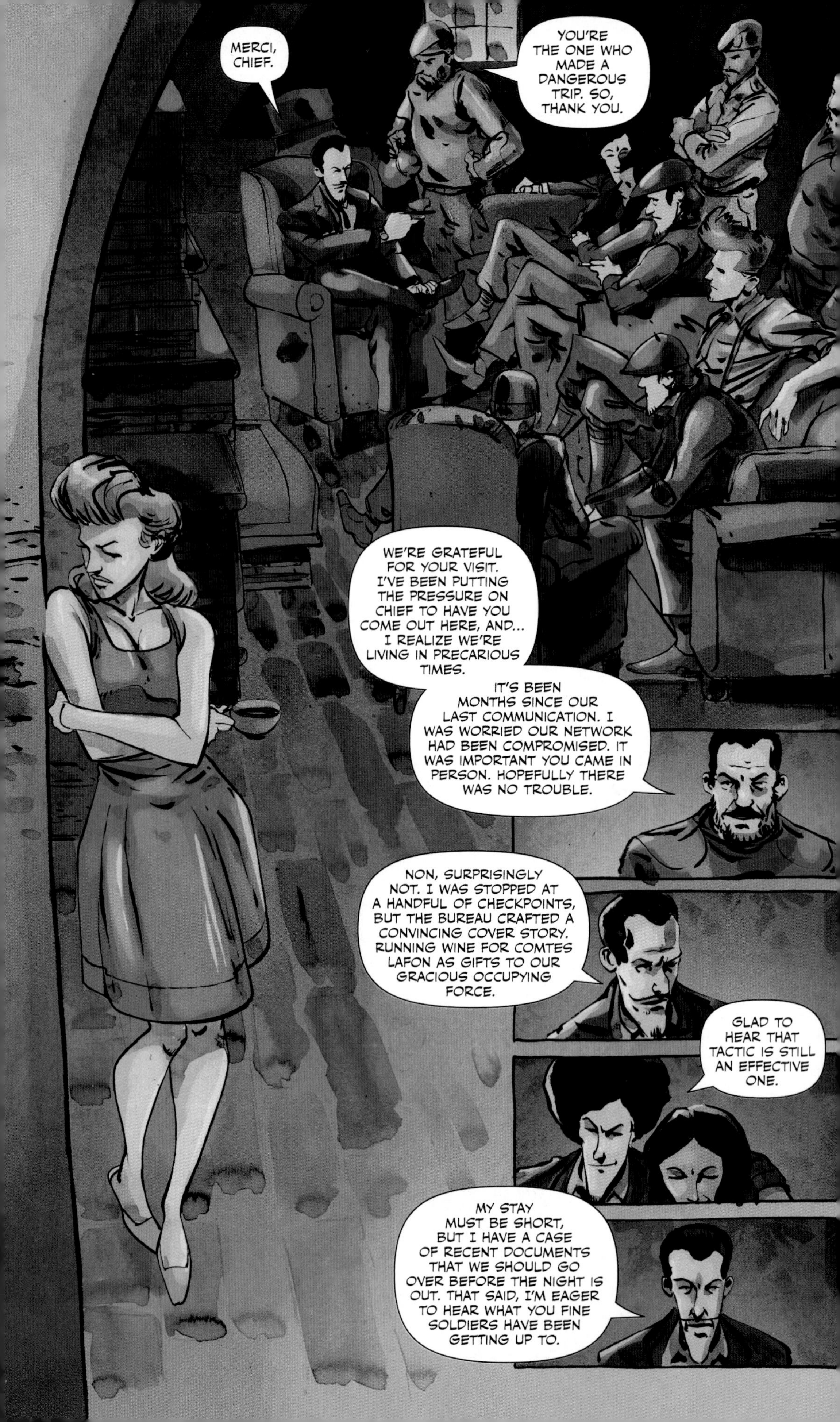
MERCI, CHIEF.
YOU'RE THE ONE WHO MADE A DANGEROUS TRIP. SO, THANK YOU.
WE'RE GRATEFUL FOR YOUR VISIT. I'VE BEEN PUTTING THE PRESSURE ON CHIEF TO HAVE YOU COME OUT HERE, AND... I REALIZE WE'RE LIVING IN PRECARIOUS TIMES.
IT'S BEEN MONTHS SINCE OUR LAST COMMUNICATION. I WAS WORRIED OUR NETWORK HAD BEEN COMPROMISED. IT WAS IMPORTANT YOU CAME IN PERSON. HOPEFULLY THERE WAS NO TROUBLE.
NON, SURPRISINGLY NOT. I WAS STOPPED AT A HANDFUL OF CHECKPOINTS, BUT THE BUREAU CRAFTED A CONVINCING COVER STORY. RUNNING WINE FOR COMTES LAFON AS GIFTS TO OUR GRACIOUS OCCUPYING FORCE.
GLAD TO HEAR THAT TACTIC IS STILL AN EFFECTIVE ONE.
MY STAY MUST BE SHORT, BUT I HAVE A CASE OF RECENT DOCUMENTS THAT WE SHOULD GO OVER BEFORE THE NIGHT IS OUT. THAT SAID, I'M EAGER TO HEAR WHAT YOU FINE SOLDIERS HAVE BEEN GETTING UP TO.

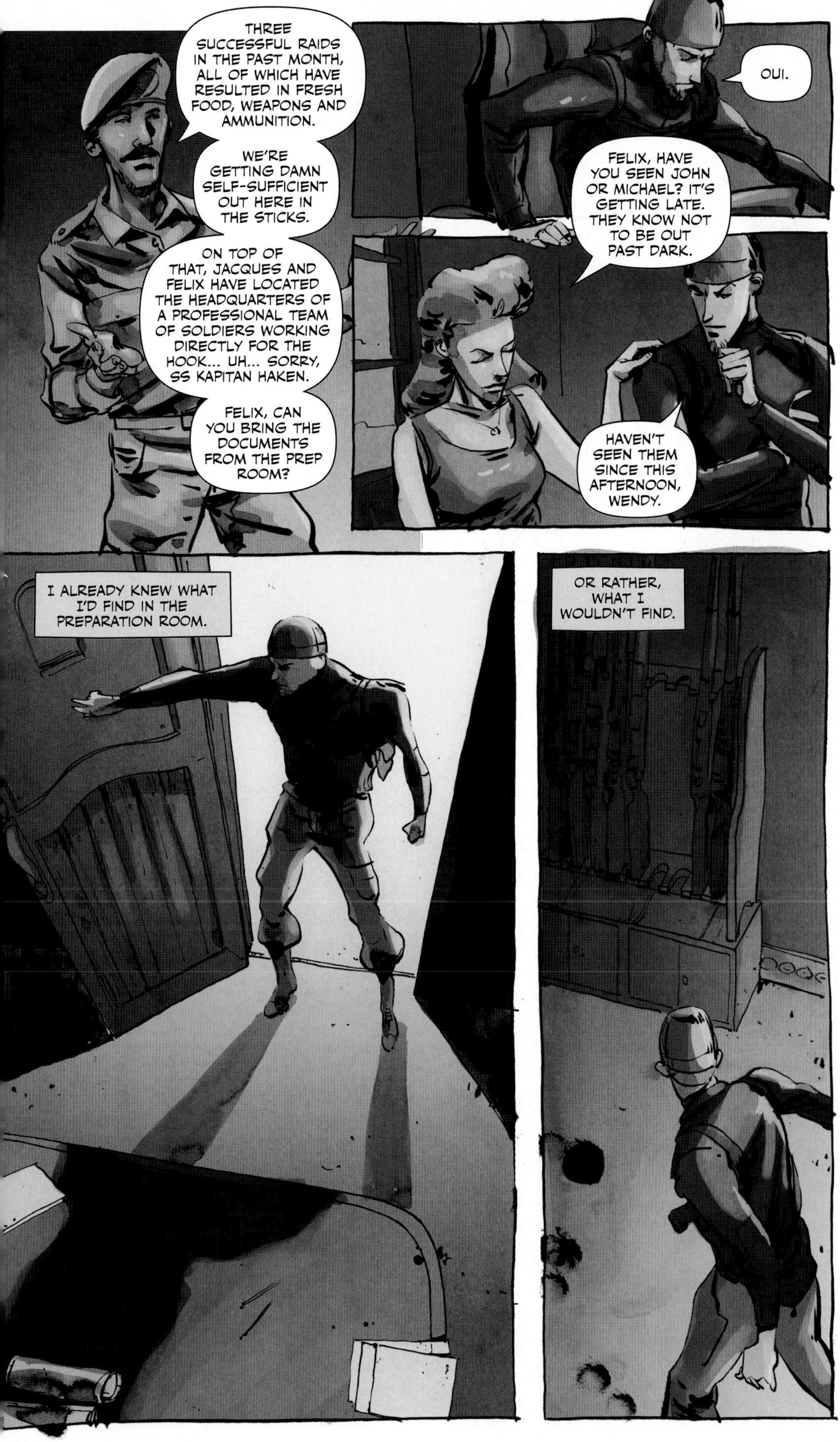
THREE SUCCESSFUL RAIDS IN THE PAST MONTH, ALL OF WHICH HAVE RESULTED IN FRESH FOOD, WEAPONS AND AMMUNITION.
WE'RE GETTING DAMN SELF-SUFFICIENT OUT HERE IN THE STICKS.
ON TOP OF THAT, JACQUES AND FELIX HAVE LOCATED THE HEADQUARTERS OF A PROFESSIONAL TEAM OF SOLDIERS WORKING DIRECTLY FOR THE HOOK... UH... SORRY, SS KAPITAN HAKEN.
FELIX, CAN YOU BRING THE DOCUMENTS FROM THE PREP ROOM?
OUI.
FELIX, HAVE YOU SEEN JOHN OR MICHAEL? IT'S GETTING LATE. THEY KNOW NOT TO BE OUT PAST DARK.
HAVEN'T SEEN THEM SINCE THIS AFTERNOON, WENDY.
I ALREADY KNEW WHAT I'D FIND IN THE PREPARATION ROOM.
OR RATHER, WHAT I WOULDN'T FIND.

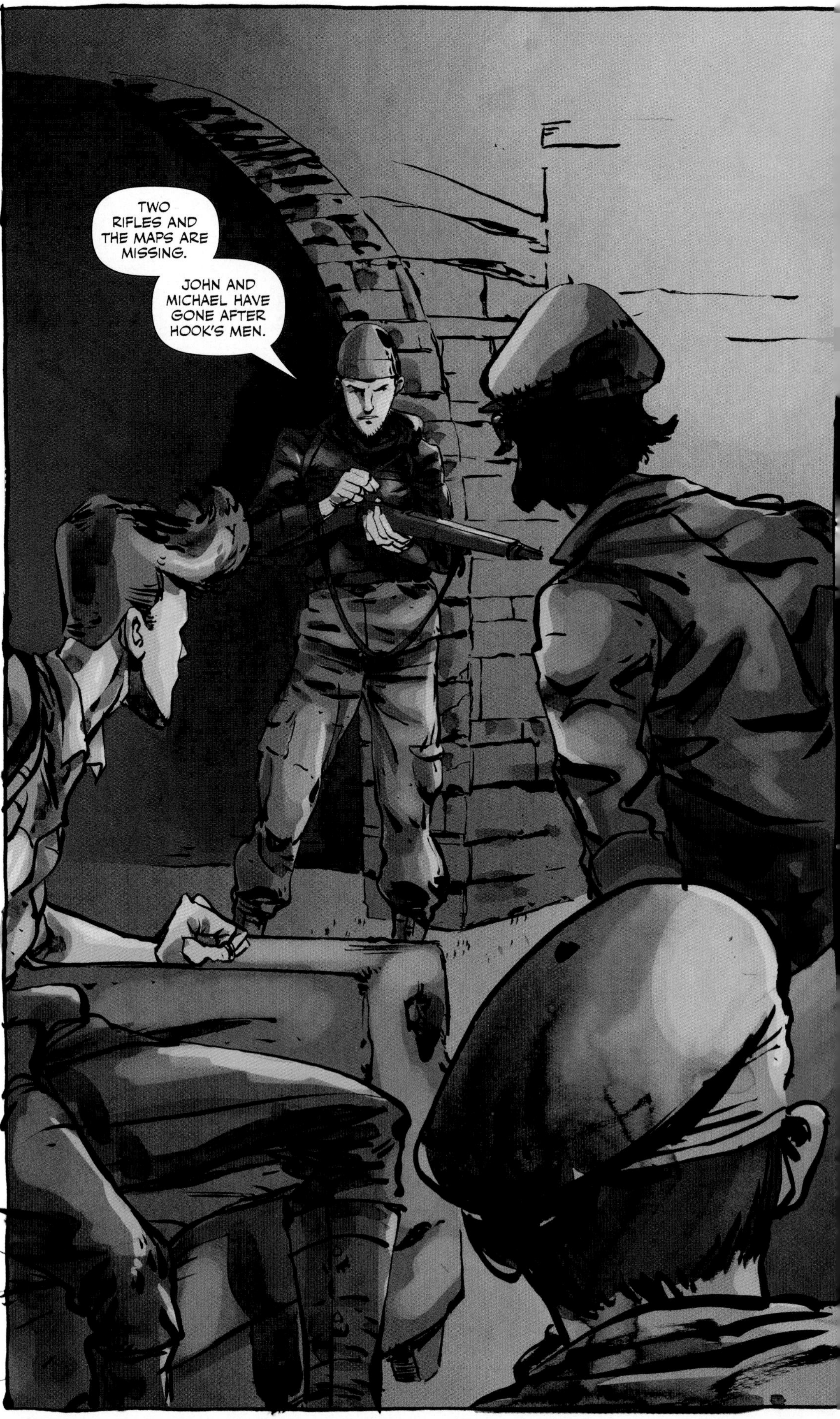
TWO RIFLES AND THE MAPS ARE MISSING.
JOHN AND MICHAEL HAVE GONE AFTER HOOK'S MEN.

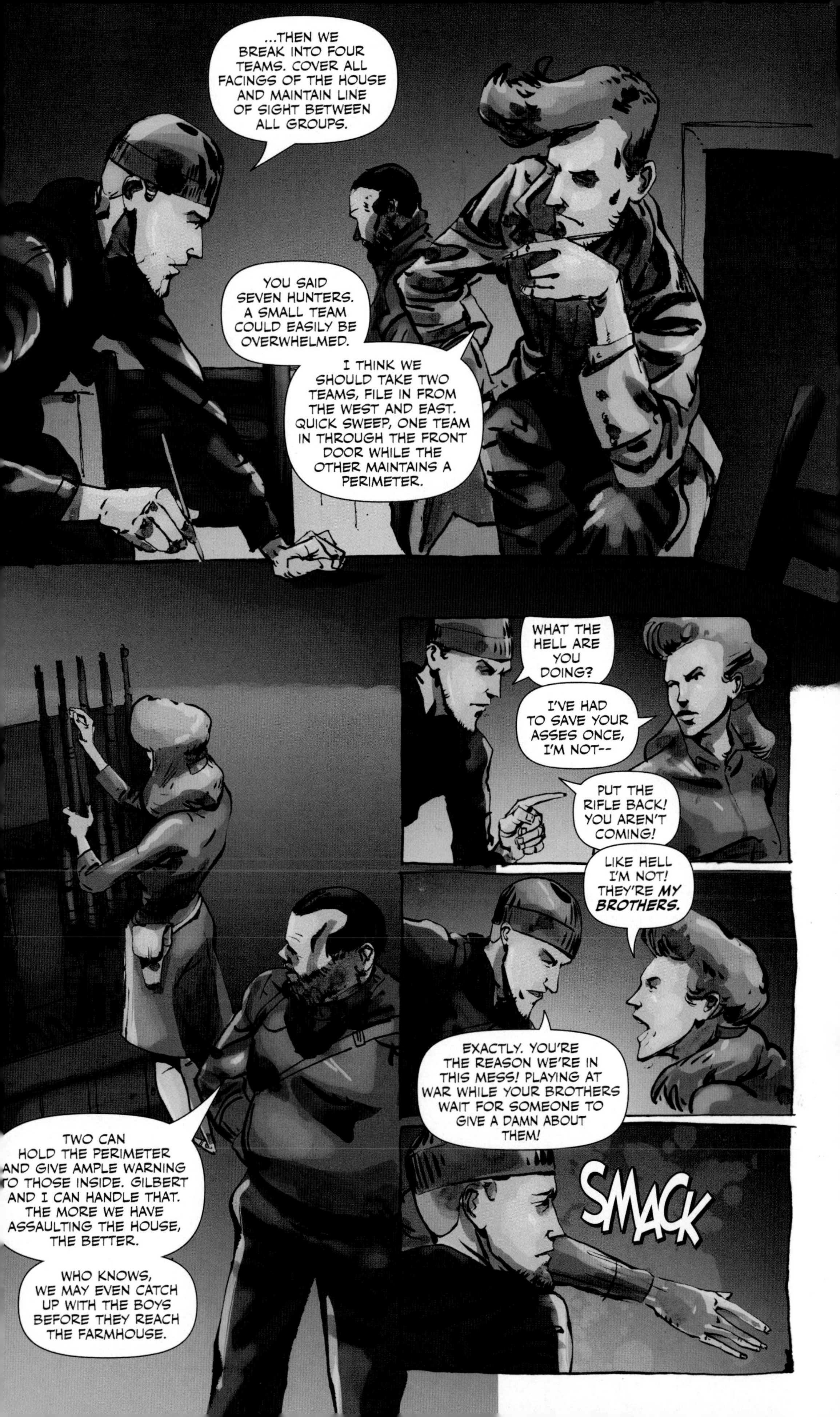
...THEN WE BREAK INTO FOUR TEAMS. COVER ALL FACINGS OF THE HOUSE AND MAINTAIN LINE OF SIGHT BETWEEN ALL GROUPS.
YOU SAID SEVEN HUNTERS. A SMALL TEAM COULD EASILY BE OVERWHELMED.
I THINK WE SHOULD TAKE TWO TEAMS, FILE IN FROM THE WEST AND EAST. QUICK SWEEP, ONE TEAM IN THROUGH THE FRONT DOOR WHILE THE OTHER MAINTAINS A PERIMETER.
TWO CAN HOLD THE PERIMETER AND GIVE AMPLE WARNING TO THOSE INSIDE. GILBERT AND I CAN HANDLE THAT. THE MORE WE HAVE ASSAULTING THE HOUSE, THE BETTER.
WHO KNOWS, WE MAY EVEN CATCH UP WITH THE BOYS BEFORE THEY REACH THE FARMHOUSE.
WHAT THE HELL ARE YOU DOING?
I'VE HAD TO SAVE YOUR ASSES ONCE, I'M NOT--
PUT THE RIFLE BACK! YOU AREN'T COMING!
LIKE HELL I'M NOT! THEY'RE *MY BROTHERS.*
EXACTLY. YOU'RE THE REASON WE'RE IN THIS MESS! PLAYING AT WAR WHILE YOUR BROTHERS WAIT FOR SOMEONE TO GIVE A DAMN ABOUT THEM!
SMACK

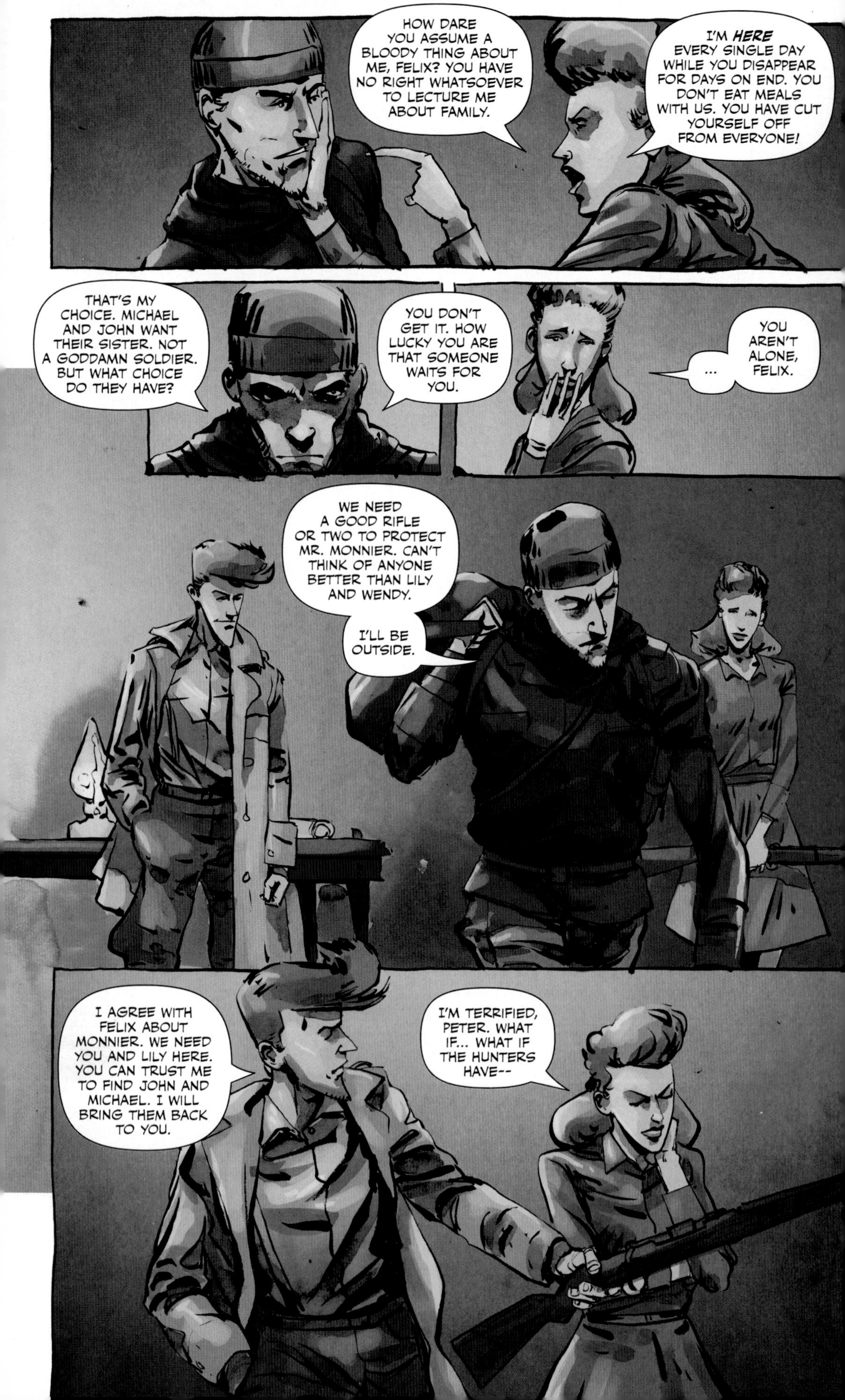
HOW DARE YOU ASSUME A BLOODY THING ABOUT ME, FELIX? YOU HAVE NO RIGHT WHATSOEVER TO LECTURE ME ABOUT FAMILY.
I'M ***HERE*** EVERY SINGLE DAY WHILE YOU DISAPPEAR FOR DAYS ON END. YOU DON'T EAT MEALS WITH US. YOU HAVE CUT YOURSELF OFF FROM EVERYONE!
THAT'S MY CHOICE. MICHAEL AND JOHN WANT THEIR SISTER. NOT A GODDAMN SOLDIER. BUT WHAT CHOICE DO THEY HAVE?
YOU DON'T GET IT. HOW LUCKY YOU ARE THAT SOMEONE WAITS FOR YOU.
...
YOU AREN'T ALONE, FELIX.
WE NEED A GOOD RIFLE OR TWO TO PROTECT MR. MONNIER. CAN'T THINK OF ANYONE BETTER THAN LILY AND WENDY.
I'LL BE OUTSIDE.
I AGREE WITH FELIX ABOUT MONNIER. WE NEED YOU AND LILY HERE. YOU CAN TRUST ME TO FIND JOHN AND MICHAEL. I WILL BRING THEM BACK TO YOU.
I'M TERRIFIED, PETER. WHAT IF... WHAT IF THE HUNTERS HAVE--

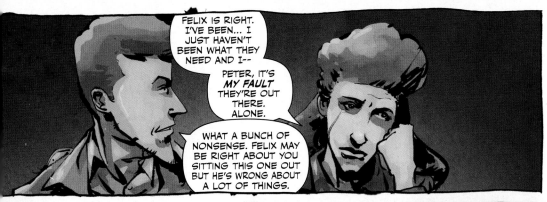

FELIX IS RIGHT. I'VE BEEN... I JUST HAVEN'T BEEN WHAT THEY NEED AND I--

PETER, IT'S *MY FAULT* THEY'RE OUT THERE. ALONE.

WHAT A BUNCH OF NONSENSE. FELIX MAY BE RIGHT ABOUT YOU SITTING THIS ONE OUT BUT HE'S WRONG ABOUT A LOT OF THINGS.

YOU KNOW, SOMETIMES AT NIGHT I CAN HEAR MICHAEL AND JOHN TELLING STORIES TO EACH OTHER FROM ACROSS THE HALL. ONE OF THEIR FAVOURITES IS THE ROOFTOP RESCUE AT FONTAINEBLEAU.

SOMETIMES IT'S THE TRAIN HEIST. SOMETIMES IT'S THE FARMHOUSE ESCAPE.

AND, LIKE WITH ANY STORY, THEY GET MAD AT EACH OTHER AND ARGUE OVER THE DETAILS. BUT THEY ALWAYS, AND I MEAN ALWAYS, AGREE ON THEIR FAVOURITE CHARACTER.

ME!

HAHAHA!

WE'LL ALL BE TOGETHER AGAIN BEFORE YOU KNOW IT. BE SAFE, WENDY DARLING.

BE SAFE, PETER.

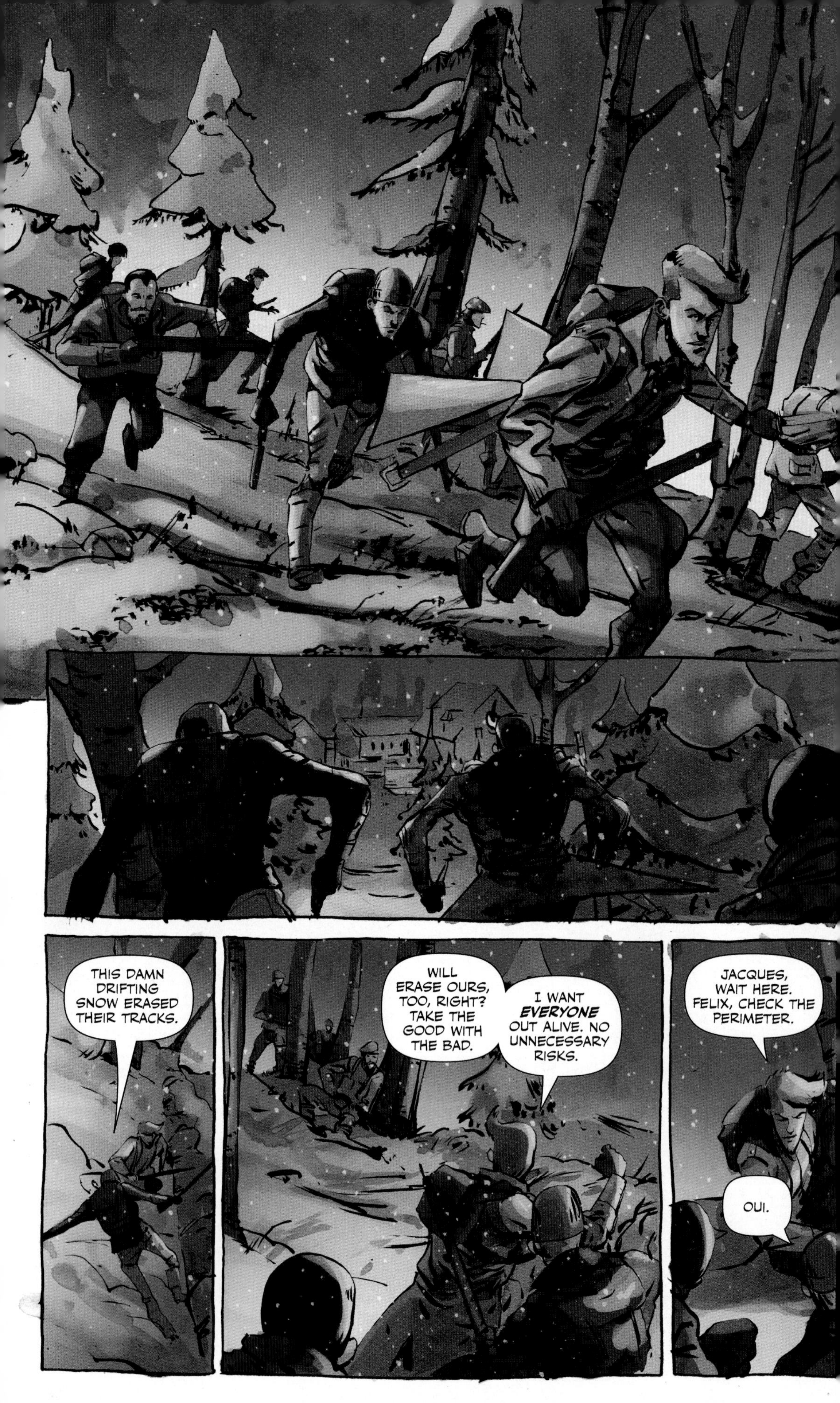
THIS DAMN DRIFTING SNOW ERASED THEIR TRACKS.
WILL ERASE OURS, TOO, RIGHT? TAKE THE GOOD WITH THE BAD.
I WANT EVERYONE OUT ALIVE. NO UNNECESSARY RISKS.
JACQUES, WAIT HERE. FELIX, CHECK THE PERIMETER.
OUI.

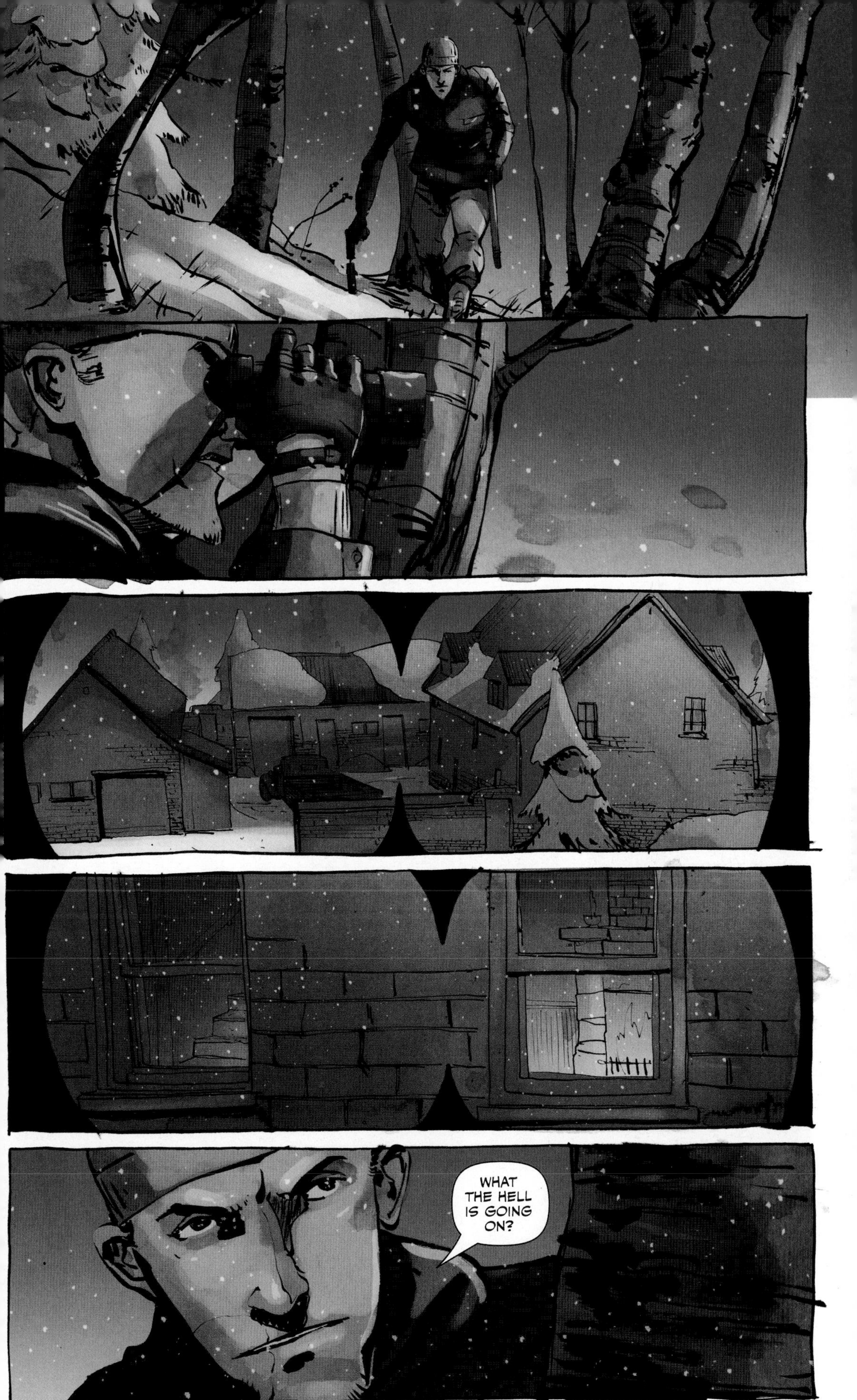
WHAT THE HELL IS GOING ON?

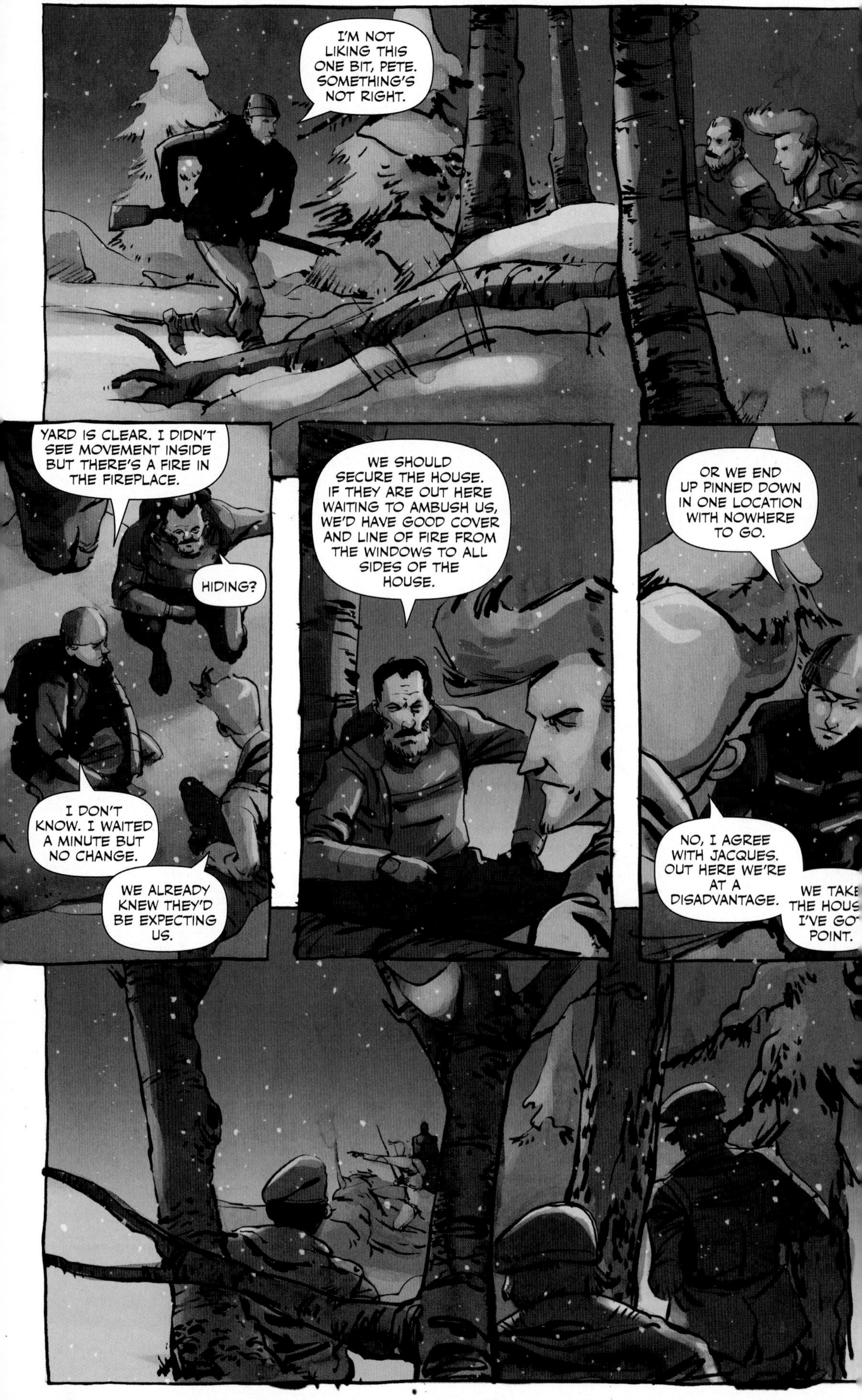
I'M NOT LIKING THIS ONE BIT, PETE. SOMETHING'S NOT RIGHT.
YARD IS CLEAR. I DIDN'T SEE MOVEMENT INSIDE BUT THERE'S A FIRE IN THE FIREPLACE.
HIDING?
I DON'T KNOW. I WAITED A MINUTE BUT NO CHANGE.
WE ALREADY KNEW THEY'D BE EXPECTING US.
WE SHOULD SECURE THE HOUSE. IF THEY ARE OUT HERE WAITING TO AMBUSH US, WE'D HAVE GOOD COVER AND LINE OF FIRE FROM THE WINDOWS TO ALL SIDES OF THE HOUSE.
OR WE END UP PINNED DOWN IN ONE LOCATION WITH NOWHERE TO GO.
NO, I AGREE WITH JACQUES. OUT HERE WE'RE AT A DISADVANTAGE.
WE TAKE THE HOUS I'VE GO POINT.

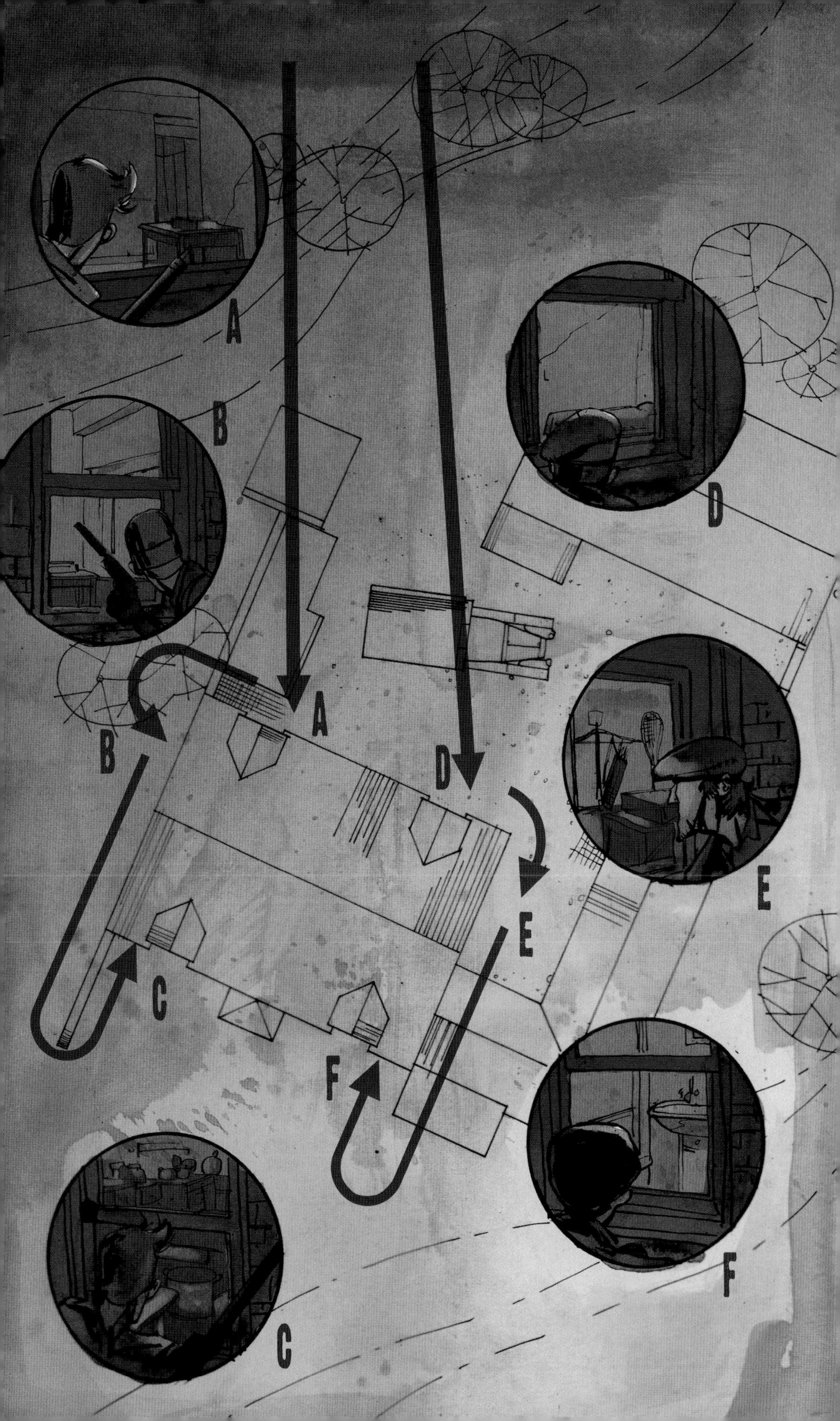
A
B
B
A
D
D
E
C
E
F
F
C

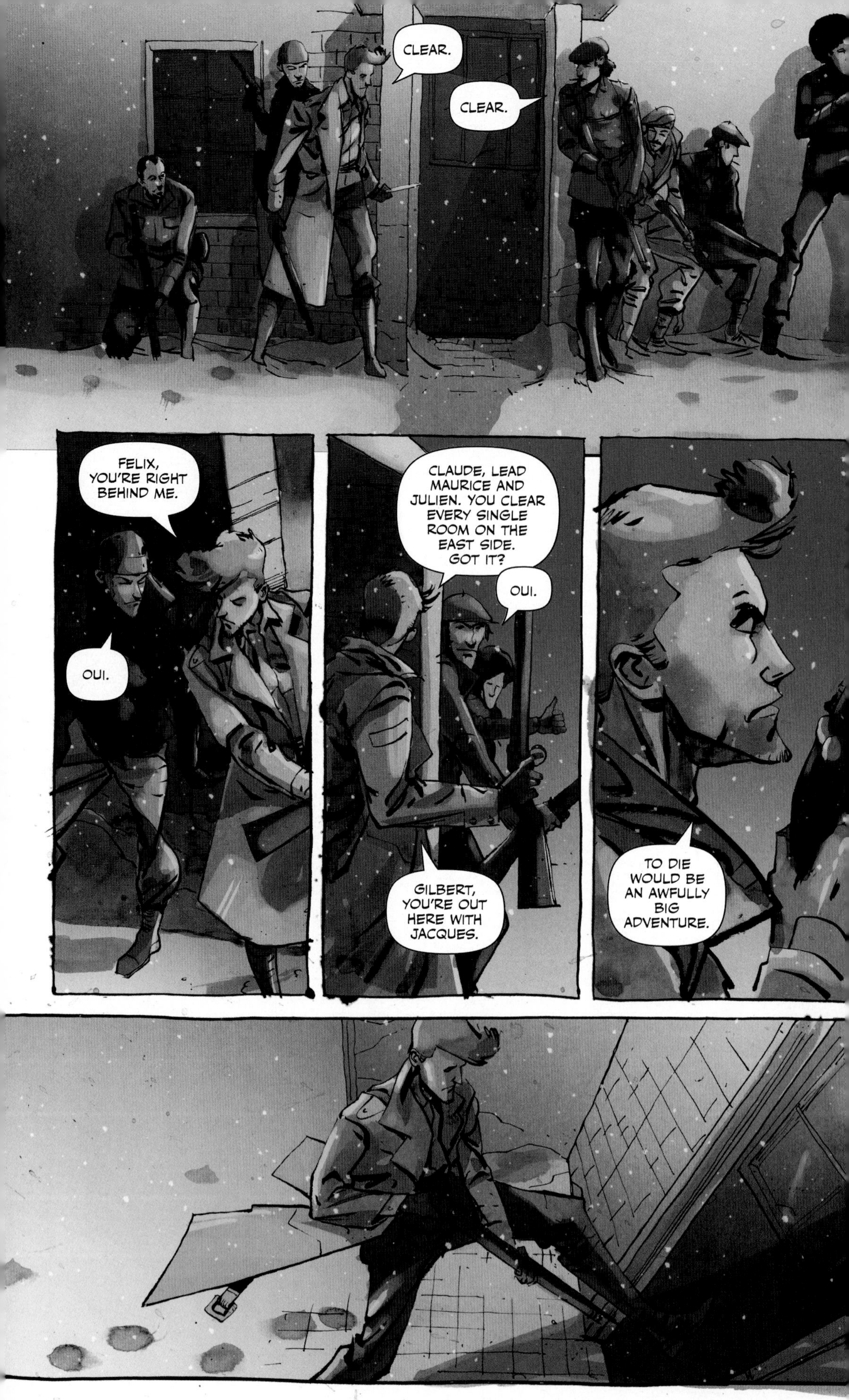

CLEAR.
CLEAR.
FELIX, YOU'RE RIGHT BEHIND ME.
OUI.
CLAUDE, LEAD MAURICE AND JULIEN. YOU CLEAR EVERY SINGLE ROOM ON THE EAST SIDE. GOT IT?
OUI.
GILBERT, YOU'RE OUT HERE WITH JACQUES.
TO DIE WOULD BE AN AWFULLY BIG ADVENTURE.

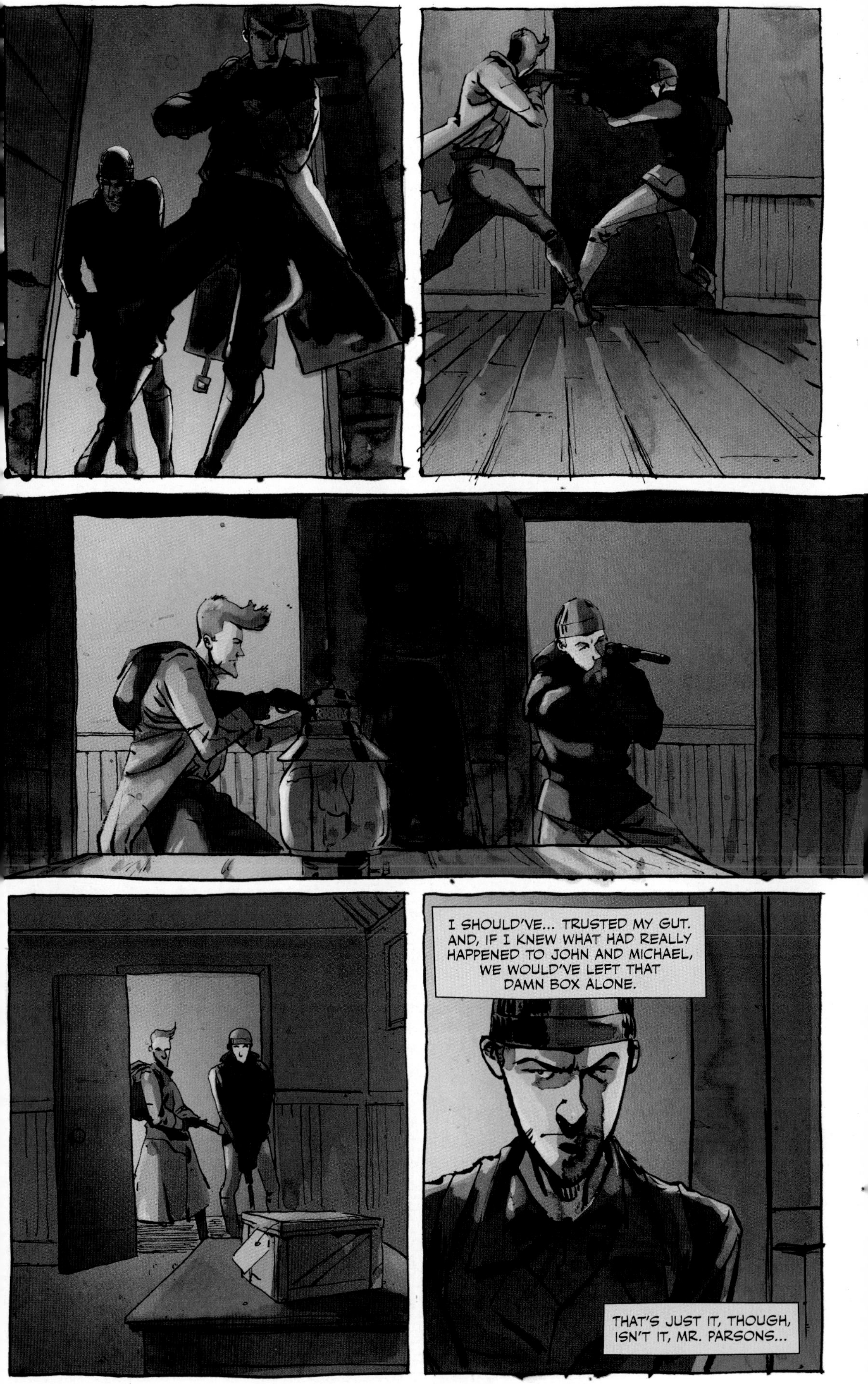
I SHOULD'VE... TRUSTED MY GUT. AND, IF I KNEW WHAT HAD REALLY HAPPENED TO JOHN AND MICHAEL, WE WOULD'VE LEFT THAT DAMN BOX ALONE.
THAT'S JUST IT, THOUGH, ISN'T IT, MR. PARSONS...

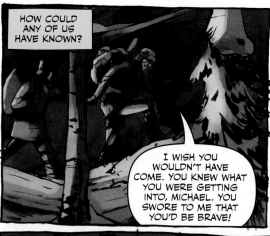

HOW COULD ANY OF US HAVE KNOWN?

I WISH YOU WOULDN'T HAVE COME. YOU KNEW WHAT YOU WERE GETTING INTO, MICHAEL. YOU SWORE TO ME THAT YOU'D BE BRAVE!

THERE, SEE IT?

YES.

YOUR CHOICE, MICHAEL. WHATEVER YOU WANT.

...

IT'S CLOSE. AND I'M COLD.

SORRY, JOHN.

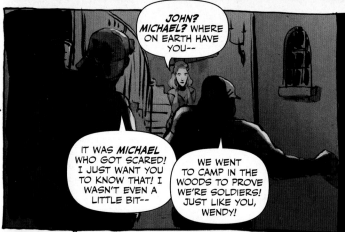

JOHN? MICHAEL? WHERE ON EARTH HAVE YOU--

IT WAS MICHAEL WHO GOT SCARED! I JUST WANT YOU TO KNOW THAT! I WASN'T EVEN A LITTLE BIT--

WE WENT TO CAMP IN THE WOODS TO PROVE WE'RE SOLDIERS! JUST LIKE YOU, WENDY!

OH MY GOD.

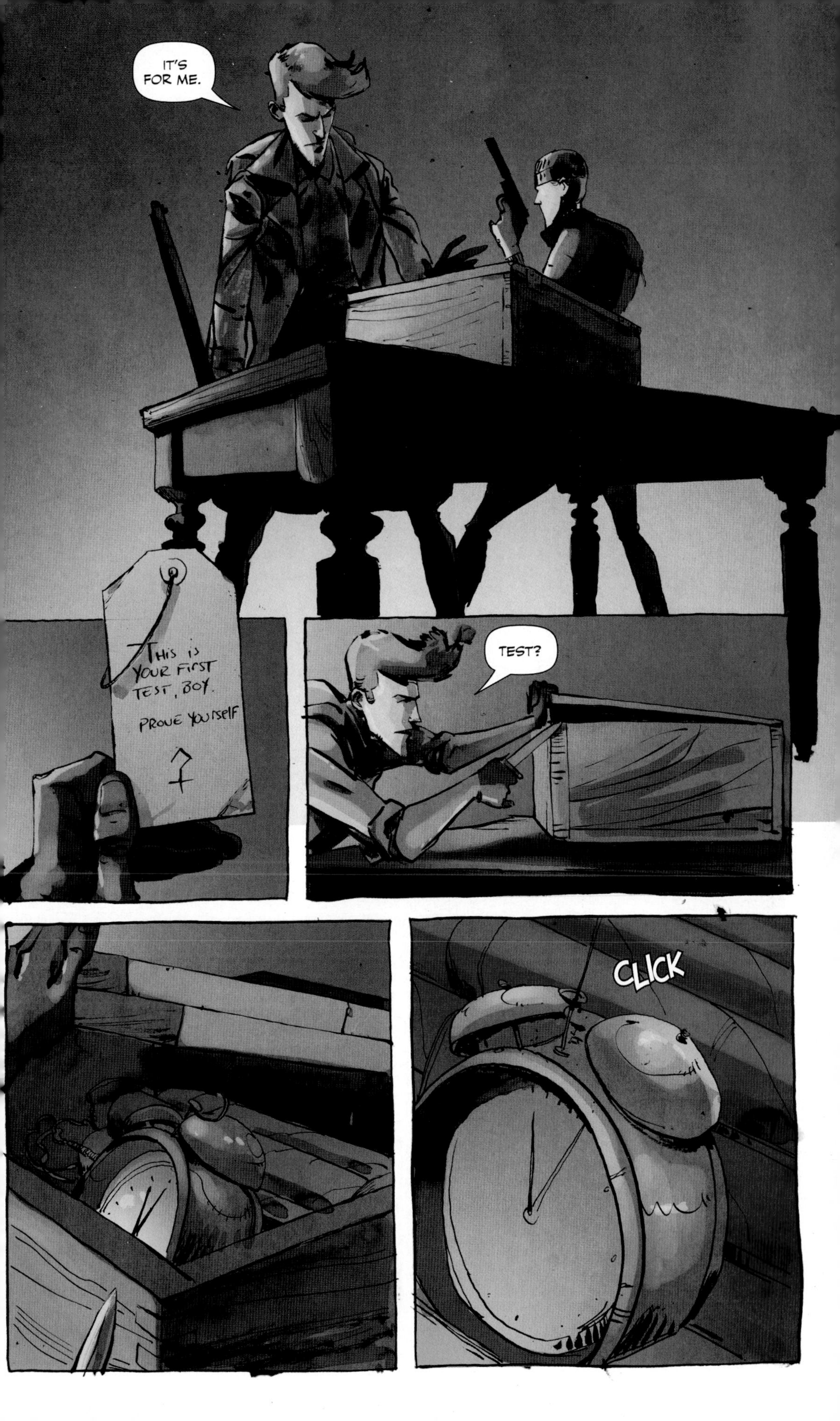
IT'S FOR ME.
THIS IS YOUR FIRST TEST, BOY. PROVE YOURSELF
TEST?
CLICK

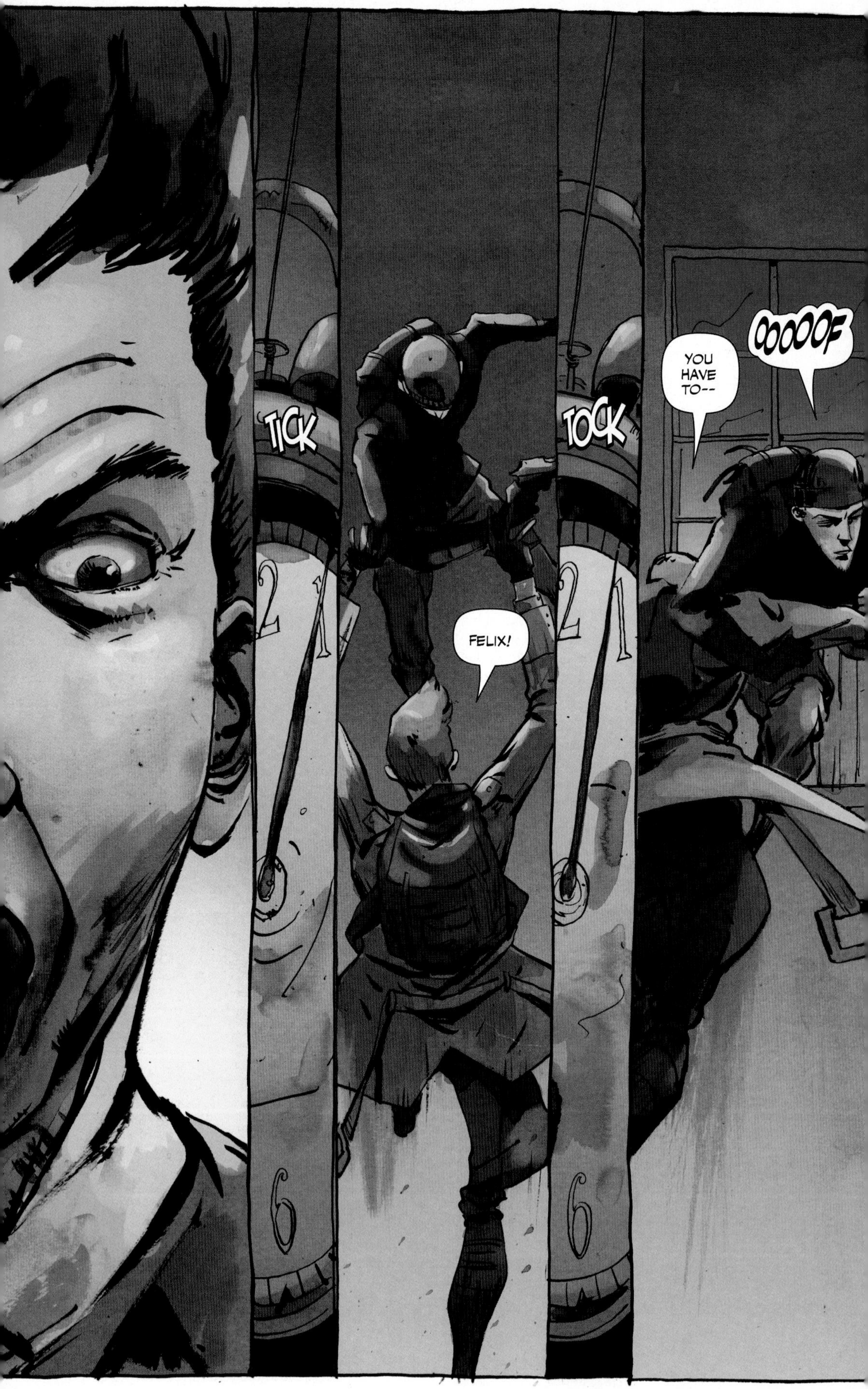
TICK
FELIX!
TOCK
YOU HAVE TO--
OOOOOF

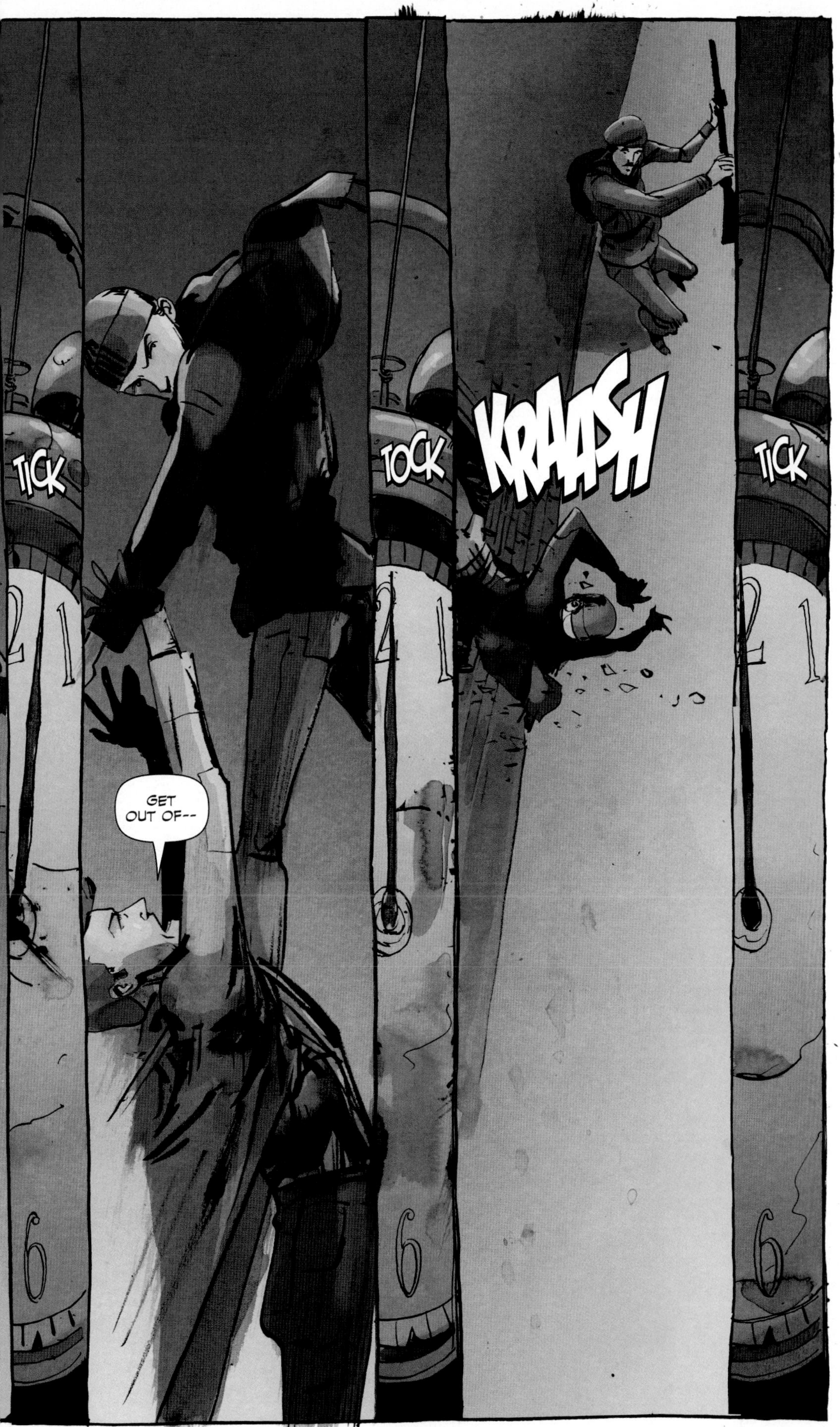
TICK
GET OUT OF--
TOCK
KRAAASH
TICK

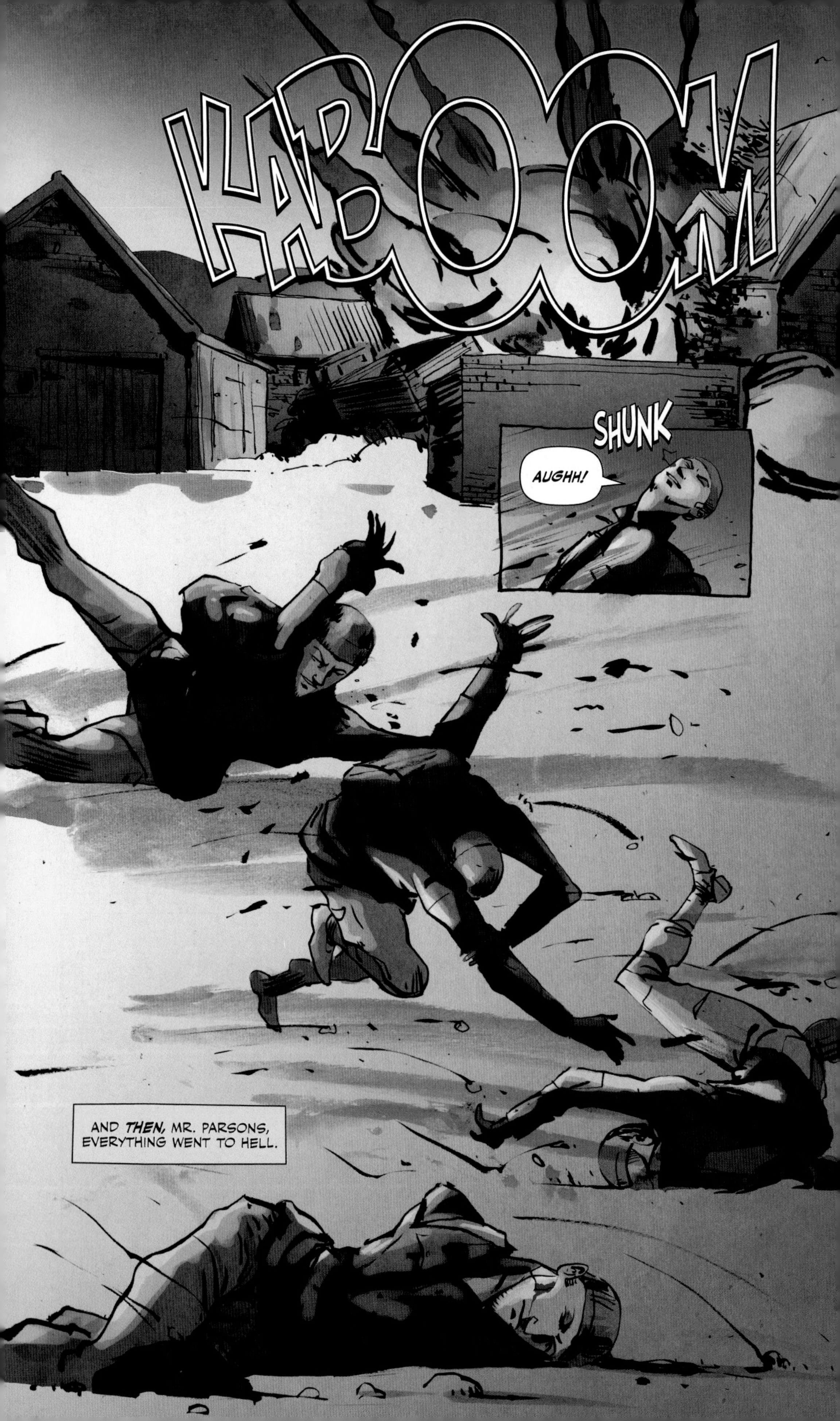
KABOOM
SHUNK
AUGHH!
AND THEN, MR. PARSONS, EVERYTHING WENT TO HELL.

CHAPTER THIRTEEN

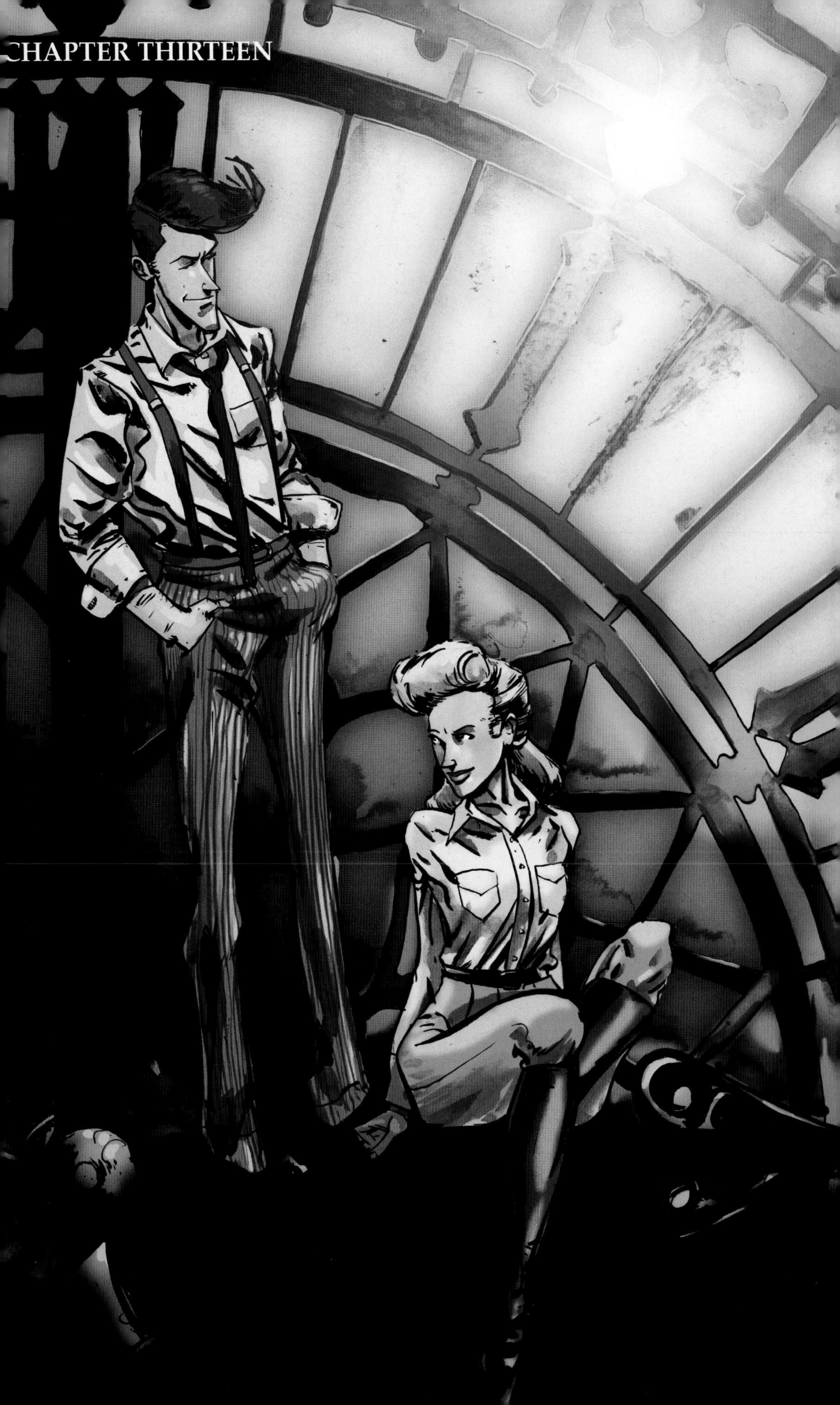

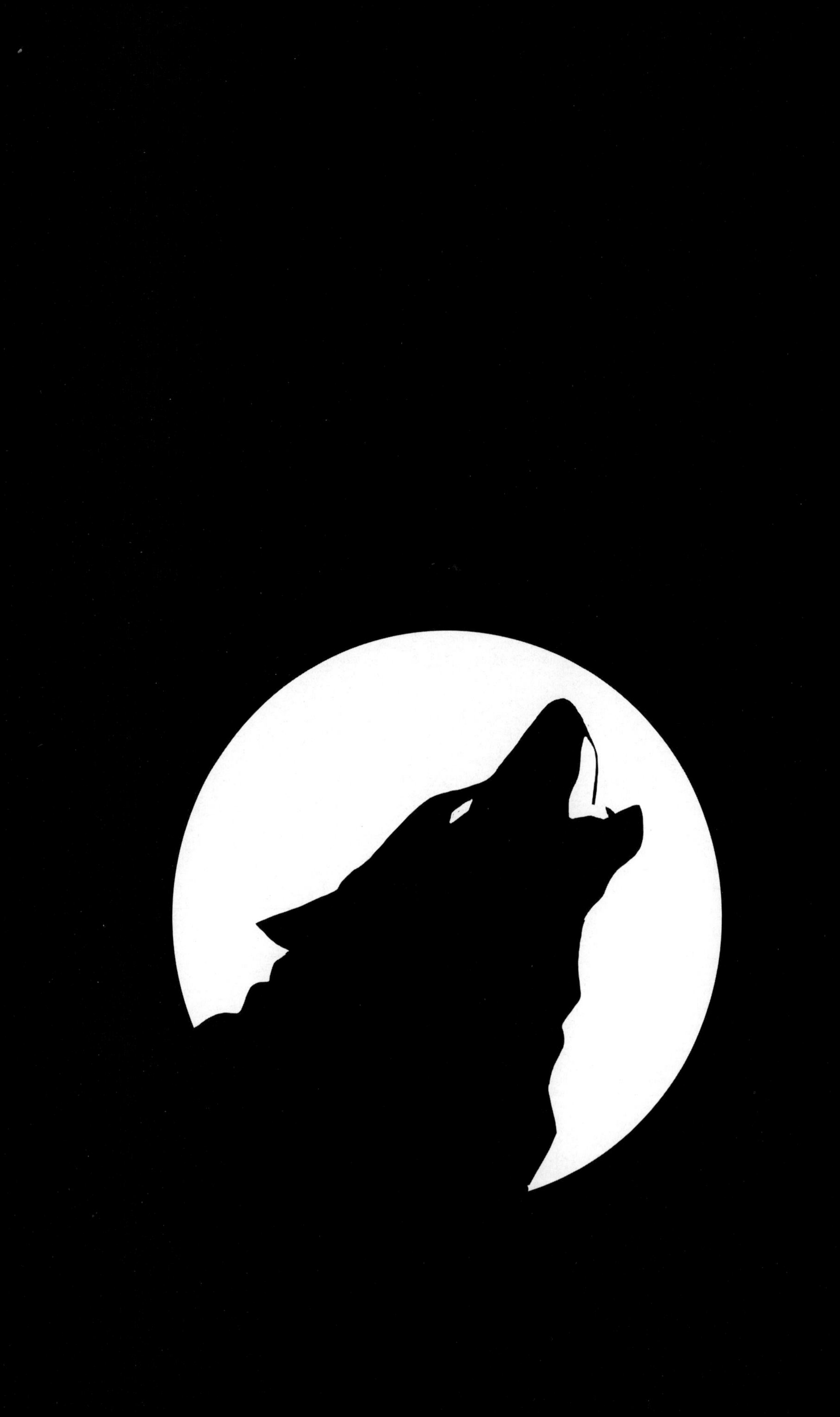

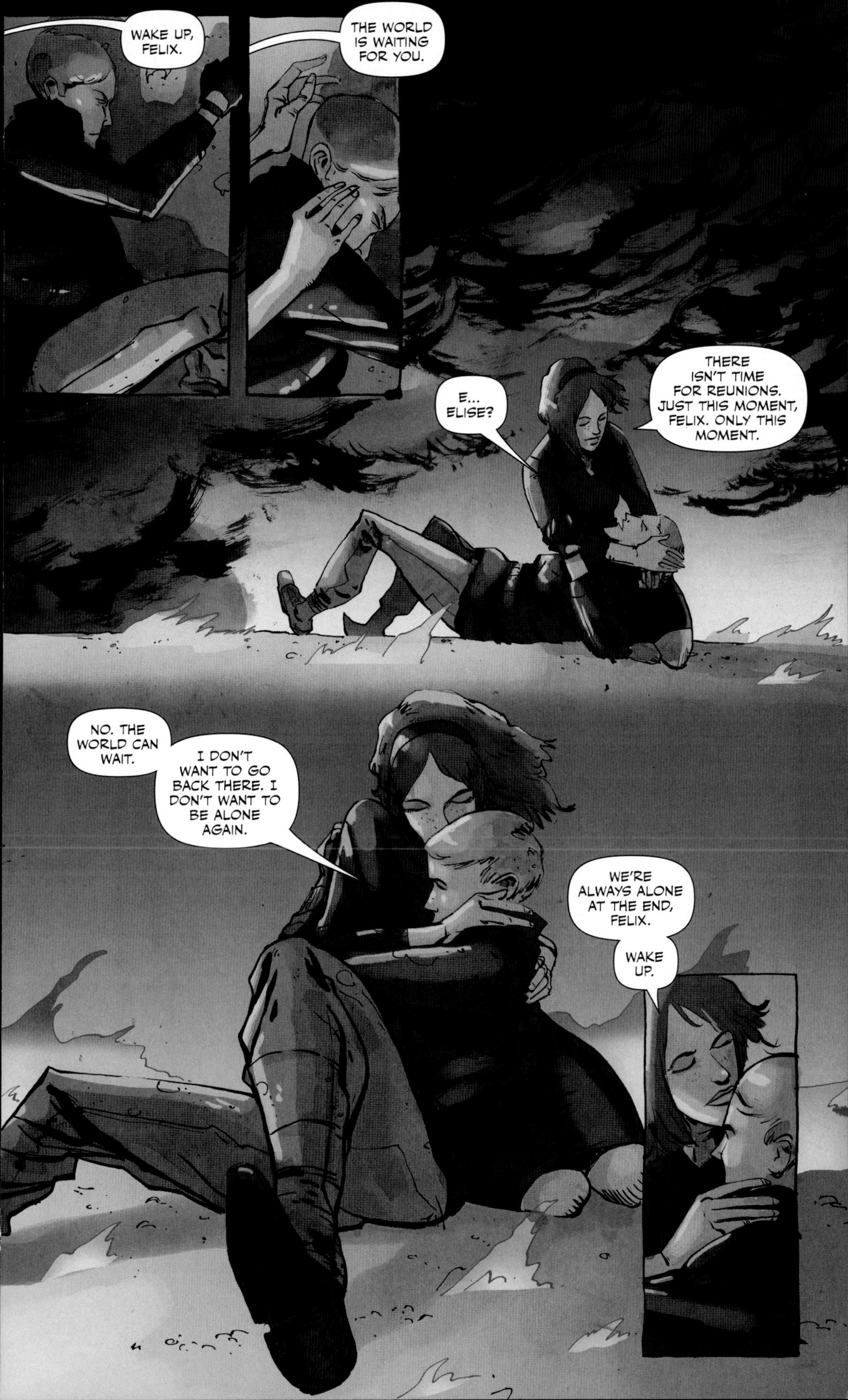
WAKE UP, FELIX.
THE WORLD IS WAITING FOR YOU.
E... ELISE?
THERE ISN'T TIME FOR REUNIONS. JUST THIS MOMENT, FELIX. ONLY THIS MOMENT.
NO. THE WORLD CAN WAIT.
I DON'T WANT TO GO BACK THERE. I DON'T WANT TO BE ALONE AGAIN.
WE'RE ALWAYS ALONE AT THE END, FELIX.
WAKE UP.

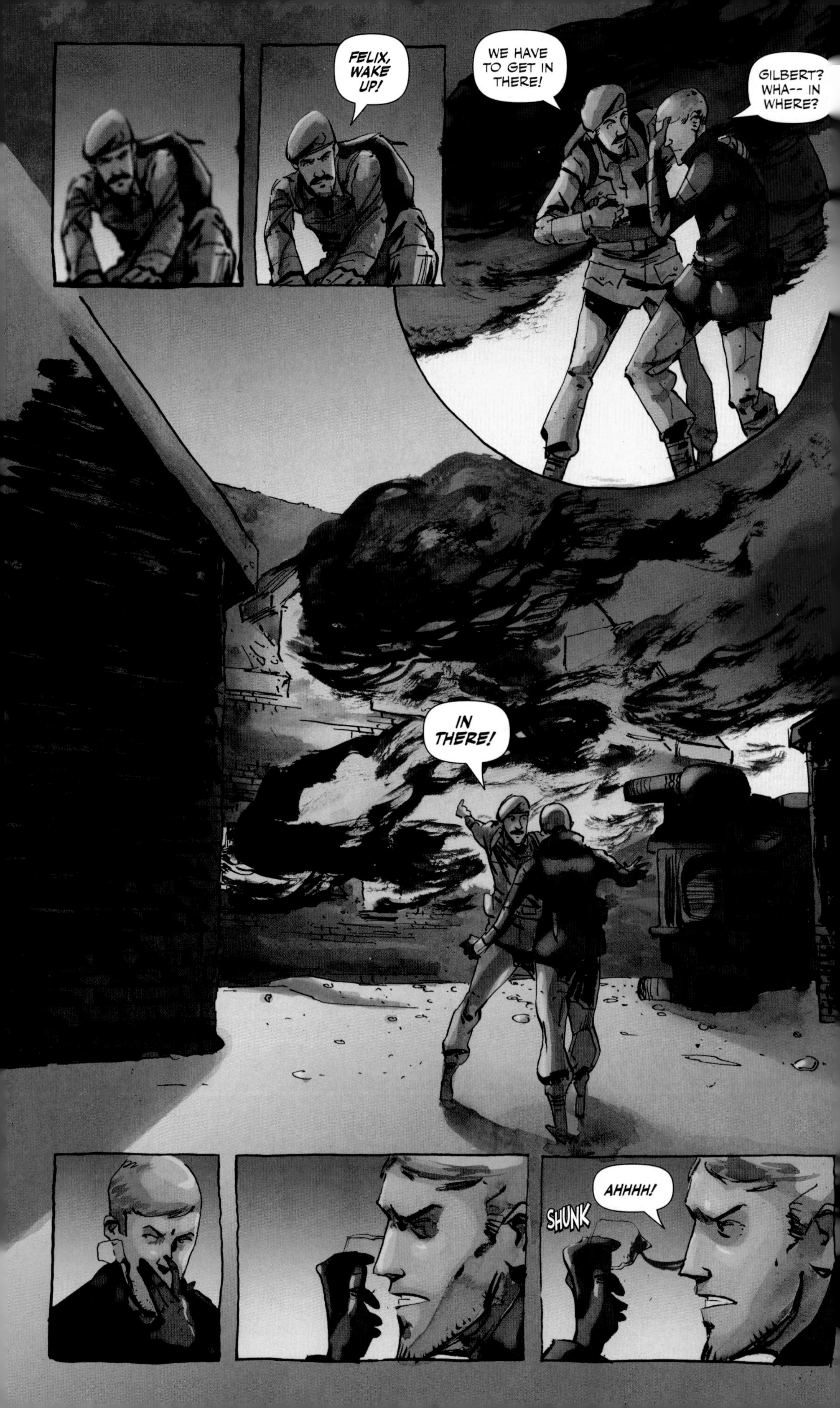
FELIX, WAKE UP!
WE HAVE TO GET IN THERE!
GILBERT? WHA-- IN WHERE?
IN THERE!
SHUNK
AHHHH!

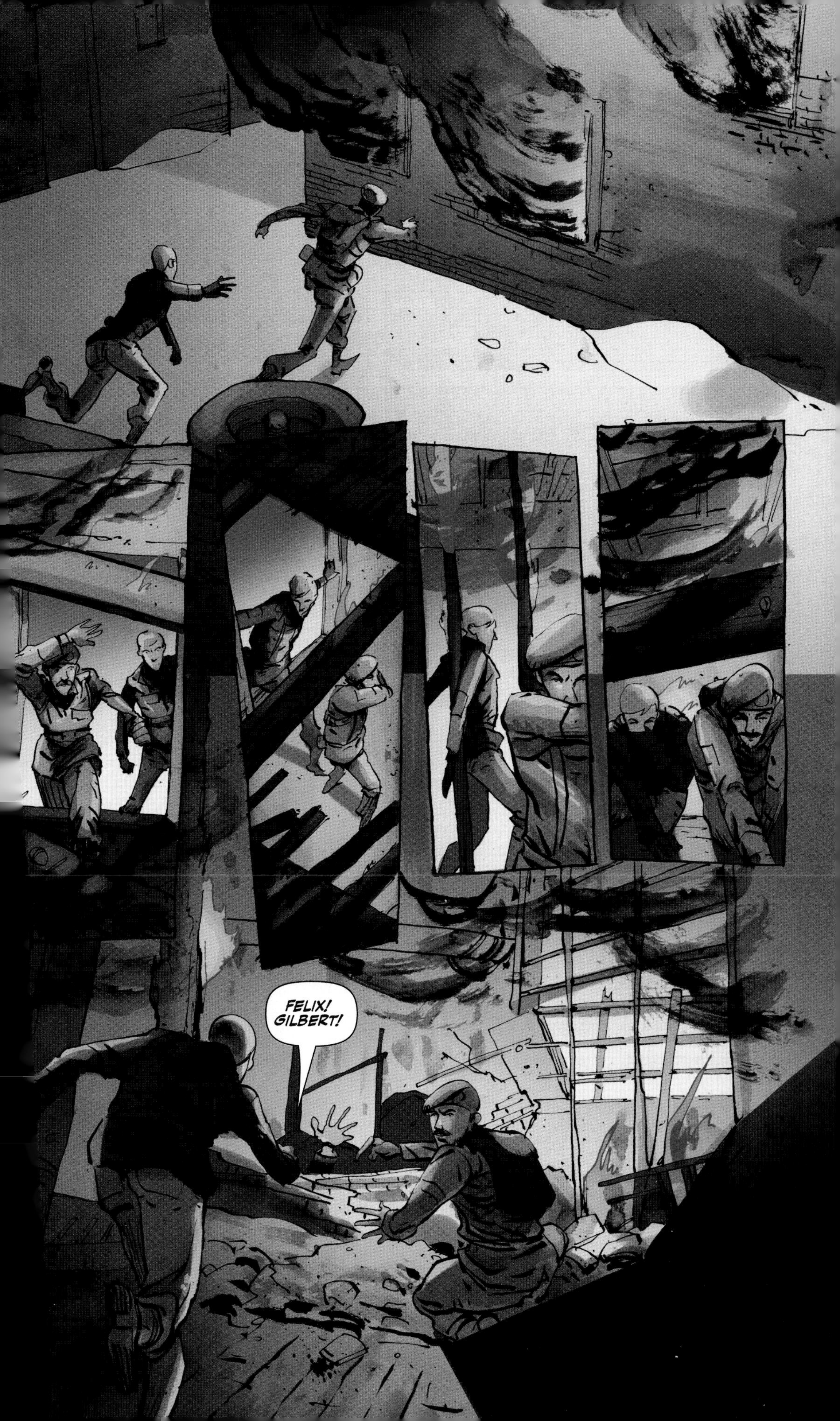
FELIX! GILBERT!

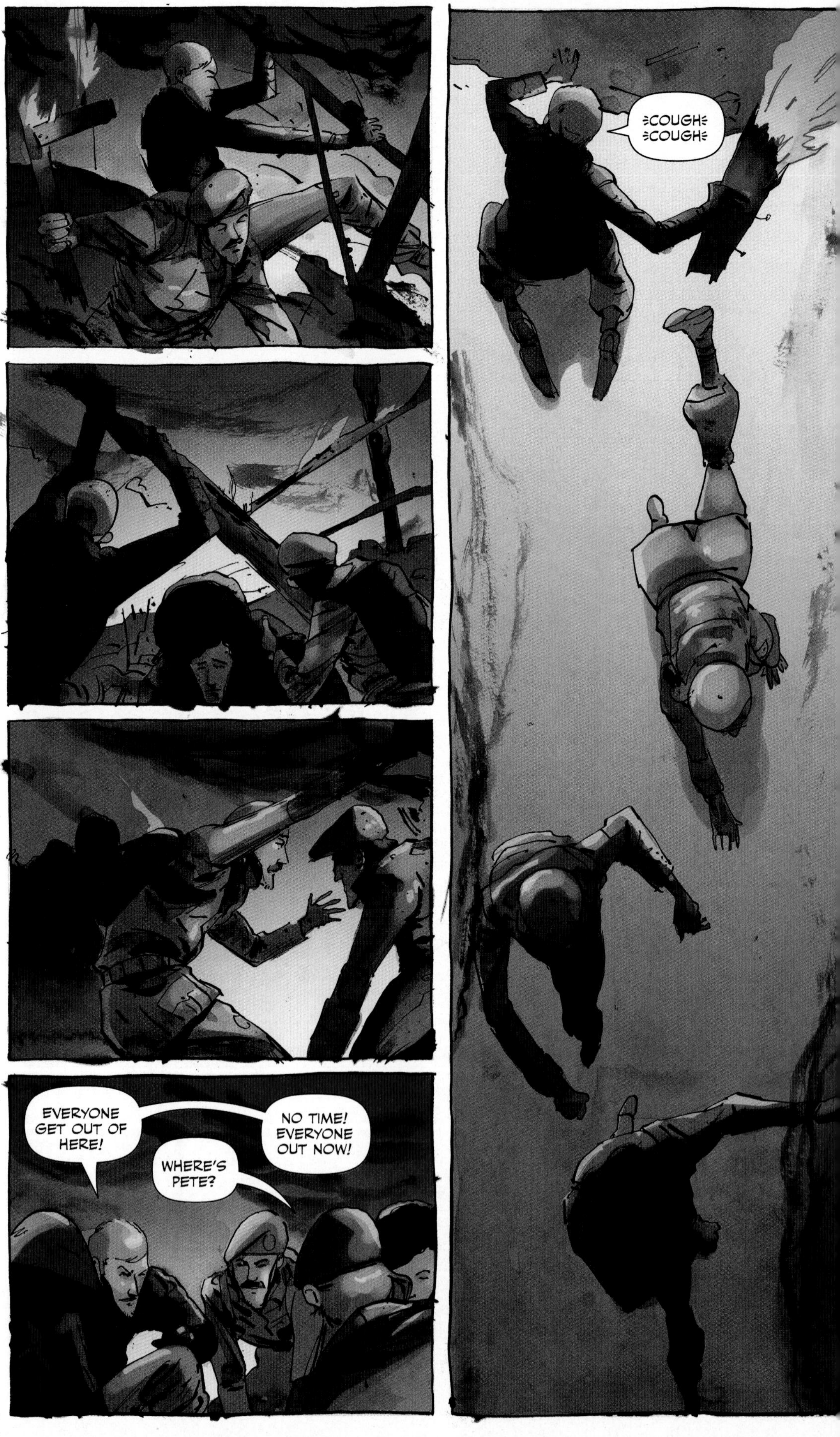
EVERYONE GET OUT OF HERE!
WHERE'S PETE?
NO TIME! EVERYONE OUT NOW!
COUGH COUGH

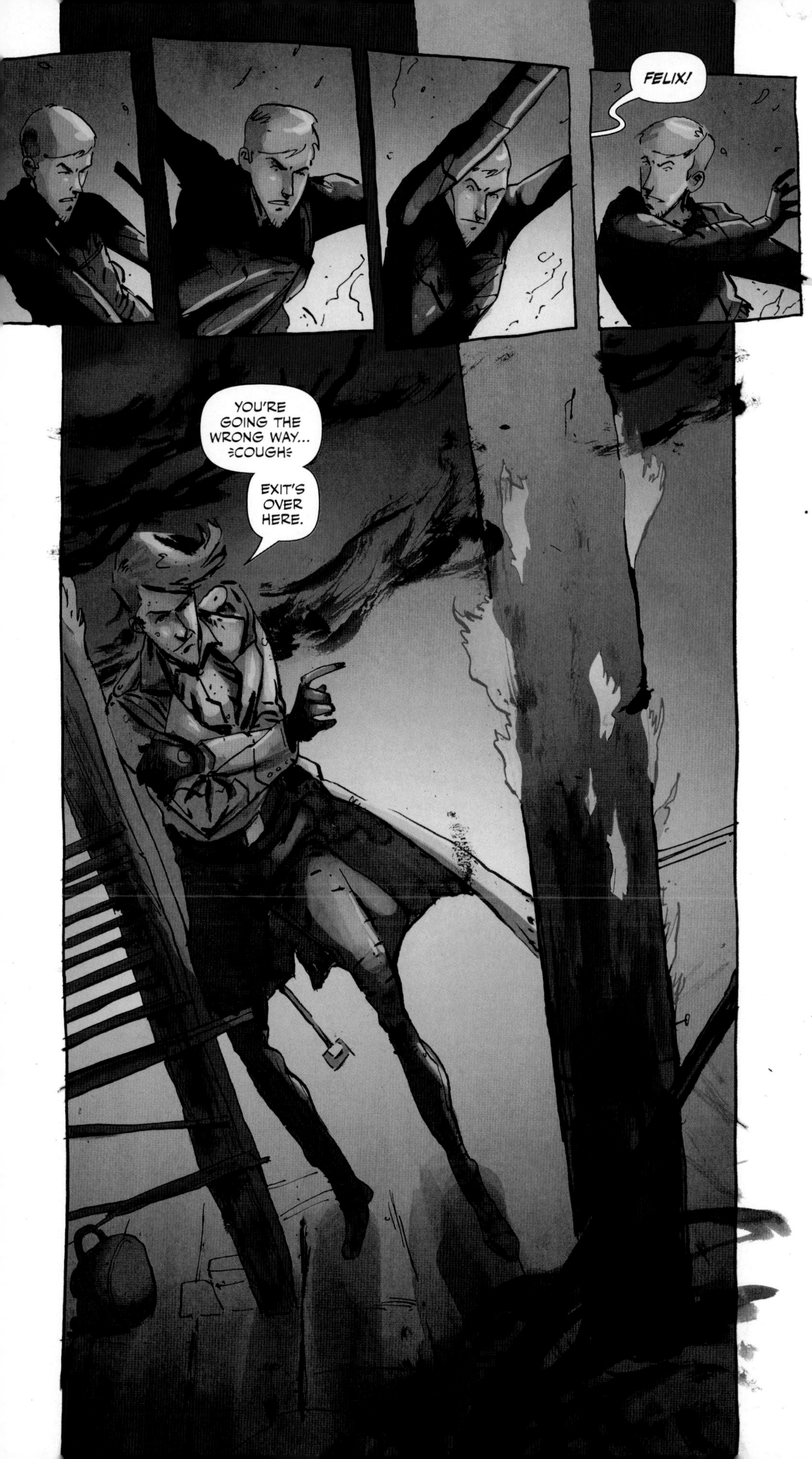
FELIX!
YOU'RE GOING THE WRONG WAY... ≡COUGH≡
EXIT'S OVER HERE.

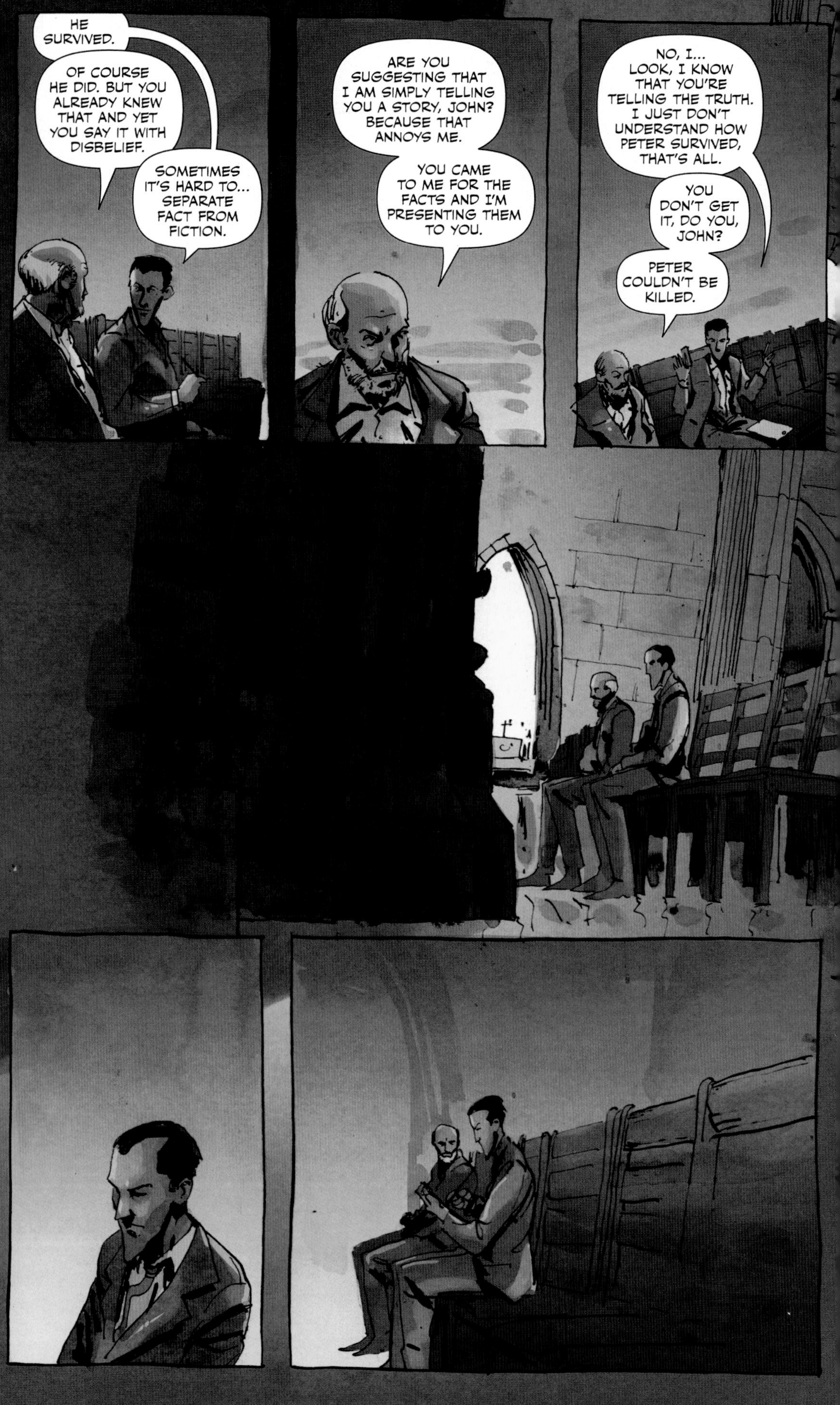
HE SURVIVED.
OF COURSE HE DID. BUT YOU ALREADY KNEW THAT AND YET YOU SAY IT WITH DISBELIEF.
SOMETIMES IT'S HARD TO... SEPARATE FACT FROM FICTION.
ARE YOU SUGGESTING THAT I AM SIMPLY TELLING YOU A STORY, JOHN? BECAUSE THAT ANNOYS ME.
YOU CAME TO ME FOR THE FACTS AND I'M PRESENTING THEM TO YOU.
NO, I... LOOK, I KNOW THAT YOU'RE TELLING THE TRUTH. I JUST DON'T UNDERSTAND HOW PETER SURVIVED, THAT'S ALL.
YOU DON'T GET IT, DO YOU, JOHN?
PETER COULDN'T BE KILLED.

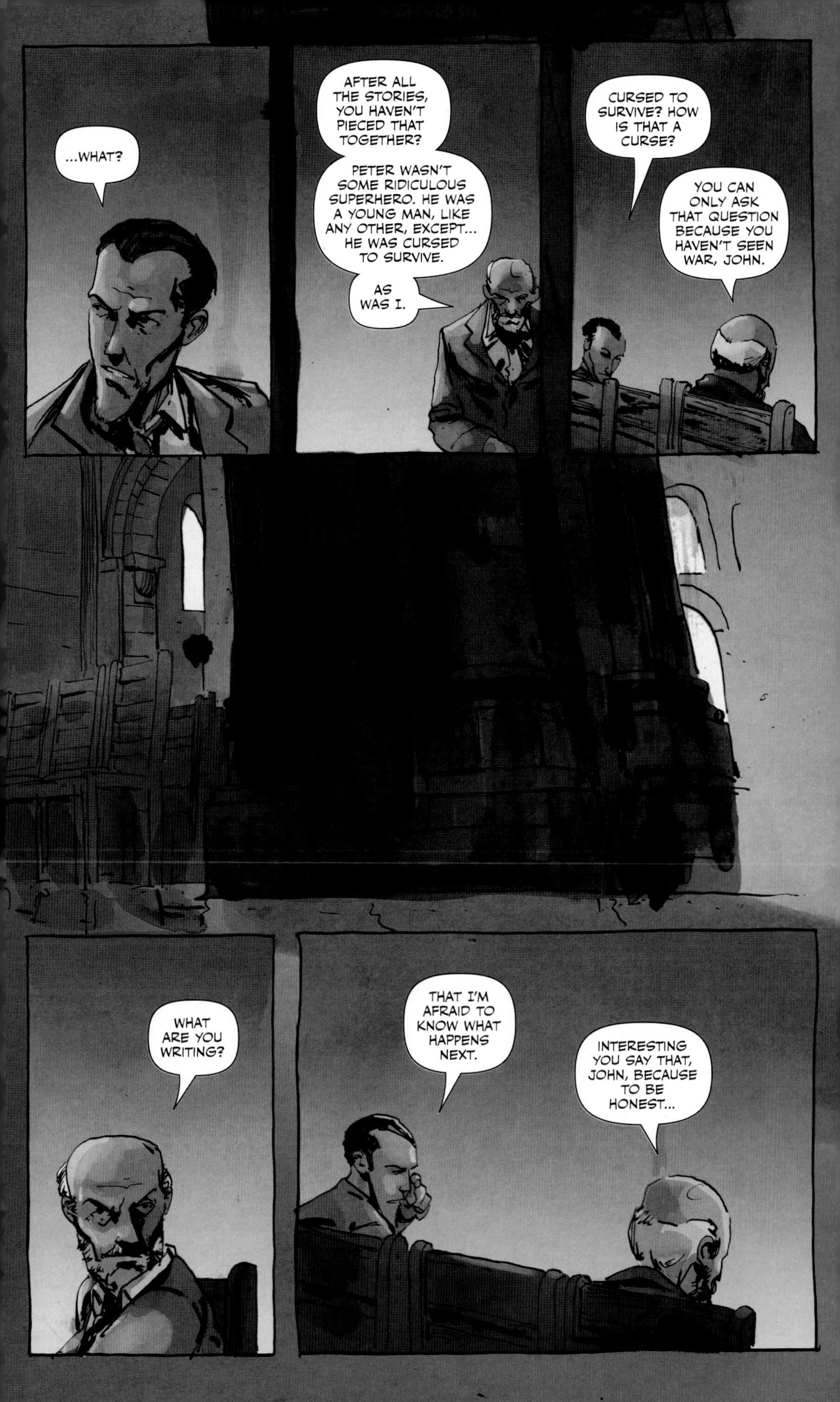
...WHAT?
AFTER ALL THE STORIES, YOU HAVEN'T PIECED THAT TOGETHER?
PETER WASN'T SOME RIDICULOUS SUPERHERO. HE WAS A YOUNG MAN, LIKE ANY OTHER, EXCEPT... HE WAS CURSED TO SURVIVE.
AS WAS I.
CURSED TO SURVIVE? HOW IS THAT A CURSE?
YOU CAN ONLY ASK THAT QUESTION BECAUSE YOU HAVEN'T SEEN WAR, JOHN.
WHAT ARE YOU WRITING?
THAT I'M AFRAID TO KNOW WHAT HAPPENS NEXT.
INTERESTING YOU SAY THAT, JOHN, BECAUSE TO BE HONEST...

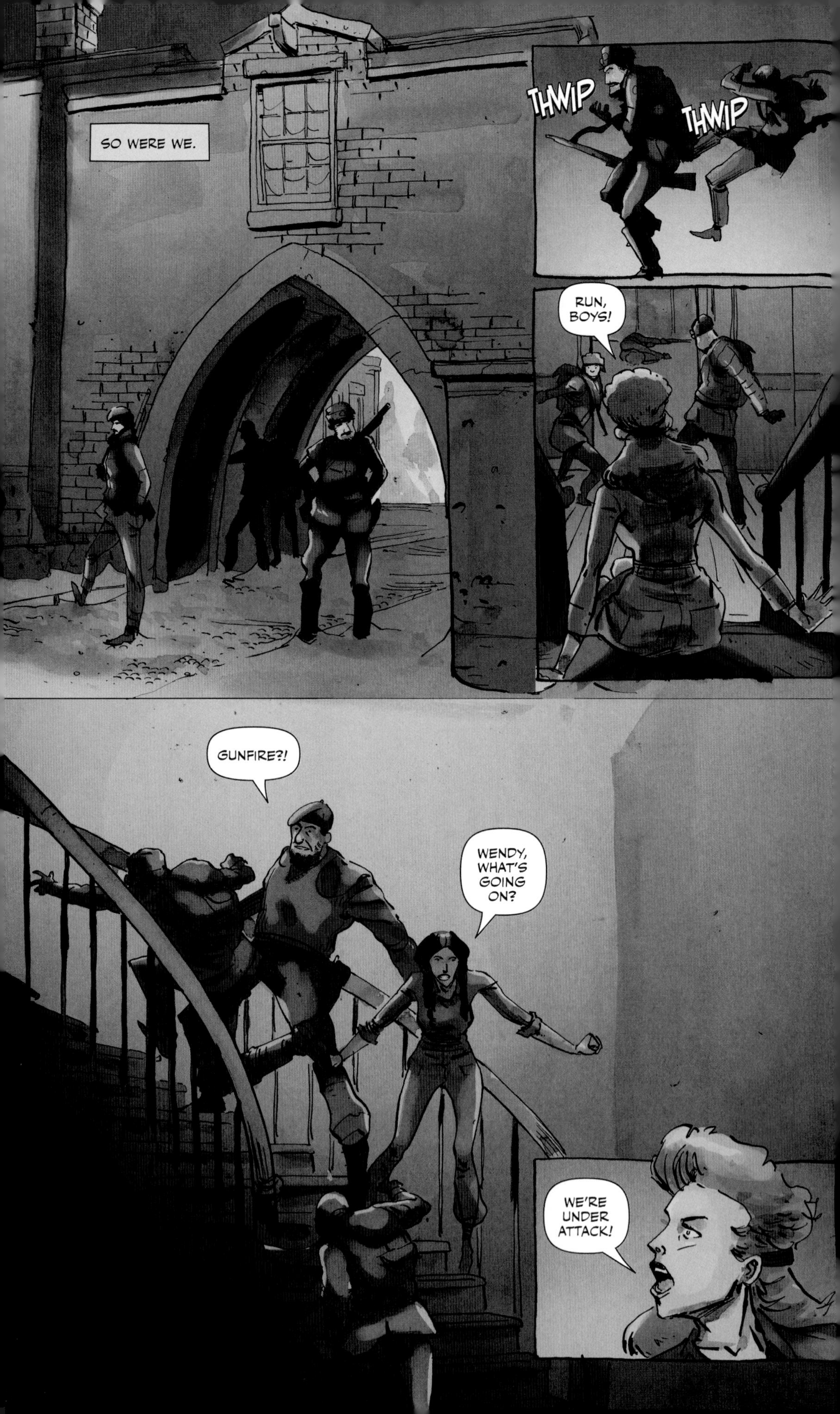
SO WERE WE.
THWIP
THWIP
RUN, BOYS!
GUNFIRE?!
WENDY, WHAT'S GOING ON?
WE'RE UNDER ATTACK!

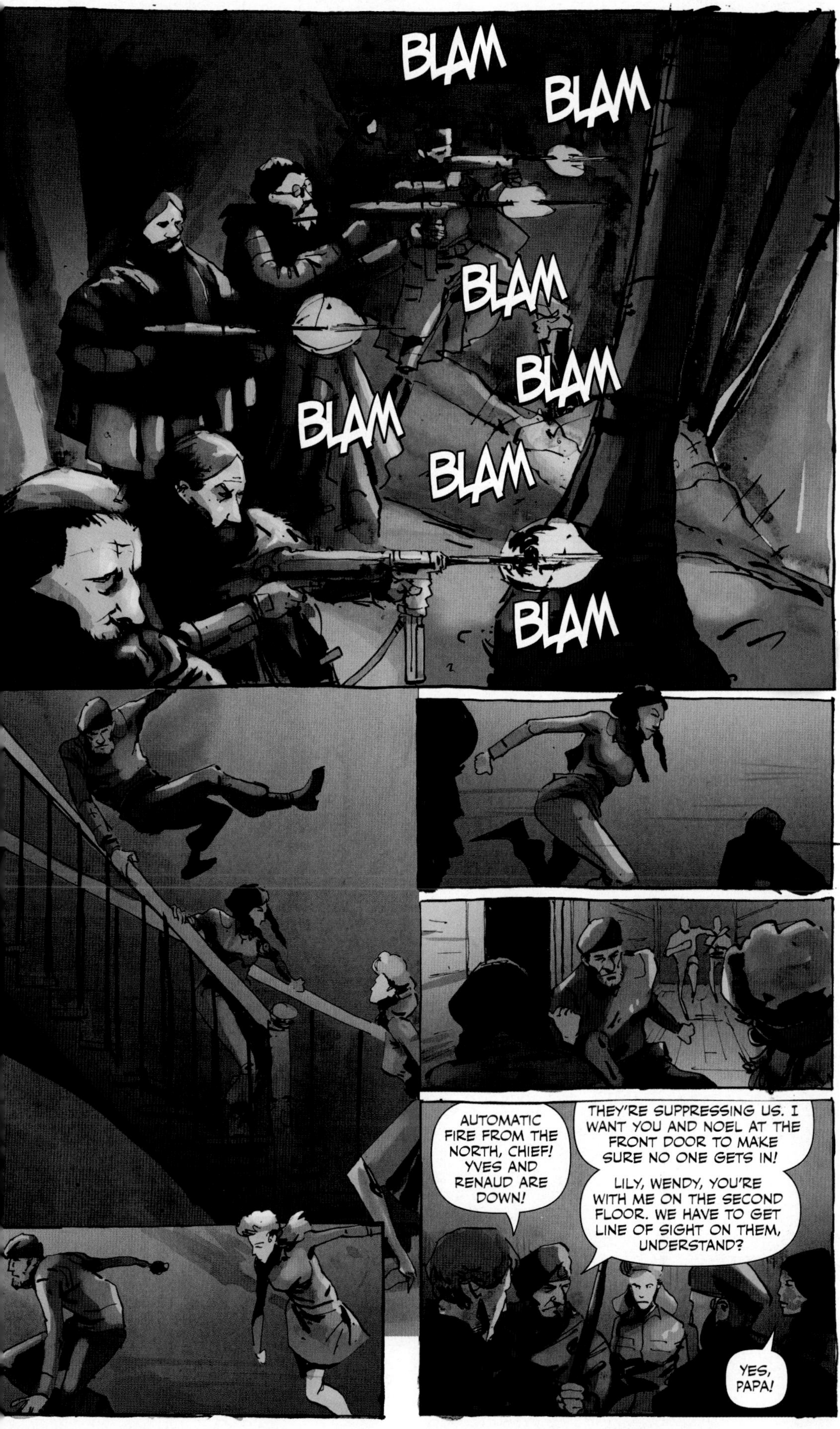
BLAM
BLAM
BLAM
BLAM
BLAM
BLAM
BLAM
AUTOMATIC FIRE FROM THE NORTH, CHIEF! YVES AND RENAUD ARE DOWN!
THEY'RE SUPPRESSING US. I WANT YOU AND NOEL AT THE FRONT DOOR TO MAKE SURE NO ONE GETS IN!
LILY, WENDY, YOU'RE WITH ME ON THE SECOND FLOOR. WE HAVE TO GET LINE OF SIGHT ON THEM, UNDERSTAND?
YES, PAPA!

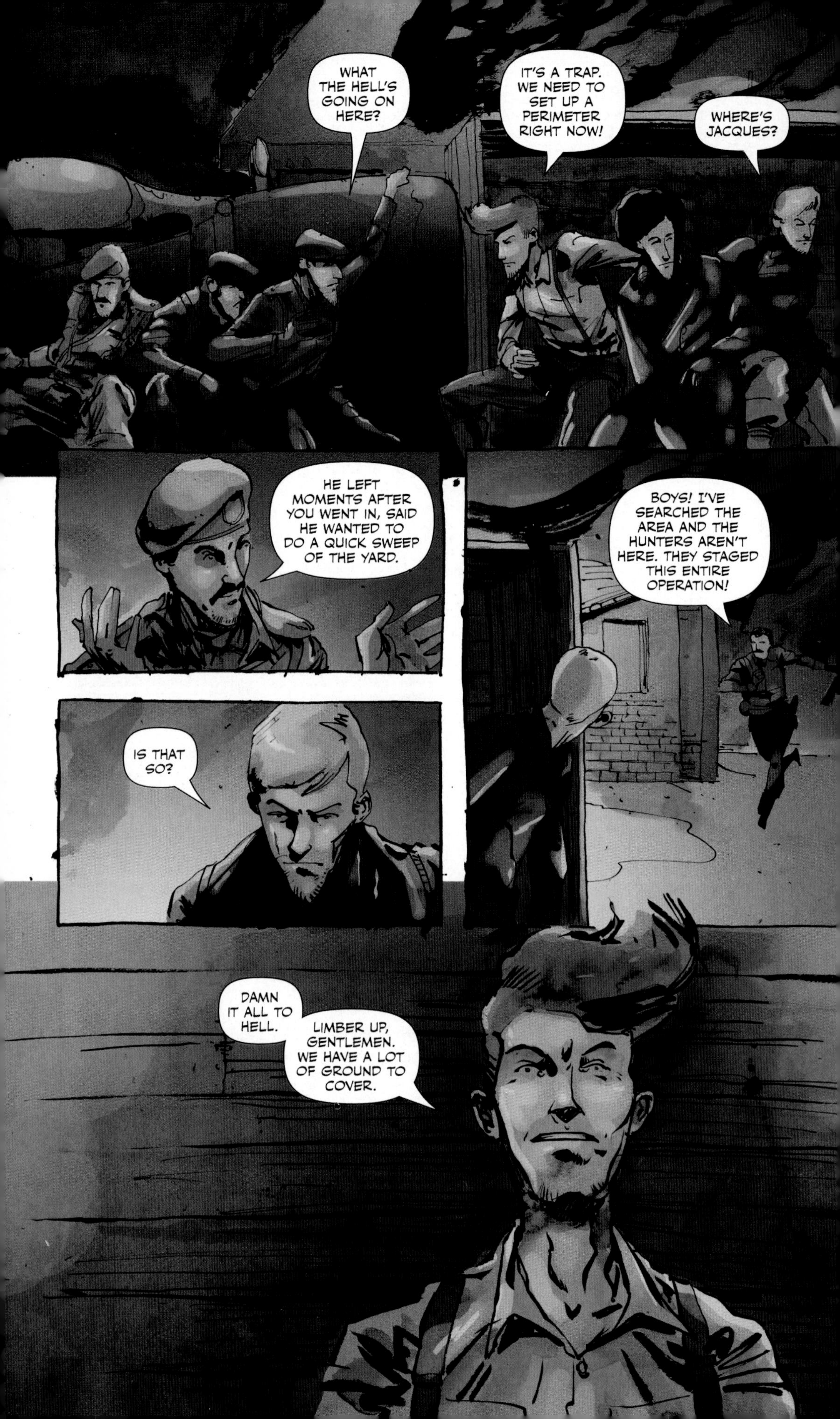
WHAT THE HELL'S GOING ON HERE?
IT'S A TRAP. WE NEED TO SET UP A PERIMETER RIGHT NOW!
WHERE'S JACQUES?
HE LEFT MOMENTS AFTER YOU WENT IN, SAID HE WANTED TO DO A QUICK SWEEP OF THE YARD.
IS THAT SO?
BOYS! I'VE SEARCHED THE AREA AND THE HUNTERS AREN'T HERE. THEY STAGED THIS ENTIRE OPERATION!
DAMN IT ALL TO HELL.
LIMBER UP, GENTLEMEN. WE HAVE A LOT OF GROUND TO COVER.

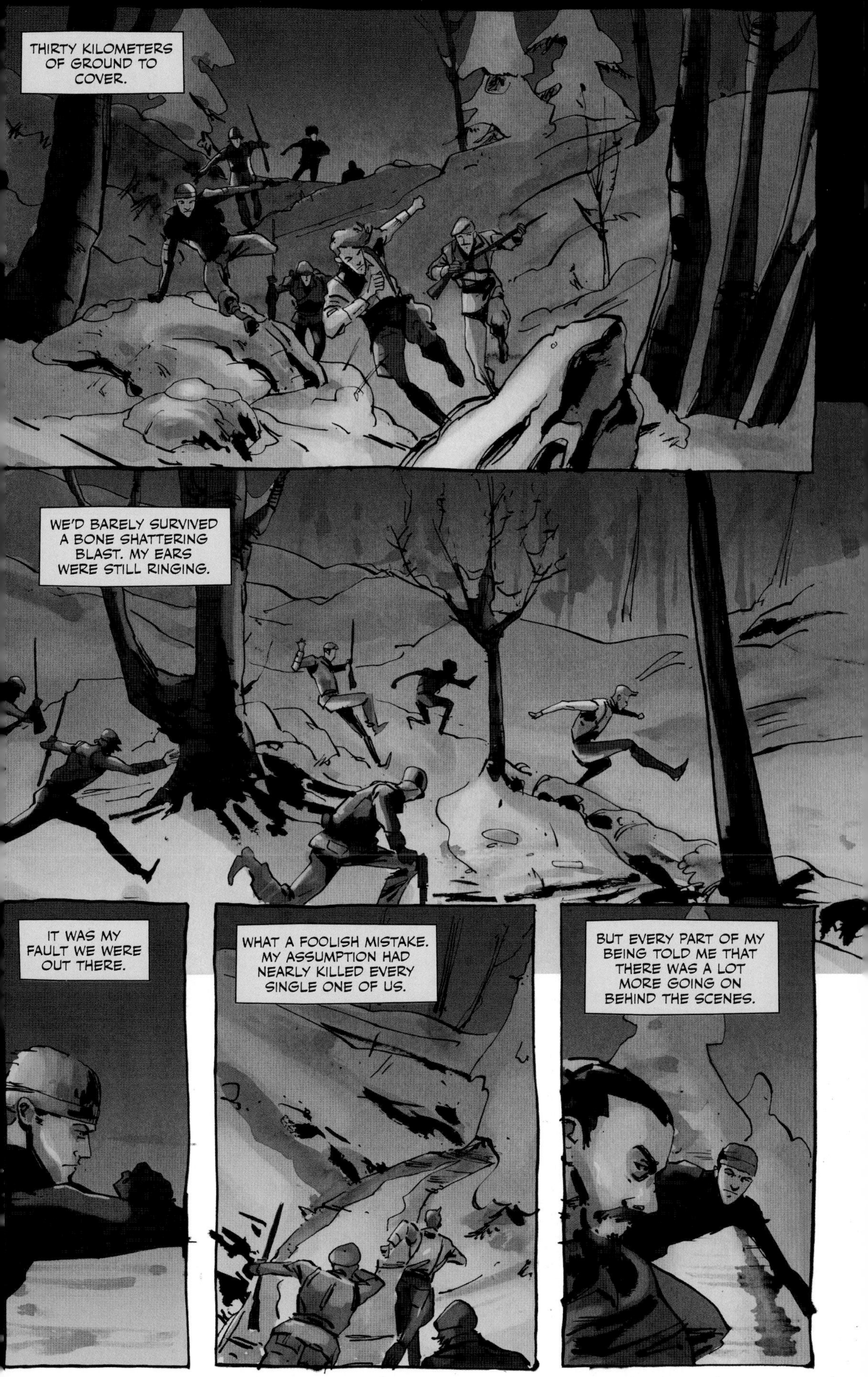

THIRTY KILOMETERS OF GROUND TO COVER.
WE'D BARELY SURVIVED A BONE SHATTERING BLAST. MY EARS WERE STILL RINGING.
IT WAS MY FAULT WE WERE OUT THERE.
WHAT A FOOLISH MISTAKE. MY ASSUMPTION HAD NEARLY KILLED EVERY SINGLE ONE OF US.
BUT EVERY PART OF MY BEING TOLD ME THAT THERE WAS A LOT MORE GOING ON BEHIND THE SCENES.

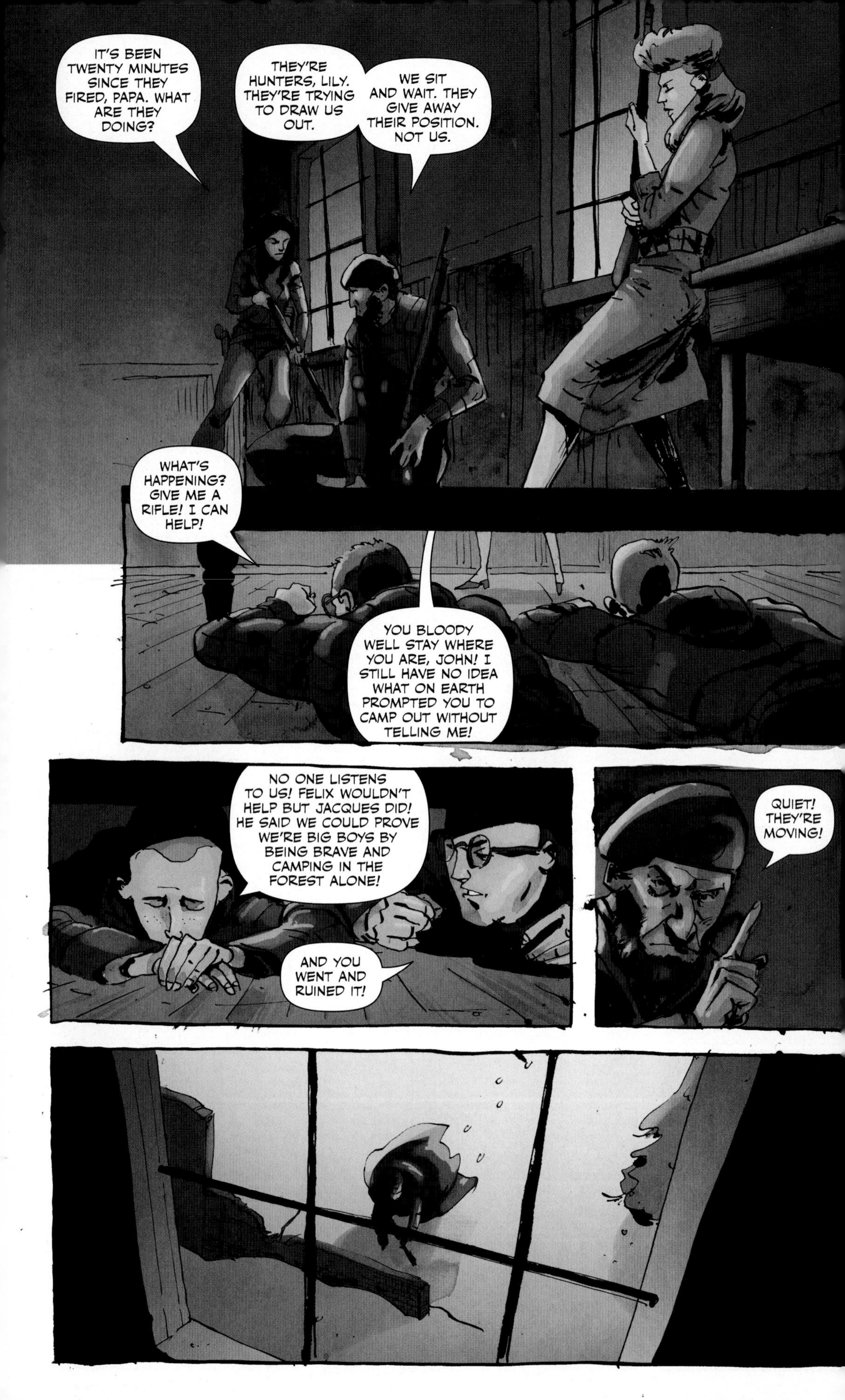
IT'S BEEN TWENTY MINUTES SINCE THEY FIRED, PAPA. WHAT ARE THEY DOING?
THEY'RE HUNTERS, LILY. THEY'RE TRYING TO DRAW US OUT.
WE SIT AND WAIT. THEY GIVE AWAY THEIR POSITION. NOT US.
WHAT'S HAPPENING? GIVE ME A RIFLE! I CAN HELP!
YOU BLOODY WELL STAY WHERE YOU ARE, JOHN! I STILL HAVE NO IDEA WHAT ON EARTH PROMPTED YOU TO CAMP OUT WITHOUT TELLING ME!
NO ONE LISTENS TO US! FELIX WOULDN'T HELP BUT JACQUES DID! HE SAID WE COULD PROVE WE'RE BIG BOYS BY BEING BRAVE AND CAMPING IN THE FOREST ALONE!
AND YOU WENT AND RUINED IT!
QUIET! THEY'RE MOVING!

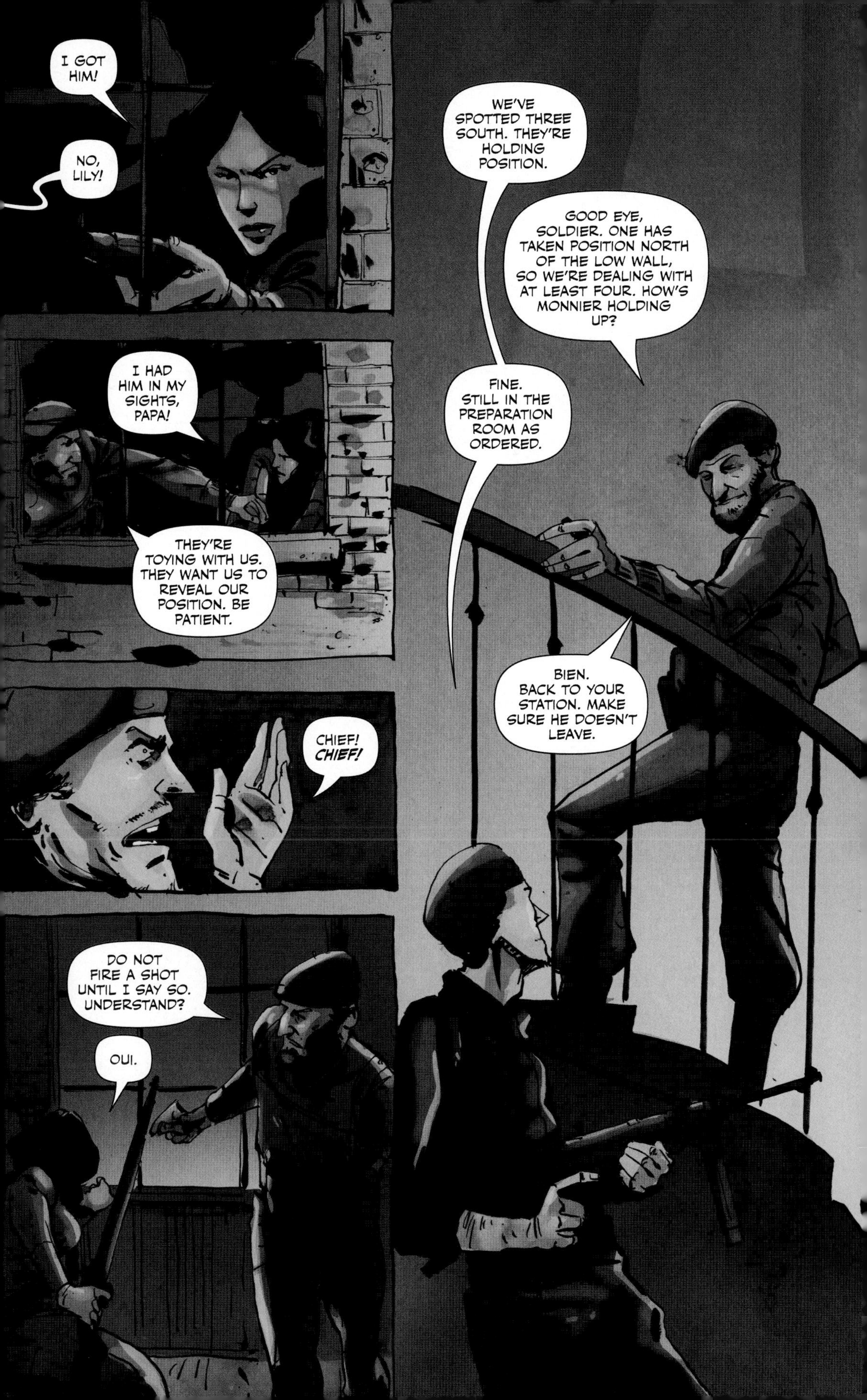
I GOT HIM!
NO, LILY!
WE'VE SPOTTED THREE SOUTH. THEY'RE HOLDING POSITION.
GOOD EYE, SOLDIER. ONE HAS TAKEN POSITION NORTH OF THE LOW WALL, SO WE'RE DEALING WITH AT LEAST FOUR. HOW'S MONNIER HOLDING UP?
FINE. STILL IN THE PREPARATION ROOM AS ORDERED.
BIEN. BACK TO YOUR STATION. MAKE SURE HE DOESN'T LEAVE.
I HAD HIM IN MY SIGHTS, PAPA!
THEY'RE TOYING WITH US. THEY WANT US TO REVEAL OUR POSITION. BE PATIENT.
CHIEF! CHIEF!
DO NOT FIRE A SHOT UNTIL I SAY SO. UNDERSTAND?
OUI.

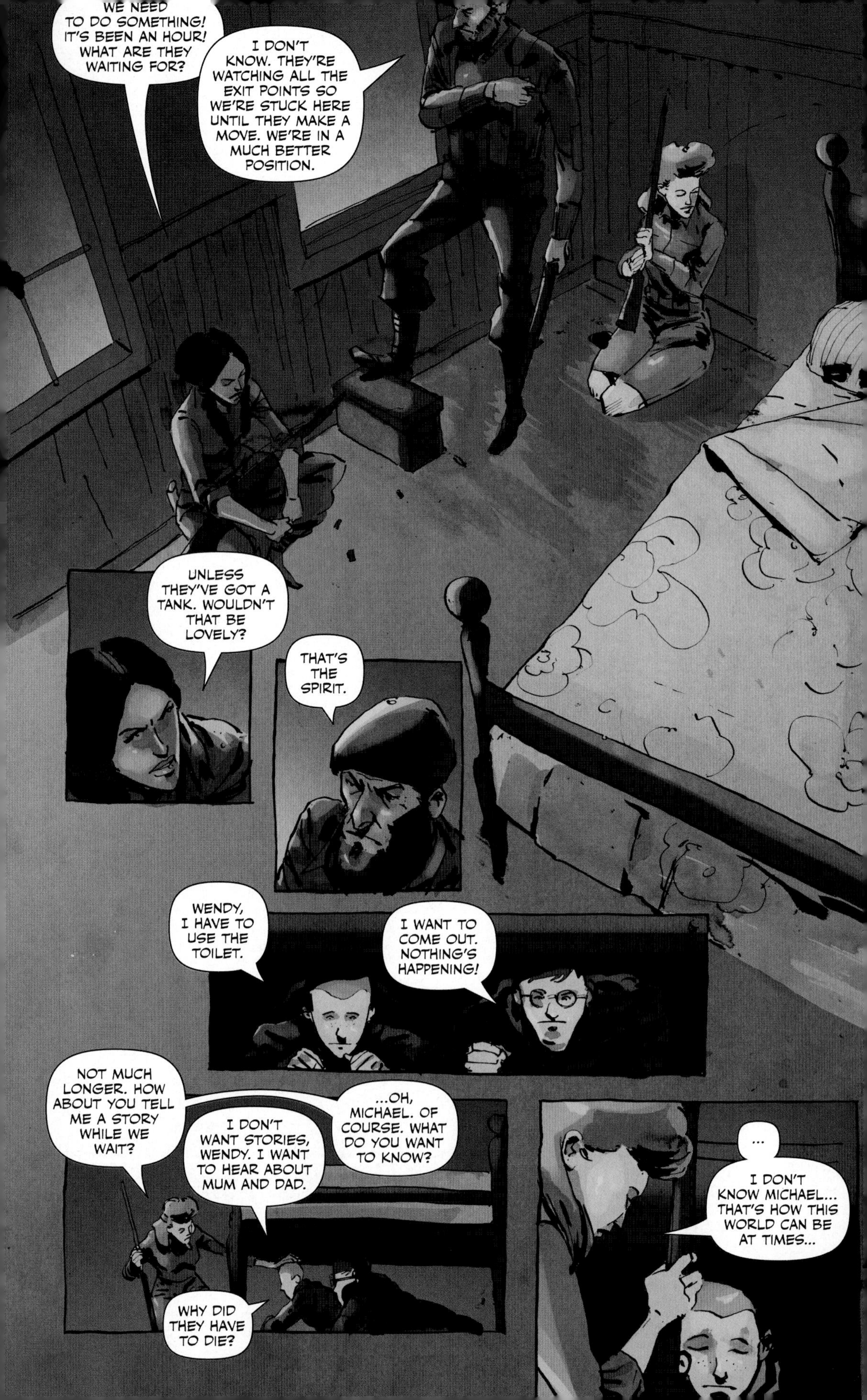
WE NEED TO DO SOMETHING! IT'S BEEN AN HOUR! WHAT ARE THEY WAITING FOR?
I DON'T KNOW. THEY'RE WATCHING ALL THE EXIT POINTS SO WE'RE STUCK HERE UNTIL THEY MAKE A MOVE. WE'RE IN A MUCH BETTER POSITION.
UNLESS THEY'VE GOT A TANK. WOULDN'T THAT BE LOVELY?
THAT'S THE SPIRIT.
WENDY, I HAVE TO USE THE TOILET.
I WANT TO COME OUT. NOTHING'S HAPPENING!
NOT MUCH LONGER. HOW ABOUT YOU TELL ME A STORY WHILE WE WAIT?
I DON'T WANT STORIES, WENDY. I WANT TO HEAR ABOUT MUM AND DAD.
WHY DID THEY HAVE TO DIE?
...OH, MICHAEL. OF COURSE. WHAT DO YOU WANT TO KNOW?
...
I DON'T KNOW MICHAEL... THAT'S HOW THIS WORLD CAN BE AT TIMES...

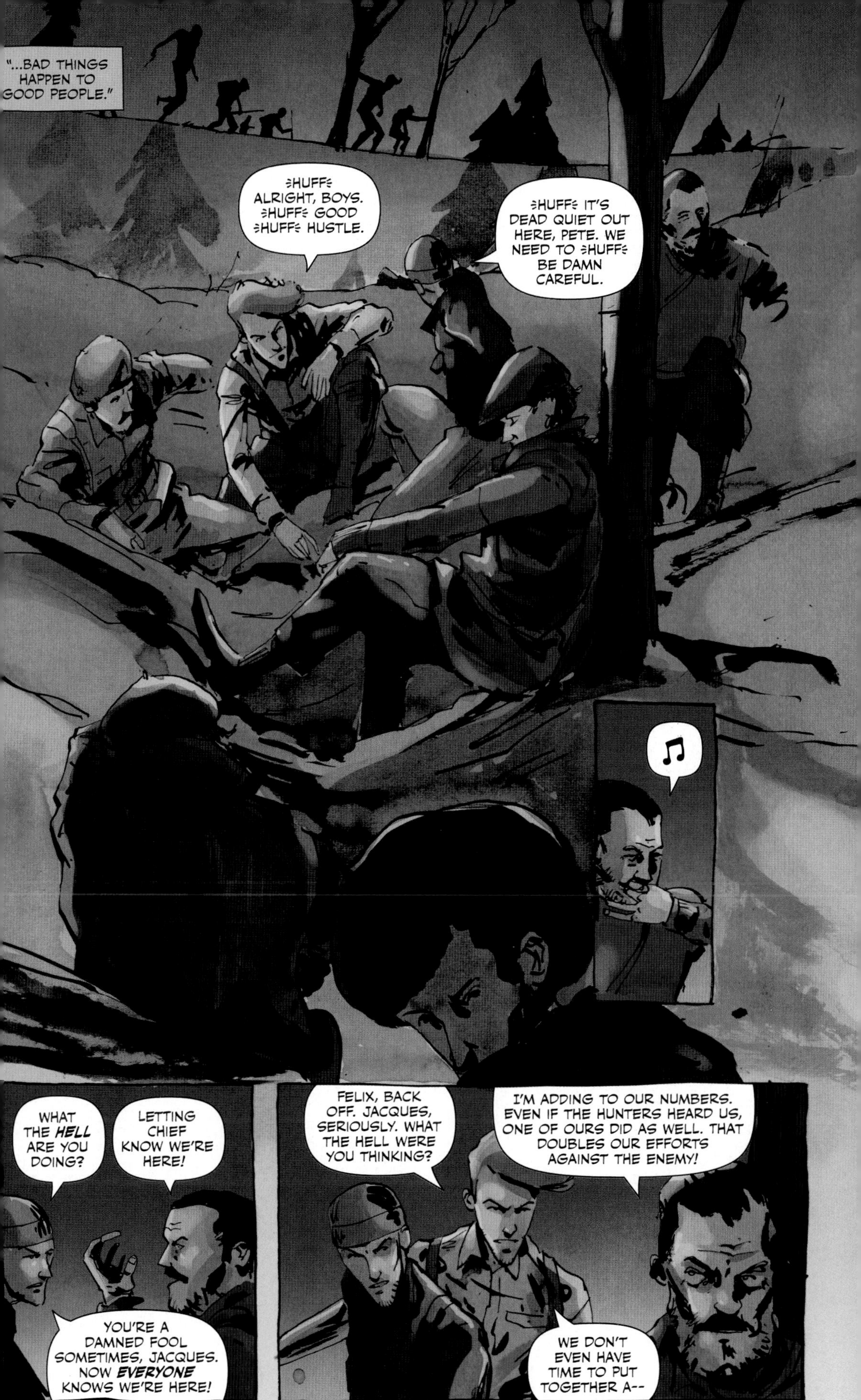
"...BAD THINGS HAPPEN TO GOOD PEOPLE."
≡HUFF≡ ALRIGHT, BOYS. ≡HUFF≡ GOOD ≡HUFF≡ HUSTLE.
≡HUFF≡ IT'S DEAD QUIET OUT HERE, PETE. WE NEED TO ≡HUFF≡ BE DAMN CAREFUL.
♫
WHAT THE *HELL* ARE YOU DOING?
LETTING CHIEF KNOW WE'RE HERE!
YOU'RE A DAMNED FOOL SOMETIMES, JACQUES. NOW *EVERYONE* KNOWS WE'RE HERE!
FELIX, BACK OFF. JACQUES, SERIOUSLY. WHAT THE HELL WERE YOU THINKING?
I'M ADDING TO OUR NUMBERS. EVEN IF THE HUNTERS HEARD US, ONE OF OURS DID AS WELL. THAT DOUBLES OUR EFFORTS AGAINST THE ENEMY!
WE DON'T EVEN HAVE TIME TO PUT TOGETHER A--

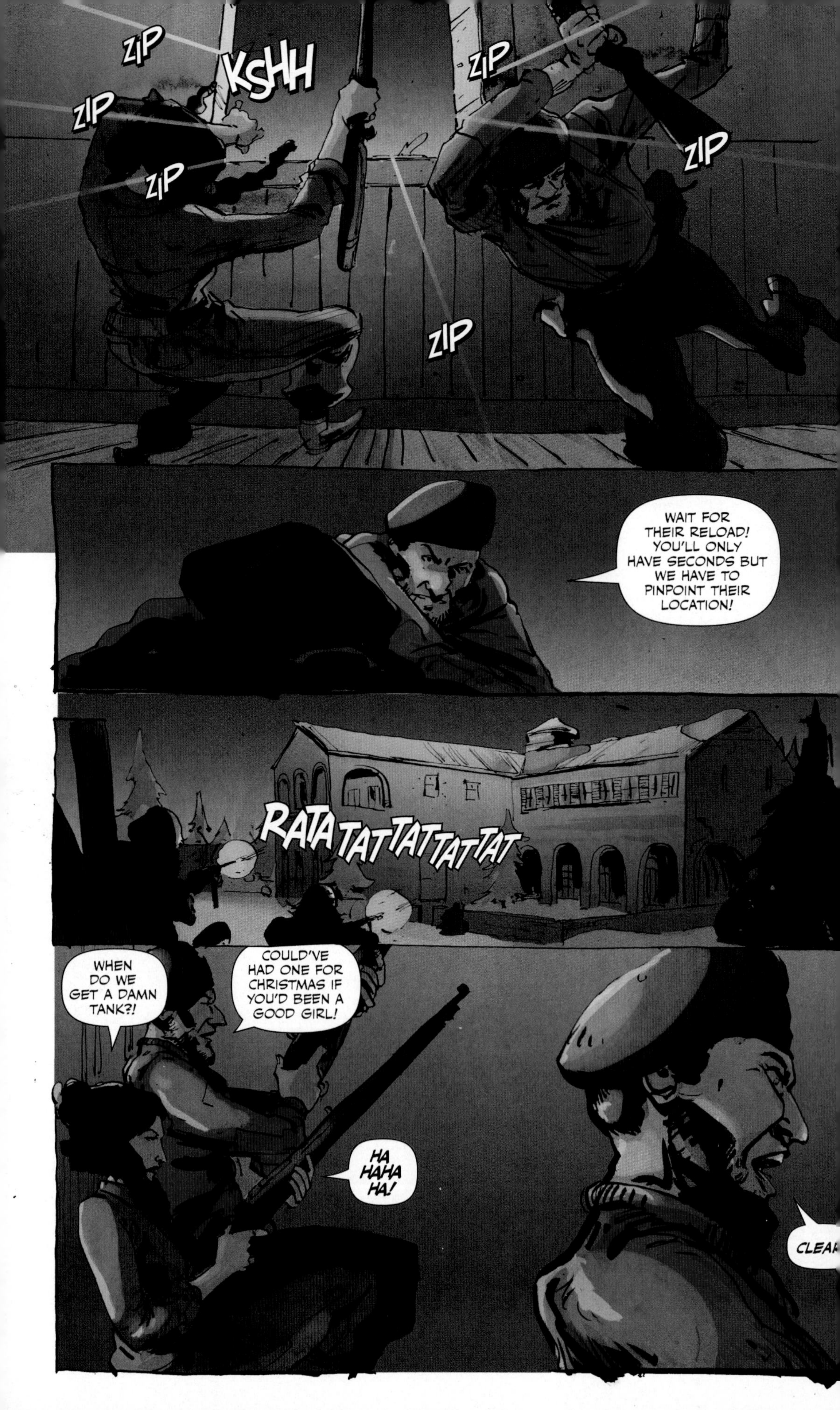
ZIP
KSHH
ZIP
ZIP
ZIP
ZIP
ZIP
WAIT FOR THEIR RELOAD! YOU'LL ONLY HAVE SECONDS BUT WE HAVE TO PINPOINT THEIR LOCATION!
RATATATTATTATTAT
WHEN DO WE GET A DAMN TANK?!
COULD'VE HAD ONE FOR CHRISTMAS IF YOU'D BEEN A GOOD GIRL!
HA HAHAHA HA!

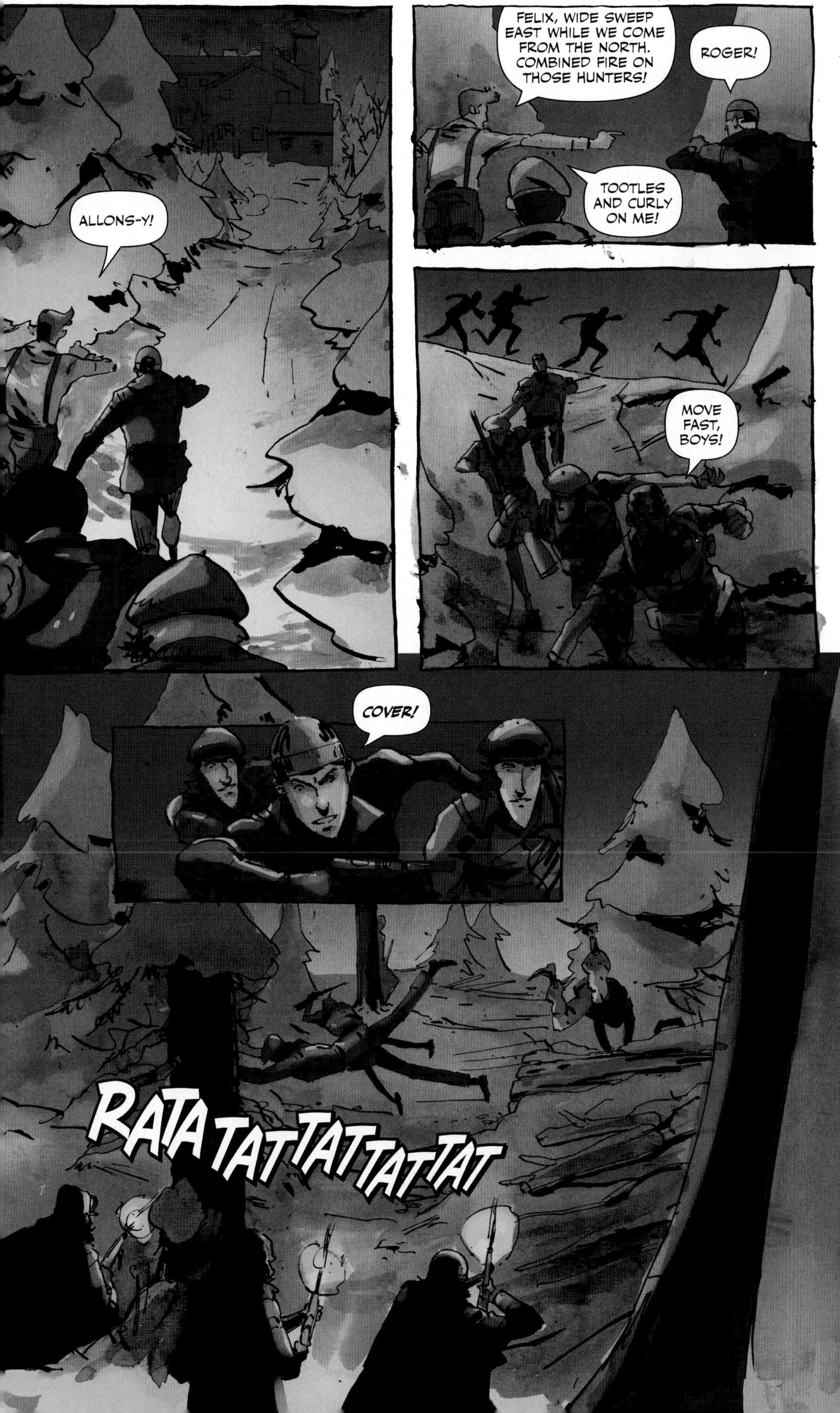
ALLONS-Y!
FELIX, WIDE SWEEP EAST WHILE WE COME FROM THE NORTH. COMBINED FIRE ON THOSE HUNTERS!
ROGER!
TOOTLES AND CURLY ON ME!
MOVE FAST, BOYS!
COVER!
RATA TAT TAT TAT TAT

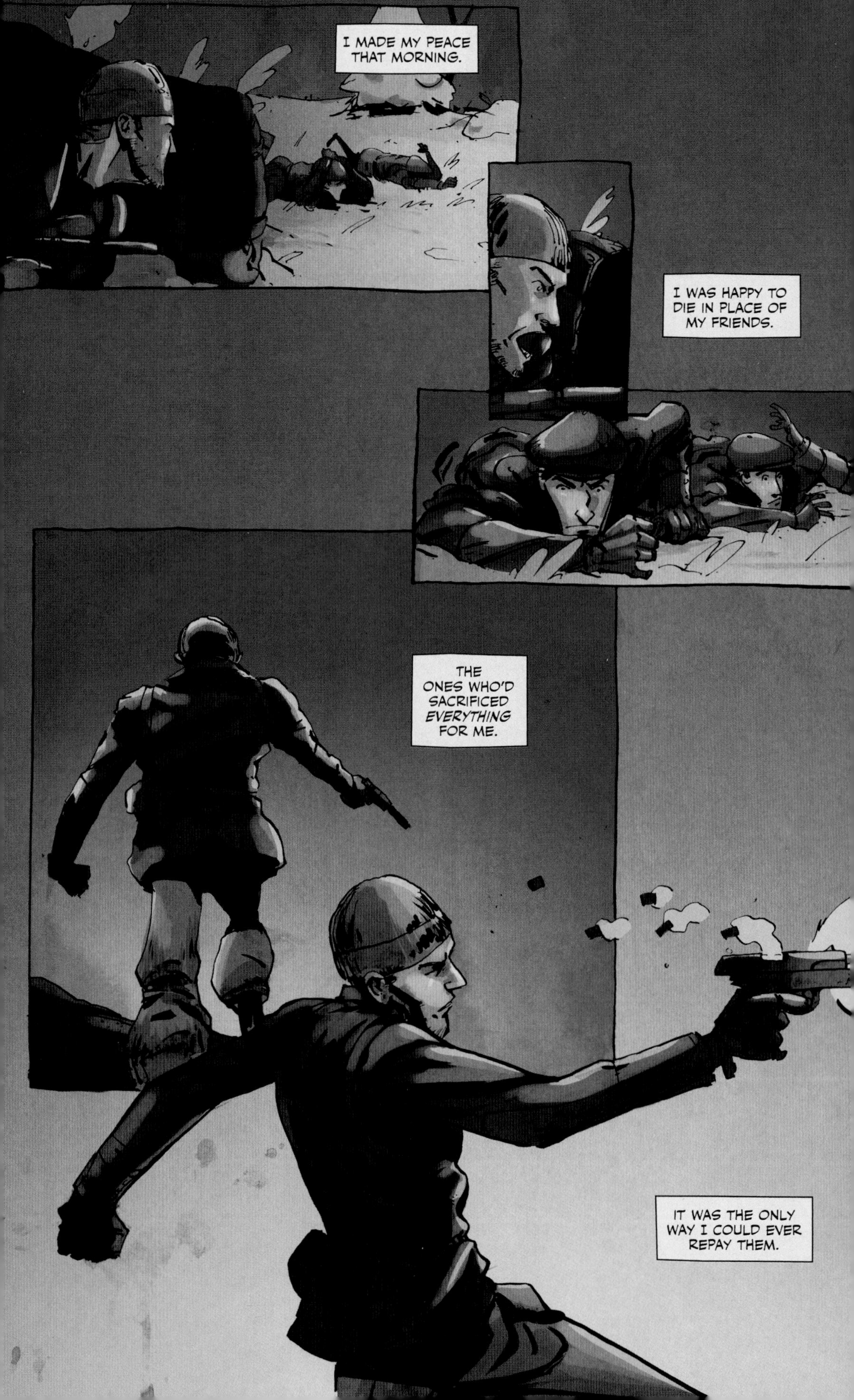

I MADE MY PEACE THAT MORNING.
I WAS HAPPY TO DIE IN PLACE OF MY FRIENDS.
THE ONES WHO'D SACRIFICED *EVERYTHING* FOR ME.
IT WAS THE ONLY WAY I COULD EVER REPAY THEM.

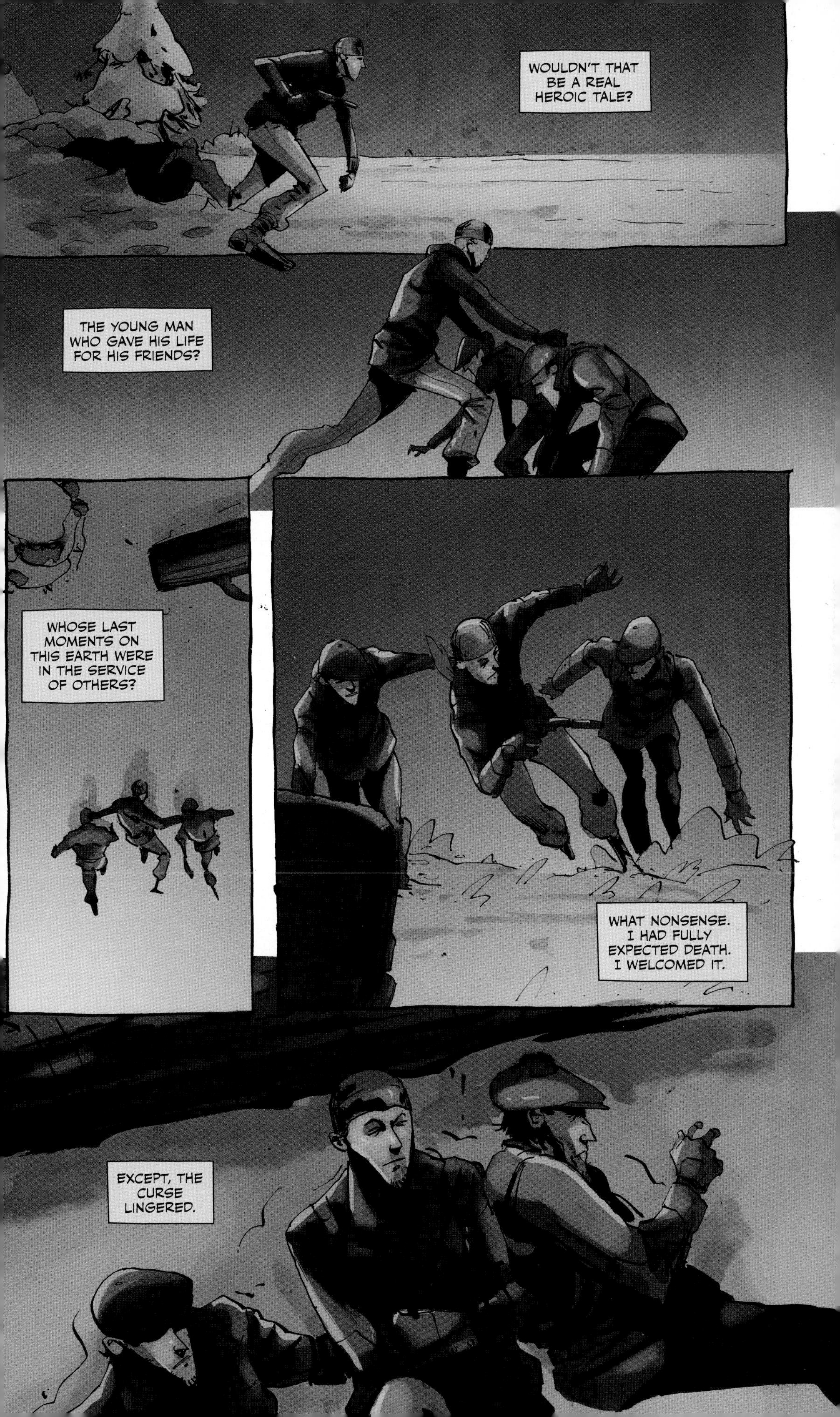
WOULDN'T THAT BE A REAL HEROIC TALE?
THE YOUNG MAN WHO GAVE HIS LIFE FOR HIS FRIENDS?
WHOSE LAST MOMENTS ON THIS EARTH WERE IN THE SERVICE OF OTHERS?
WHAT NONSENSE. I HAD FULLY EXPECTED DEATH. I WELCOMED IT.
EXCEPT, THE CURSE LINGERED.

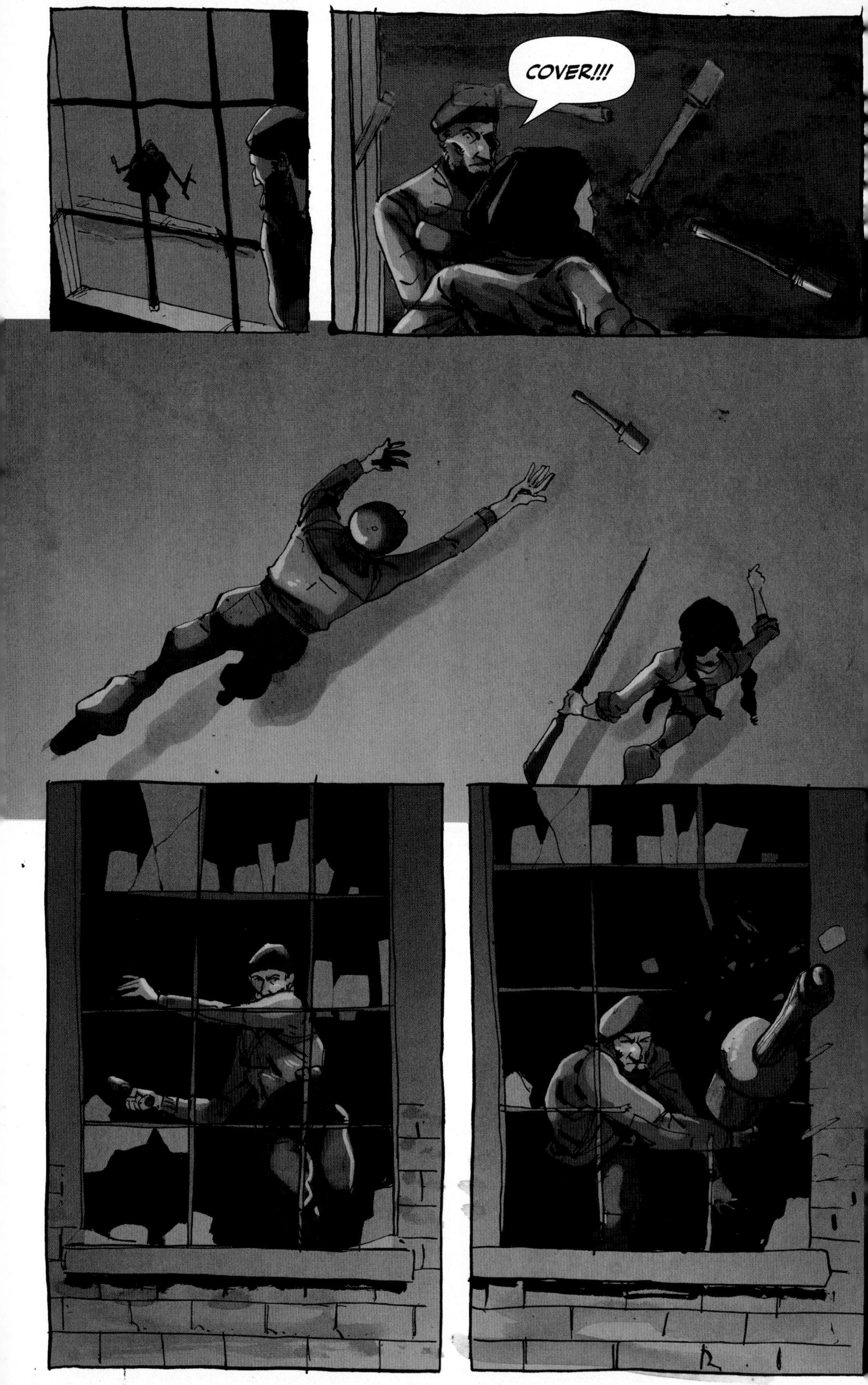
COVER!!!

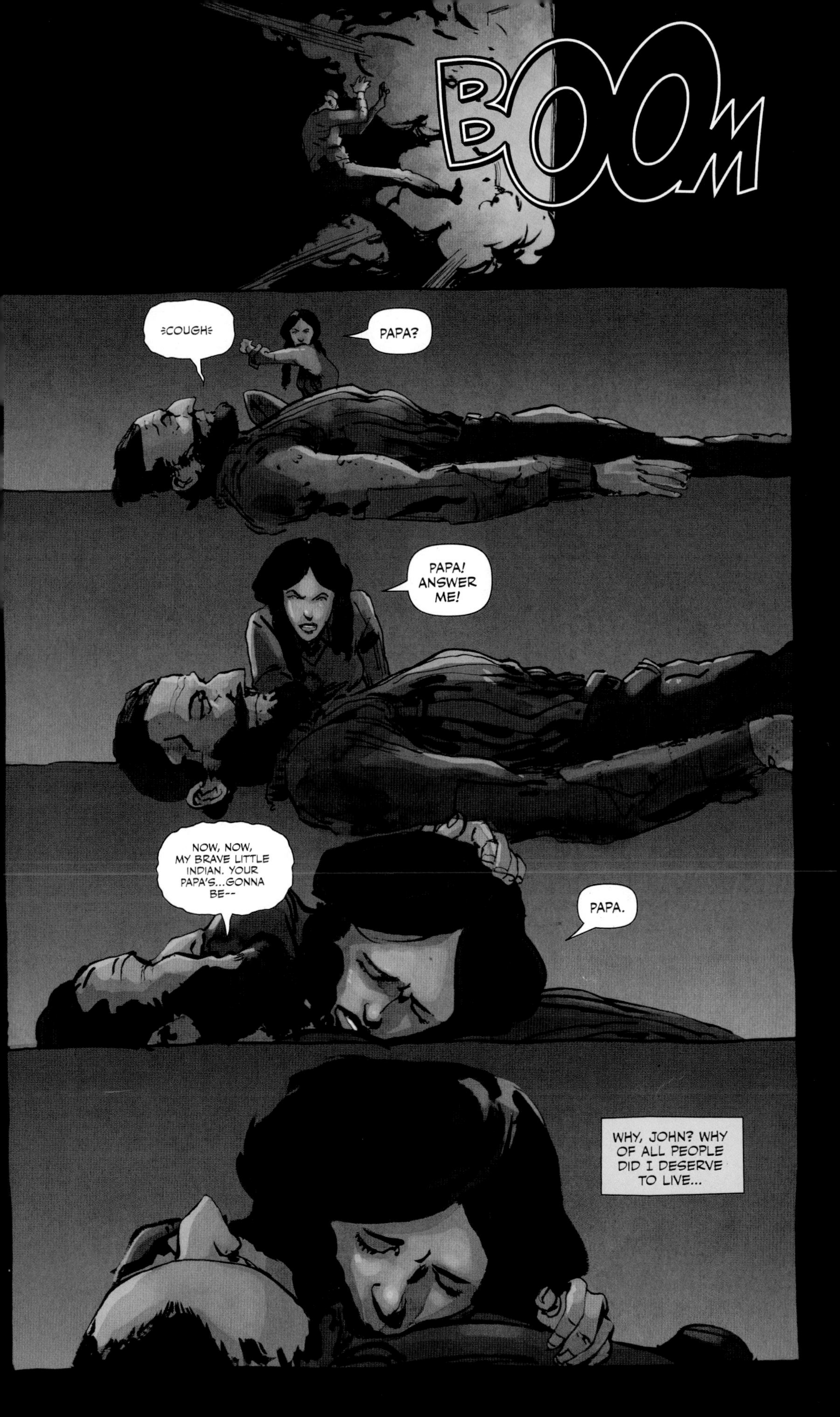
BOOM
≈COUGH≈
PAPA?
PAPA! ANSWER ME!
NOW, NOW, MY BRAVE LITTLE INDIAN. YOUR PAPA'S...GONNA BE--
PAPA.
WHY, JOHN? WHY OF ALL PEOPLE DID I DESERVE TO LIVE...

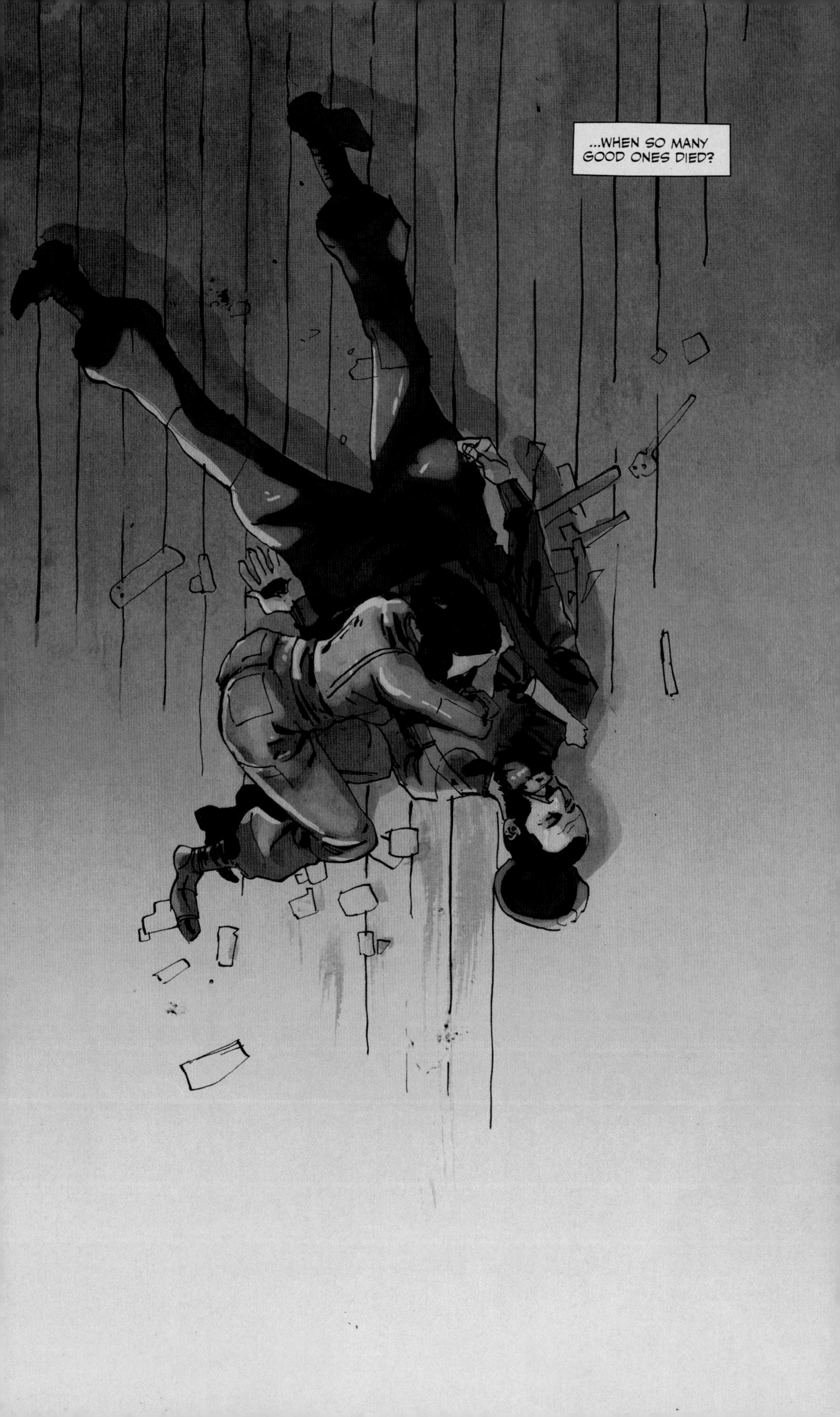
...WHEN SO MANY GOOD ONES DIED?

CHAPTER FOURTEEN

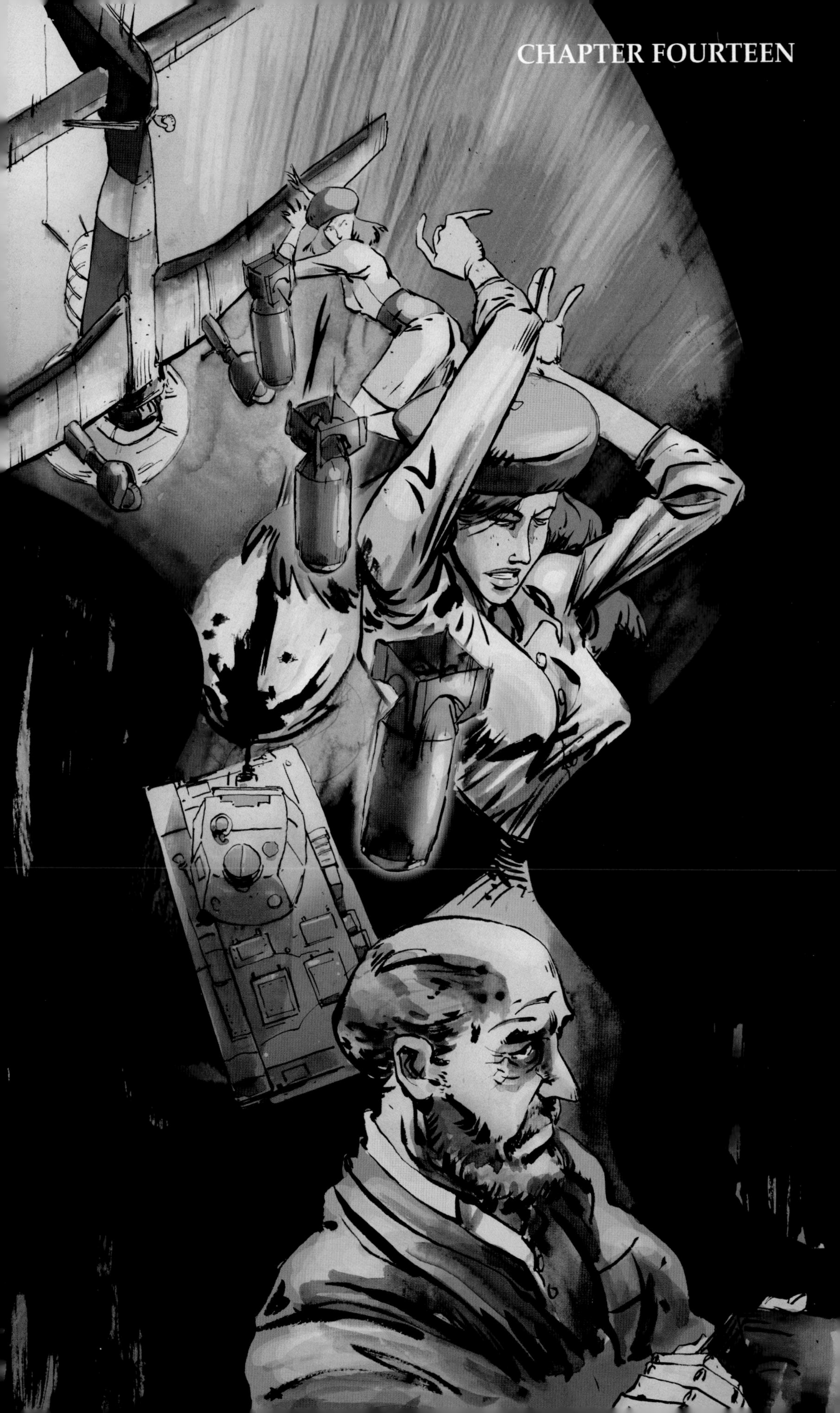

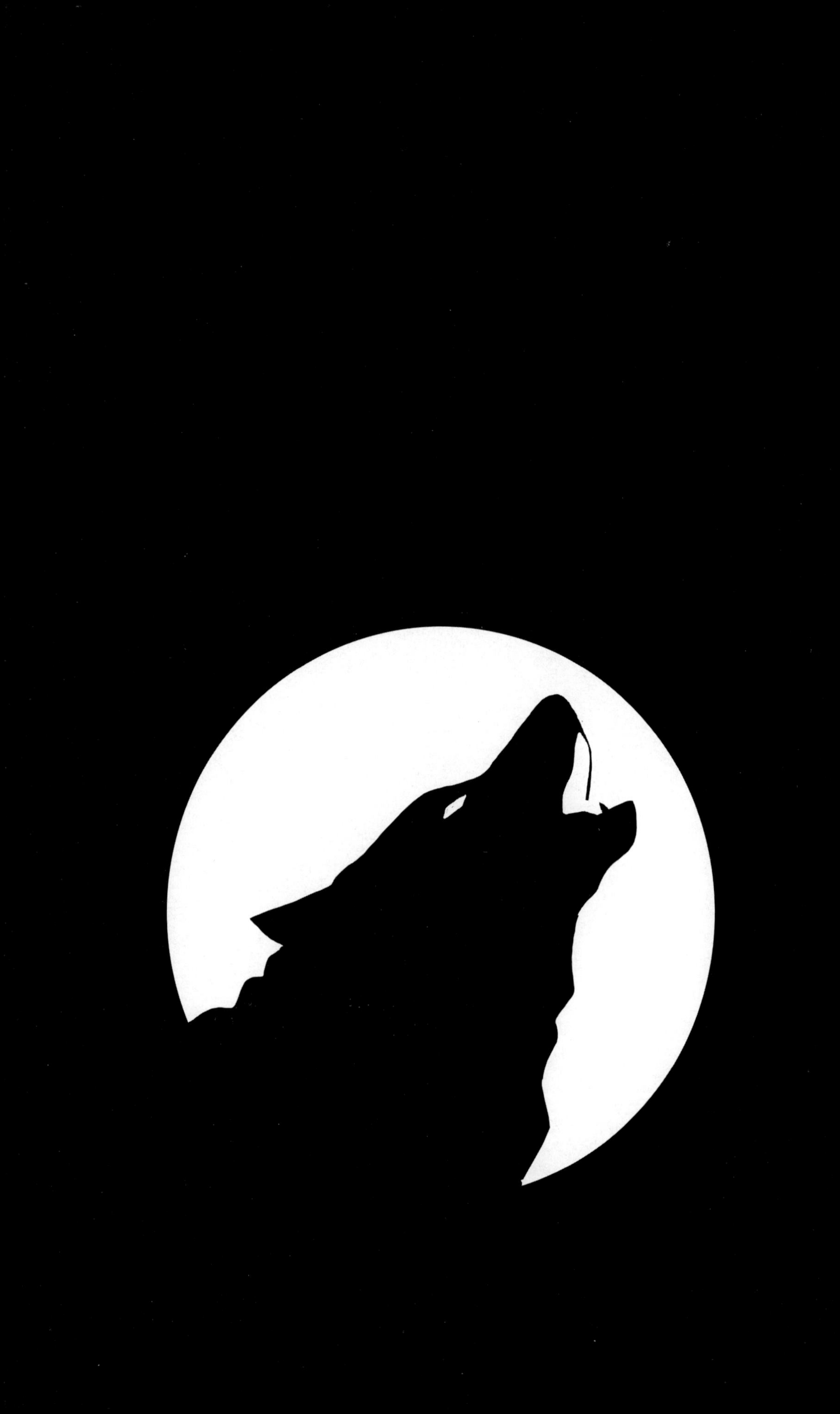

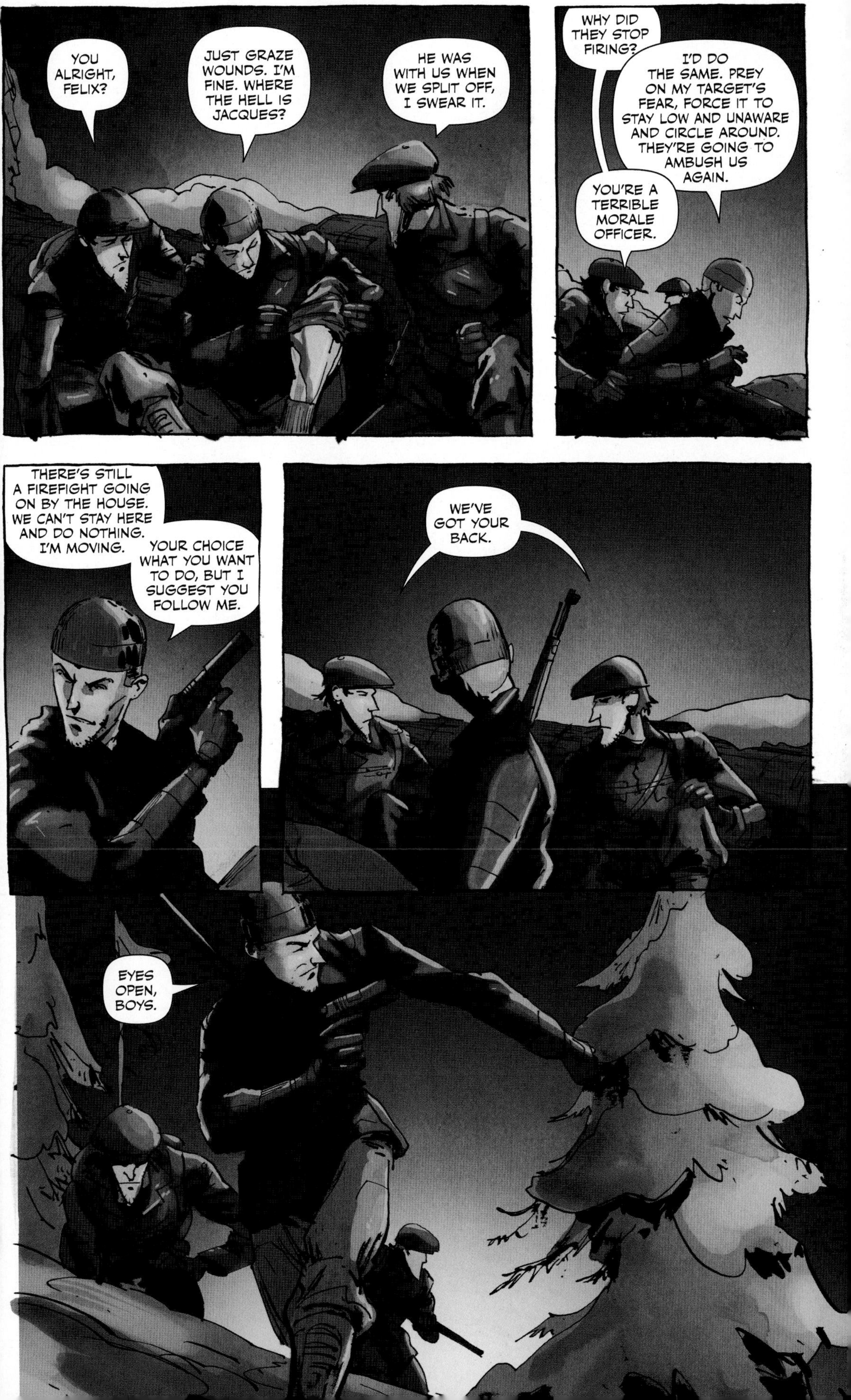
YOU ALRIGHT, FELIX?
JUST GRAZE WOUNDS. I'M FINE. WHERE THE HELL IS JACQUES?
HE WAS WITH US WHEN WE SPLIT OFF, I SWEAR IT.
WHY DID THEY STOP FIRING?
I'D DO THE SAME. PREY ON MY TARGET'S FEAR, FORCE IT TO STAY LOW AND UNAWARE AND CIRCLE AROUND. THEY'RE GOING TO AMBUSH US AGAIN.
YOU'RE A TERRIBLE MORALE OFFICER.
THERE'S STILL A FIREFIGHT GOING ON BY THE HOUSE. WE CAN'T STAY HERE AND DO NOTHING. I'M MOVING.
YOUR CHOICE WHAT YOU WANT TO DO, BUT I SUGGEST YOU FOLLOW ME.
WE'VE GOT YOUR BACK.
EYES OPEN, BOYS.

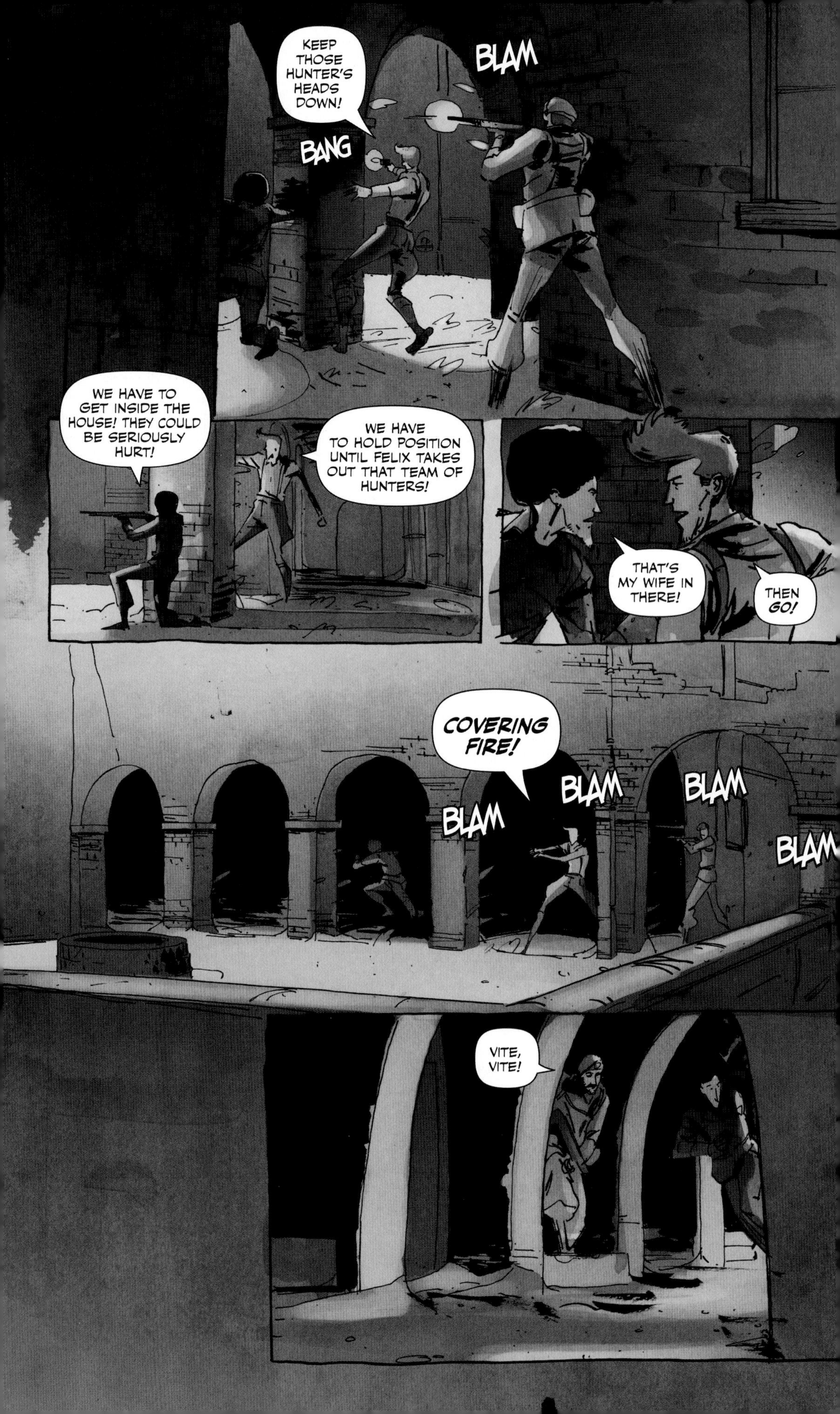
KEEP THOSE HUNTER'S HEADS DOWN!
BLAM
BANG
WE HAVE TO GET INSIDE THE HOUSE! THEY COULD BE SERIOUSLY HURT!
WE HAVE TO HOLD POSITION UNTIL FELIX TAKES OUT THAT TEAM OF HUNTERS!
THAT'S MY WIFE IN THERE!
THEN GO!
COVERING FIRE!
BLAM
BLAM
BLAM
BLAM
VITE, VITE!

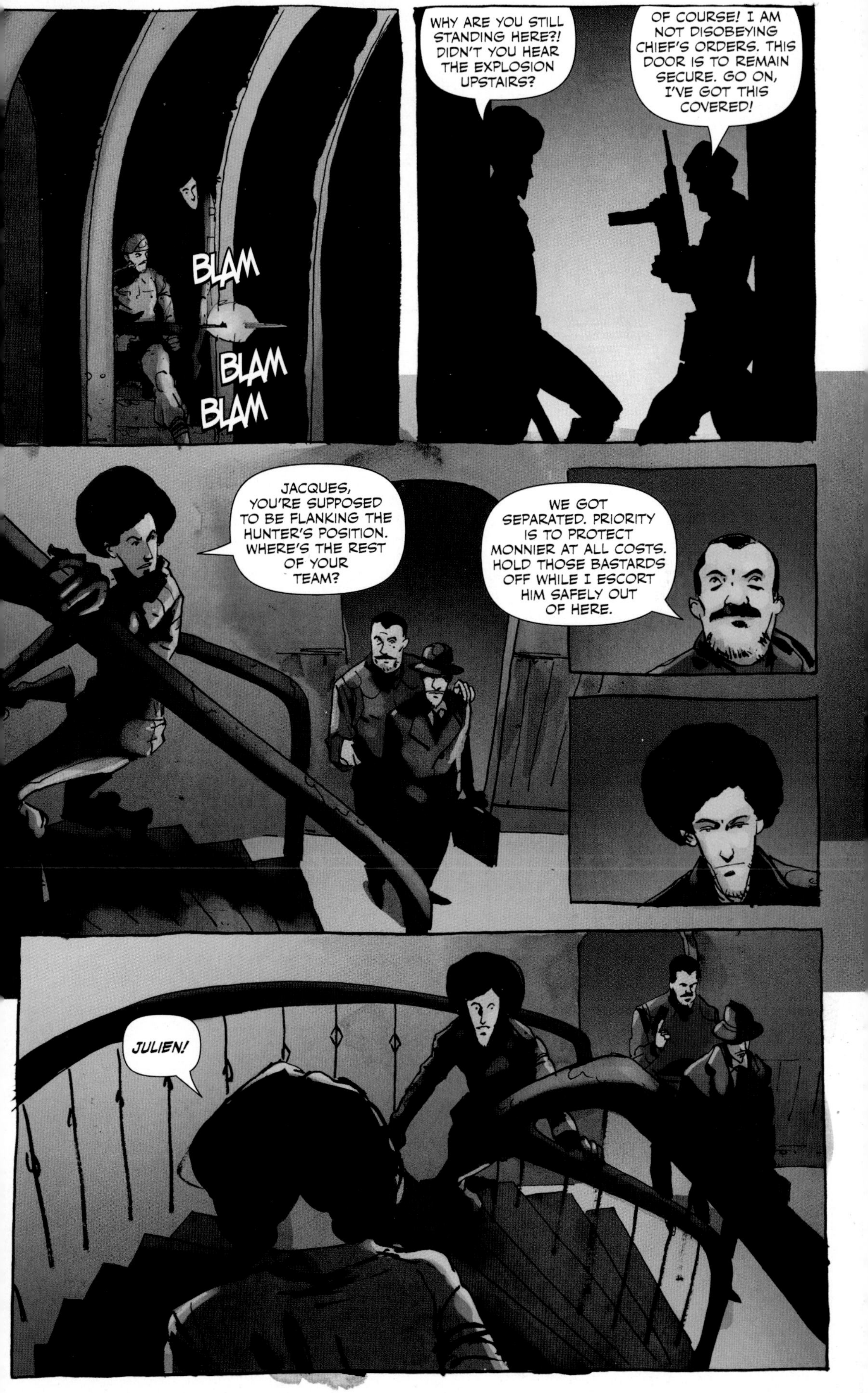
BLAM
BLAM
BLAM
WHY ARE YOU STILL STANDING HERE?! DIDN'T YOU HEAR THE EXPLOSION UPSTAIRS?
OF COURSE! I AM NOT DISOBEYING CHIEF'S ORDERS. THIS DOOR IS TO REMAIN SECURE. GO ON, I'VE GOT THIS COVERED!
JACQUES, YOU'RE SUPPOSED TO BE FLANKING THE HUNTER'S POSITION. WHERE'S THE REST OF YOUR TEAM?
WE GOT SEPARATED. PRIORITY IS TO PROTECT MONNIER AT ALL COSTS. HOLD THOSE BASTARDS OFF WHILE I ESCORT HIM SAFELY OUT OF HERE.
JULIEN!

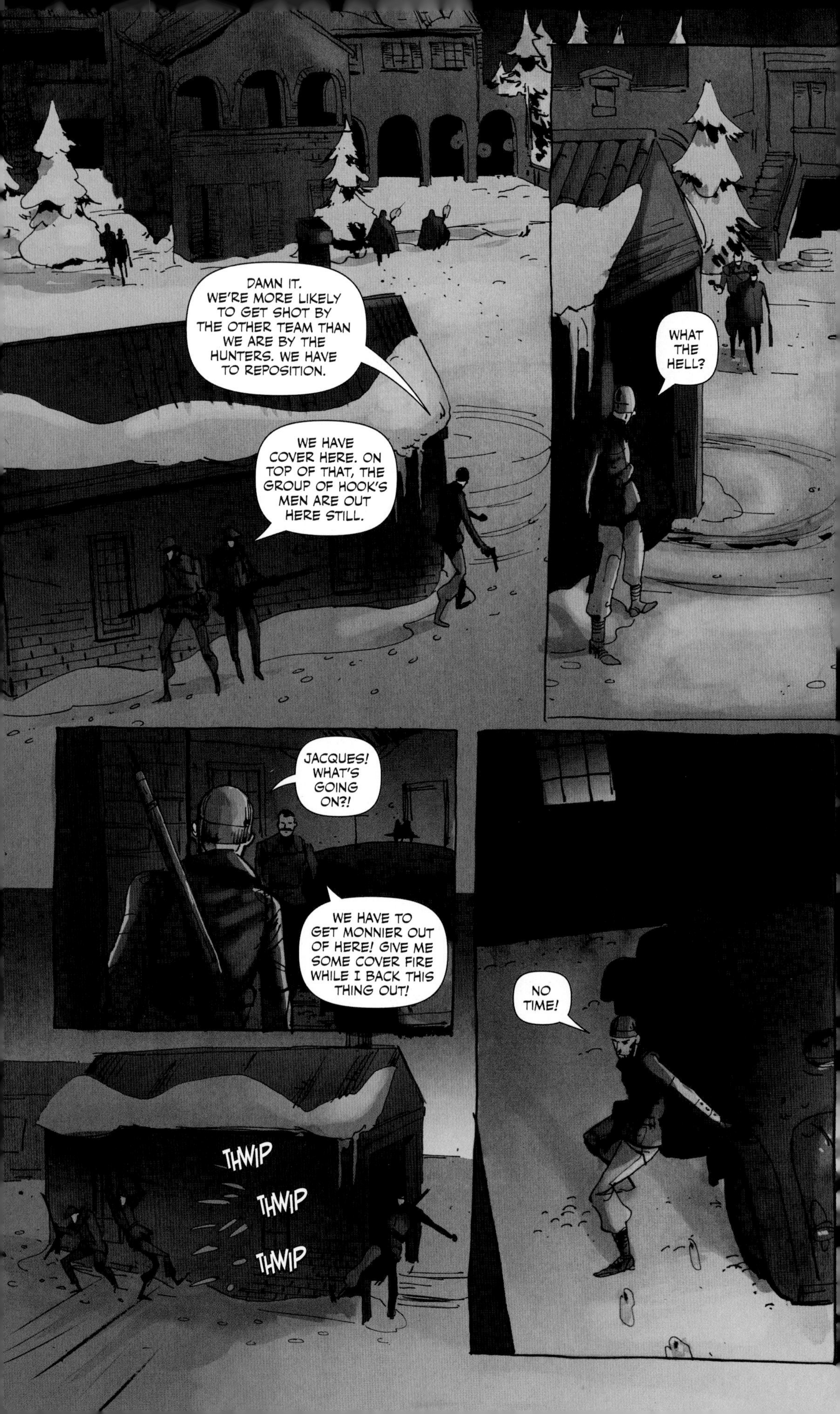
DAMN IT. WE'RE MORE LIKELY TO GET SHOT BY THE OTHER TEAM THAN WE ARE BY THE HUNTERS. WE HAVE TO REPOSITION.
WE HAVE COVER HERE. ON TOP OF THAT, THE GROUP OF HOOK'S MEN ARE OUT HERE STILL.
WHAT THE HELL?
JACQUES! WHAT'S GOING ON?!
WE HAVE TO GET MONNIER OUT OF HERE! GIVE ME SOME COVER FIRE WHILE I BACK THIS THING OUT!
NO TIME!
THWIP
THWIP
THWIP

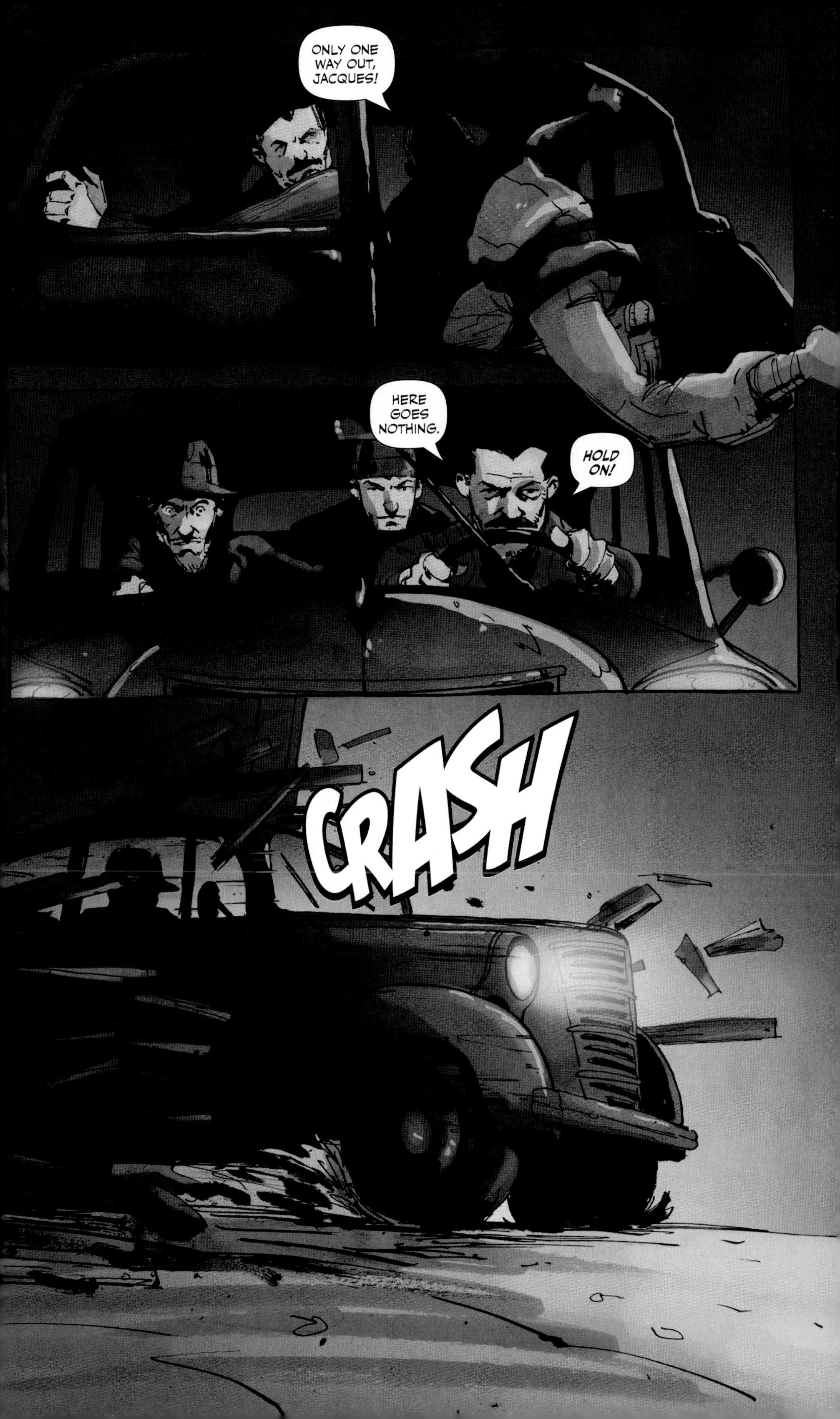
ONLY ONE WAY OUT, JACQUES!
HERE GOES NOTHING.
HOLD ON!
CRASH

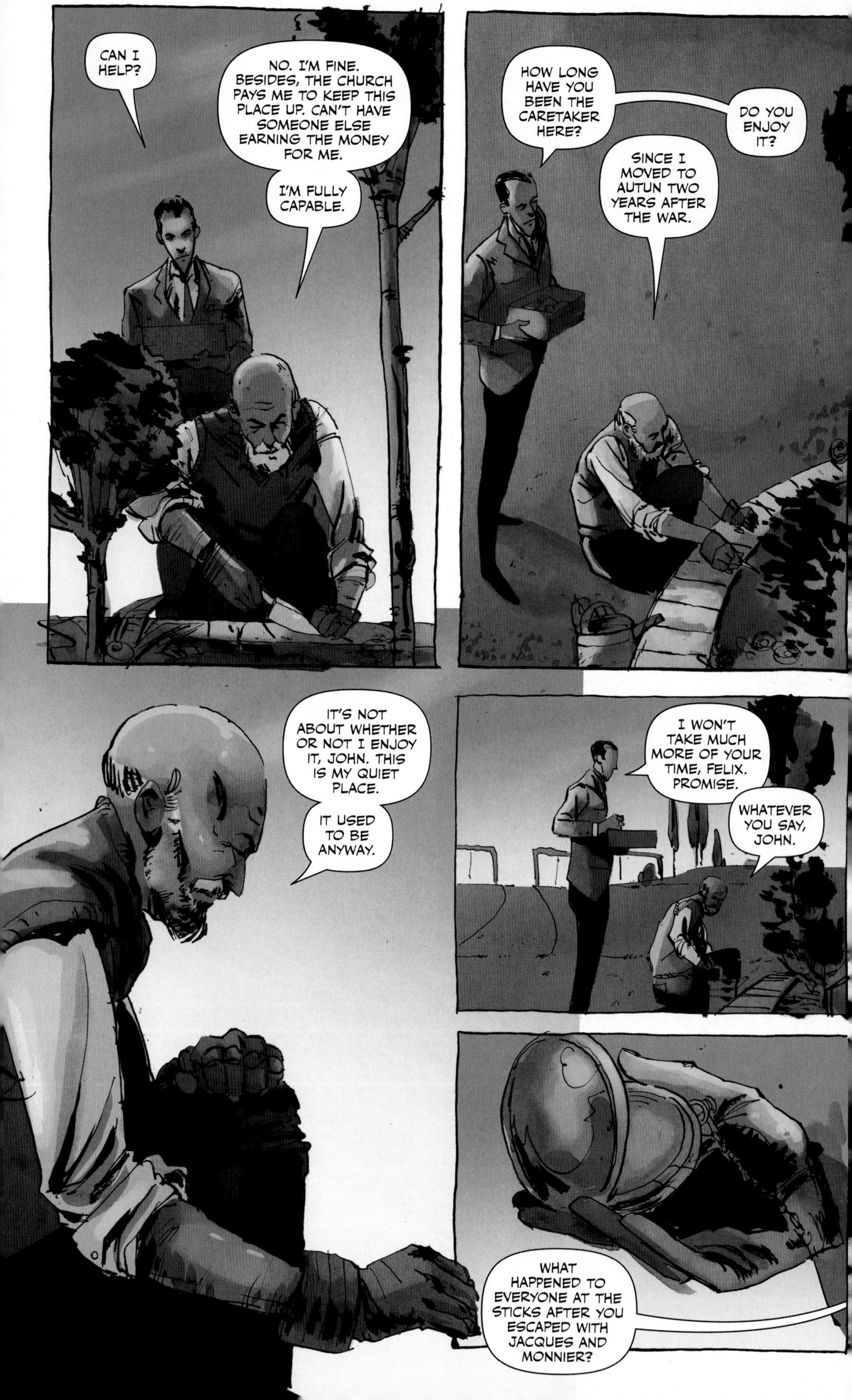
CAN I HELP?
NO. I'M FINE. BESIDES, THE CHURCH PAYS ME TO KEEP THIS PLACE UP. CAN'T HAVE SOMEONE ELSE EARNING THE MONEY FOR ME.
I'M FULLY CAPABLE.
HOW LONG HAVE YOU BEEN THE CARETAKER HERE?
DO YOU ENJOY IT?
SINCE I MOVED TO AUTUN TWO YEARS AFTER THE WAR.
IT'S NOT ABOUT WHETHER OR NOT I ENJOY IT, JOHN. THIS IS MY QUIET PLACE.
IT USED TO BE ANYWAY.
I WON'T TAKE MUCH MORE OF YOUR TIME, FELIX. PROMISE.
WHATEVER YOU SAY, JOHN.
WHAT HAPPENED TO EVERYONE AT THE STICKS AFTER YOU ESCAPED WITH JACQUES AND MONNIER?

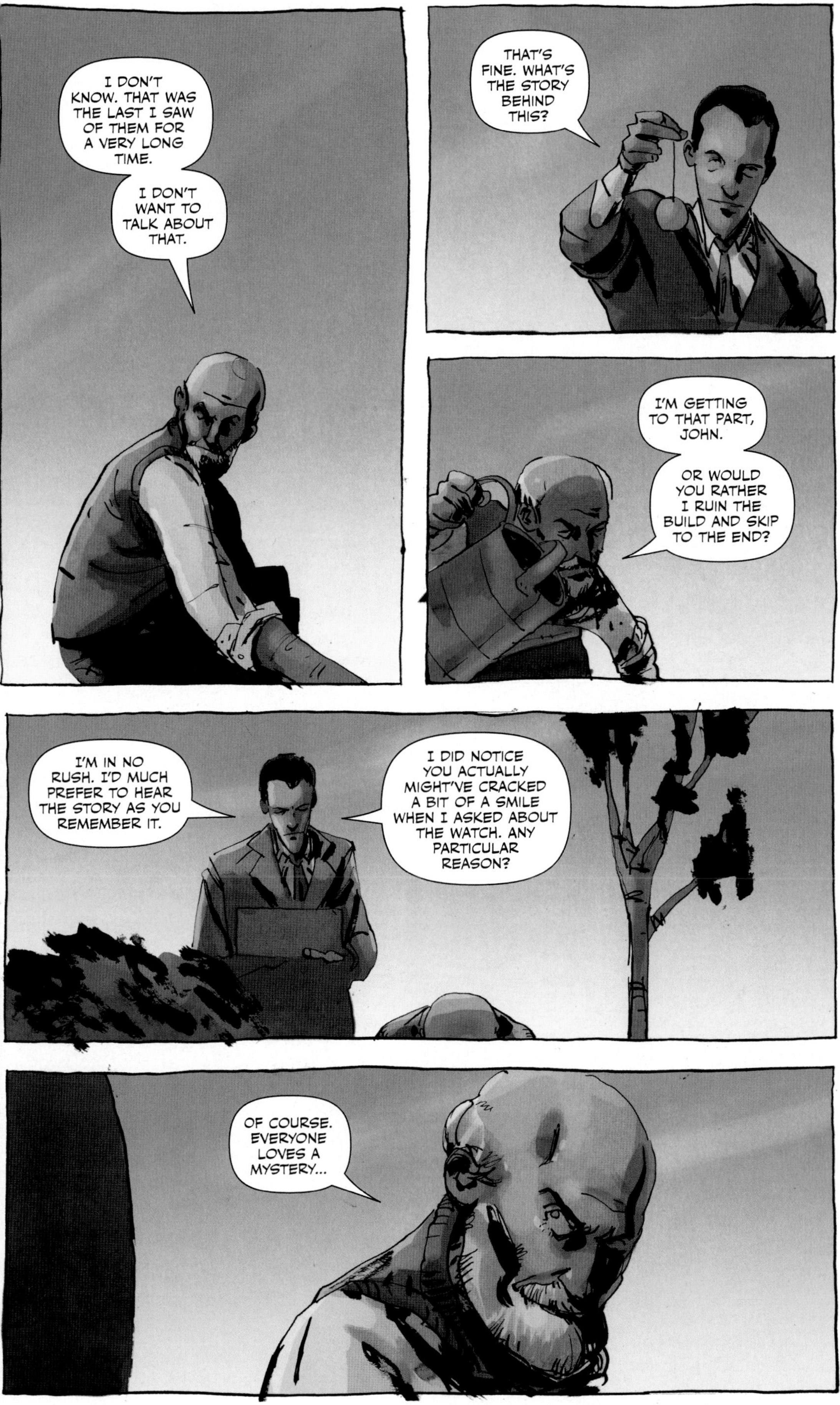
I DON'T KNOW. THAT WAS THE LAST I SAW OF THEM FOR A VERY LONG TIME.
I DON'T WANT TO TALK ABOUT THAT.
THAT'S FINE. WHAT'S THE STORY BEHIND THIS?
I'M GETTING TO THAT PART, JOHN.
OR WOULD YOU RATHER I RUIN THE BUILD AND SKIP TO THE END?
I'M IN NO RUSH. I'D MUCH PREFER TO HEAR THE STORY AS YOU REMEMBER IT.
I DID NOTICE YOU ACTUALLY MIGHT'VE CRACKED A BIT OF A SMILE WHEN I ASKED ABOUT THE WATCH. ANY PARTICULAR REASON?
OF COURSE. EVERYONE LOVES A MYSTERY...

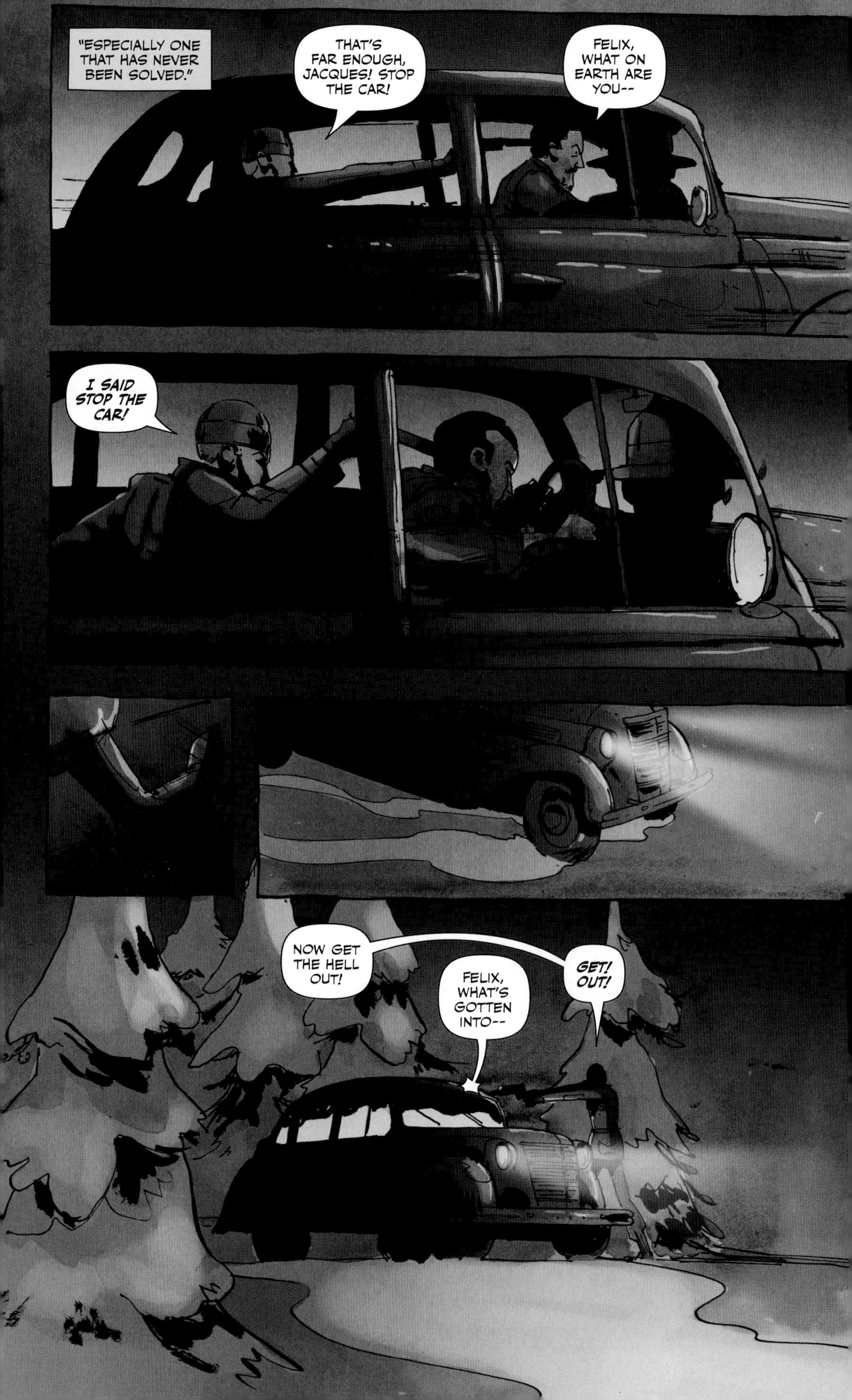
"ESPECIALLY ONE THAT HAS NEVER BEEN SOLVED."
THAT'S FAR ENOUGH, JACQUES! STOP THE CAR!
FELIX, WHAT ON EARTH ARE YOU--
I SAID STOP THE CAR!
NOW GET THE HELL OUT!
FELIX, WHAT'S GOTTEN INTO--
GET! OUT!

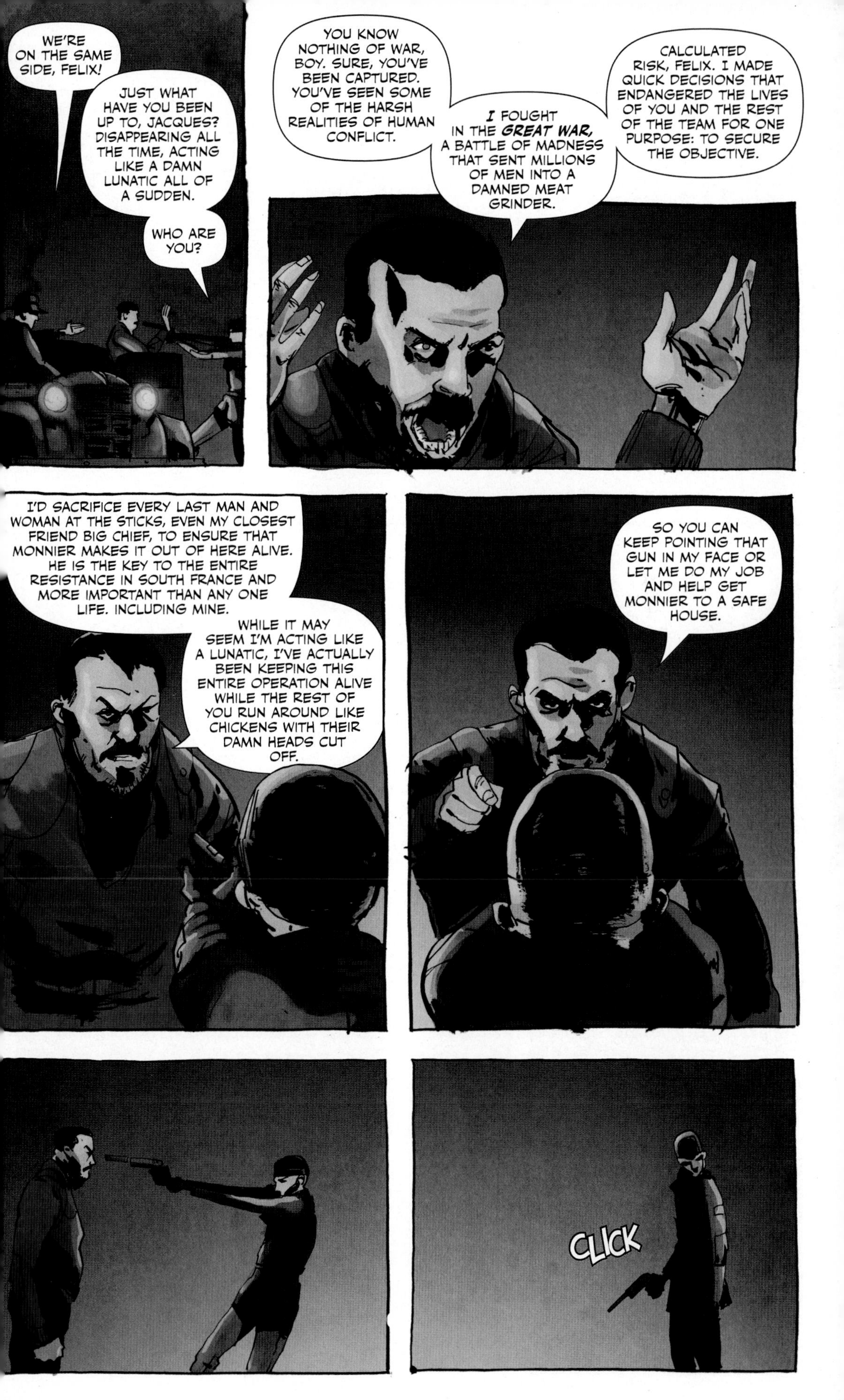
WE'RE ON THE SAME SIDE, FELIX!
JUST WHAT HAVE YOU BEEN UP TO, JACQUES? DISAPPEARING ALL THE TIME, ACTING LIKE A DAMN LUNATIC ALL OF A SUDDEN.
WHO ARE YOU?
YOU KNOW NOTHING OF WAR, BOY. SURE, YOU'VE BEEN CAPTURED. YOU'VE SEEN SOME OF THE HARSH REALITIES OF HUMAN CONFLICT.
I FOUGHT IN THE GREAT WAR, A BATTLE OF MADNESS THAT SENT MILLIONS OF MEN INTO A DAMNED MEAT GRINDER.
CALCULATED RISK, FELIX. I MADE QUICK DECISIONS THAT ENDANGERED THE LIVES OF YOU AND THE REST OF THE TEAM FOR ONE PURPOSE: TO SECURE THE OBJECTIVE.
I'D SACRIFICE EVERY LAST MAN AND WOMAN AT THE STICKS, EVEN MY CLOSEST FRIEND BIG CHIEF, TO ENSURE THAT MONNIER MAKES IT OUT OF HERE ALIVE. HE IS THE KEY TO THE ENTIRE RESISTANCE IN SOUTH FRANCE AND MORE IMPORTANT THAN ANY ONE LIFE. INCLUDING MINE.
WHILE IT MAY SEEM I'M ACTING LIKE A LUNATIC, I'VE ACTUALLY BEEN KEEPING THIS ENTIRE OPERATION ALIVE WHILE THE REST OF YOU RUN AROUND LIKE CHICKENS WITH THEIR DAMN HEADS CUT OFF.
SO YOU CAN KEEP POINTING THAT GUN IN MY FACE OR LET ME DO MY JOB AND HELP GET MONNIER TO A SAFE HOUSE.
CLICK

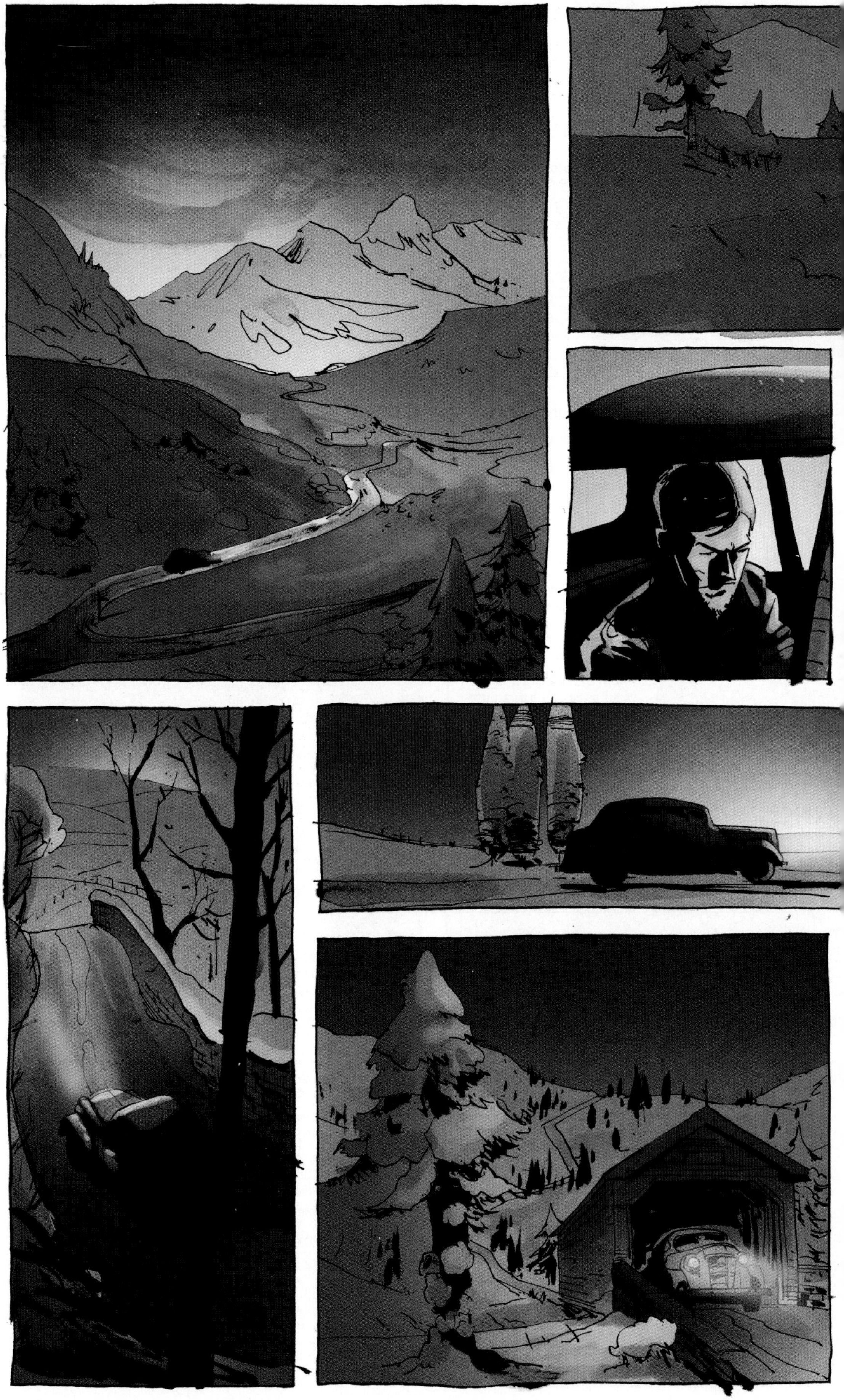

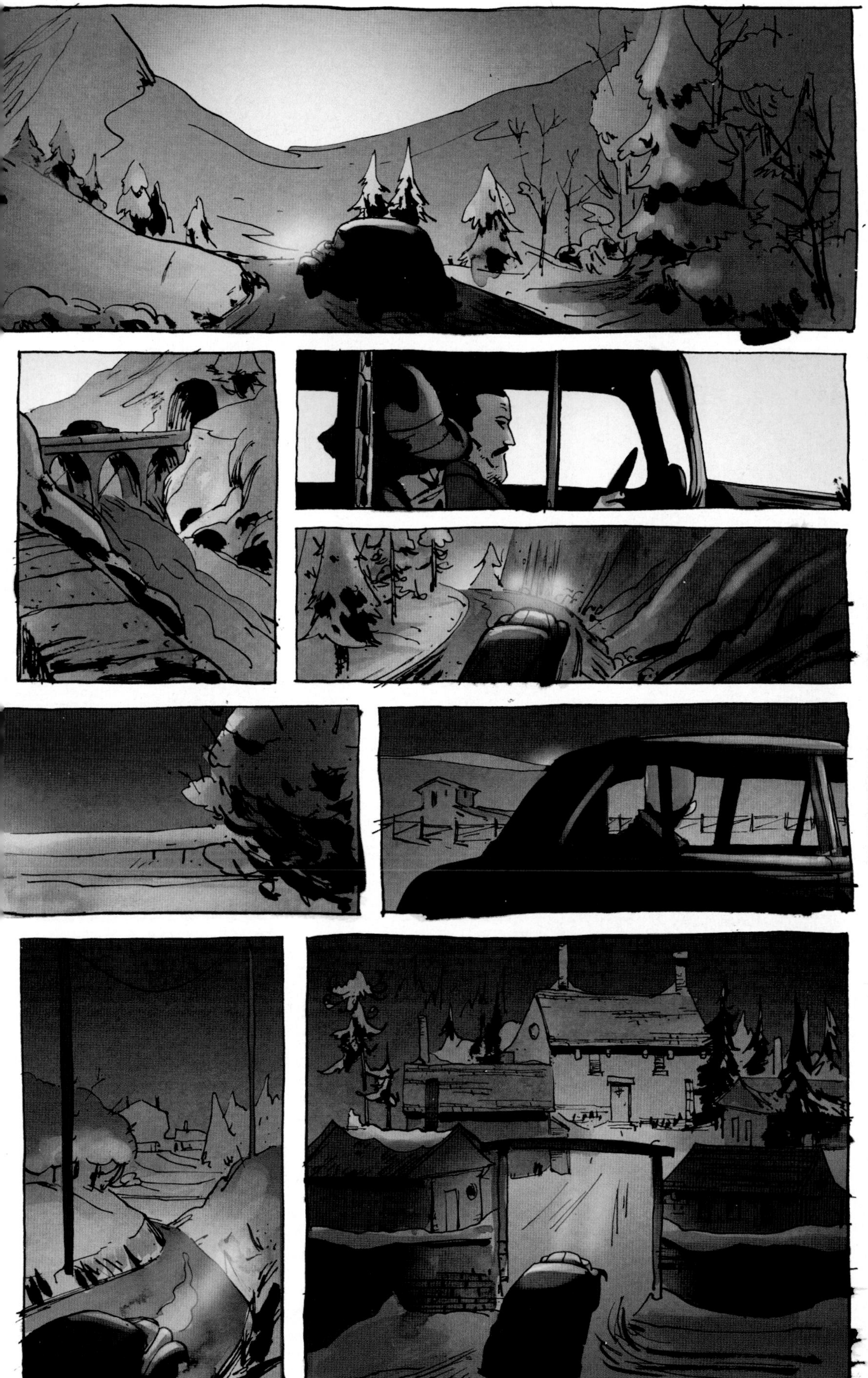

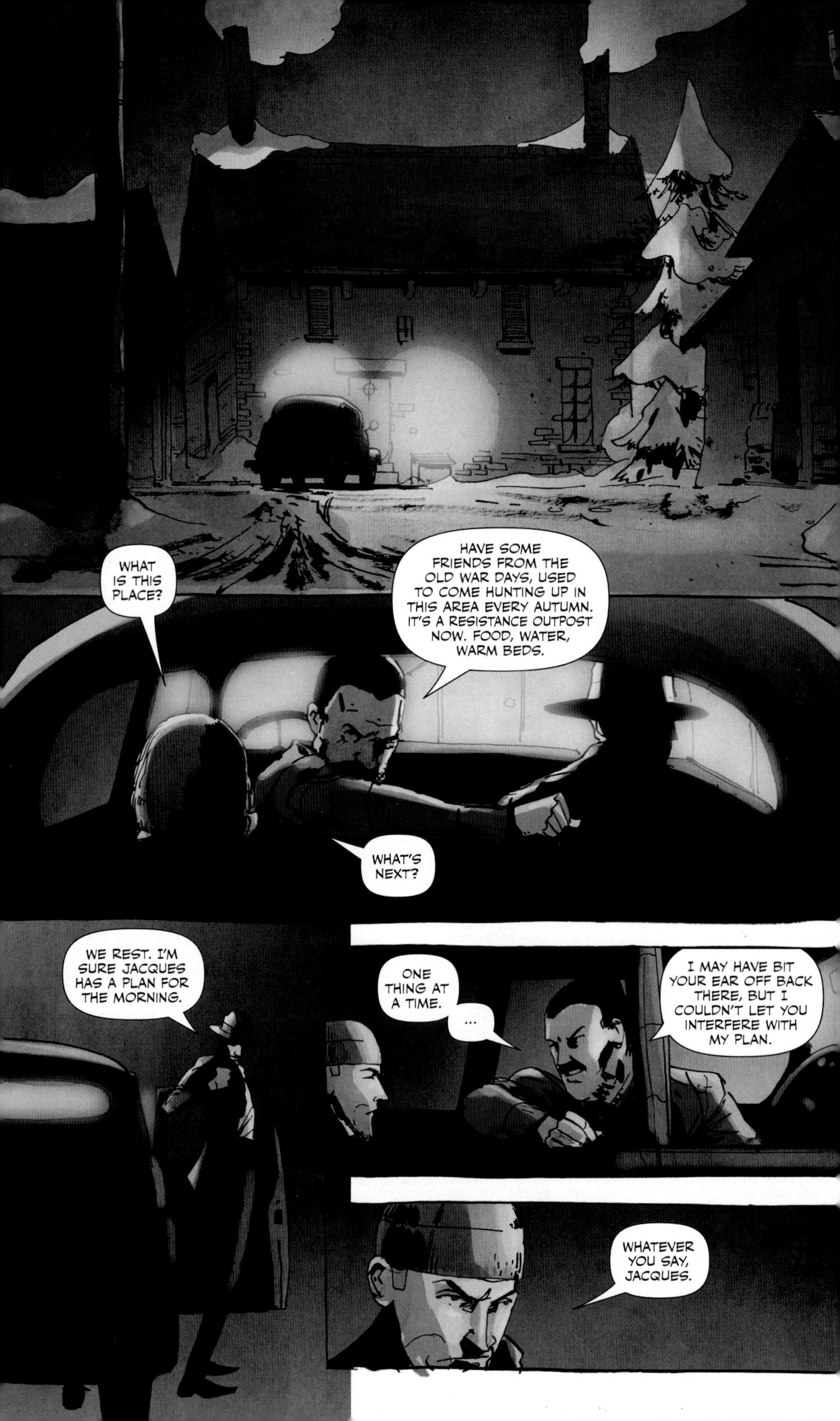

WHAT IS THIS PLACE?
HAVE SOME FRIENDS FROM THE OLD WAR DAYS, USED TO COME HUNTING UP IN THIS AREA EVERY AUTUMN. IT'S A RESISTANCE OUTPOST NOW. FOOD, WATER, WARM BEDS.
WHAT'S NEXT?
WE REST. I'M SURE JACQUES HAS A PLAN FOR THE MORNING.
ONE THING AT A TIME.
...
I MAY HAVE BIT YOUR EAR OFF BACK THERE, BUT I COULDN'T LET YOU INTERFERE WITH MY PLAN.
WHATEVER YOU SAY, JACQUES.

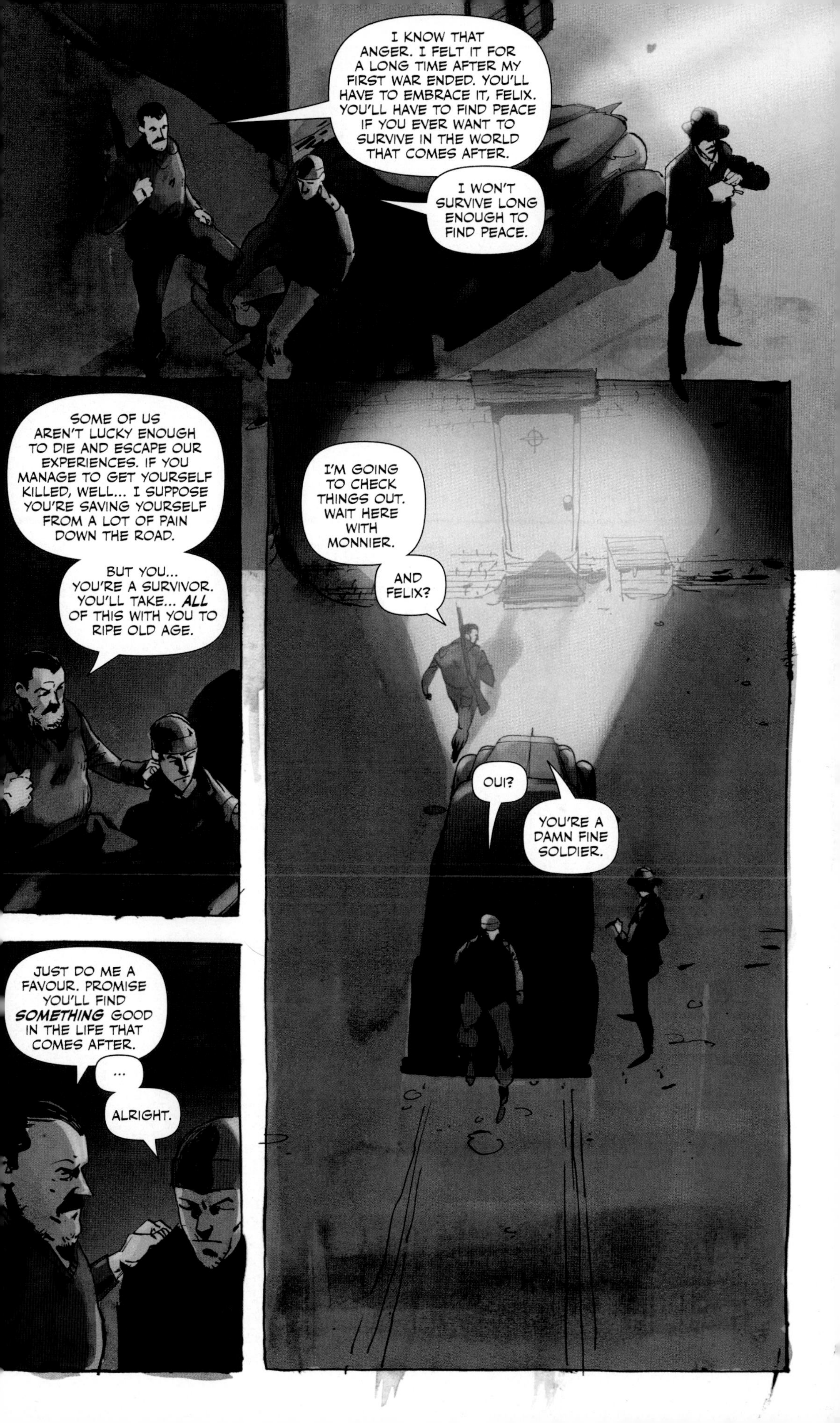
I KNOW THAT ANGER. I FELT IT FOR A LONG TIME AFTER MY FIRST WAR ENDED. YOU'LL HAVE TO EMBRACE IT, FELIX. YOU'LL HAVE TO FIND PEACE IF YOU EVER WANT TO SURVIVE IN THE WORLD THAT COMES AFTER.
I WON'T SURVIVE LONG ENOUGH TO FIND PEACE.
SOME OF US AREN'T LUCKY ENOUGH TO DIE AND ESCAPE OUR EXPERIENCES. IF YOU MANAGE TO GET YOURSELF KILLED, WELL... I SUPPOSE YOU'RE SAVING YOURSELF FROM A LOT OF PAIN DOWN THE ROAD.
BUT YOU... YOU'RE A SURVIVOR. YOU'LL TAKE... *ALL* OF THIS WITH YOU TO RIPE OLD AGE.
JUST DO ME A FAVOUR. PROMISE YOU'LL FIND ***SOMETHING*** GOOD IN THE LIFE THAT COMES AFTER.
...
ALRIGHT.
I'M GOING TO CHECK THINGS OUT. WAIT HERE WITH MONNIER.
AND FELIX?
OUI?
YOU'RE A DAMN FINE SOLDIER.

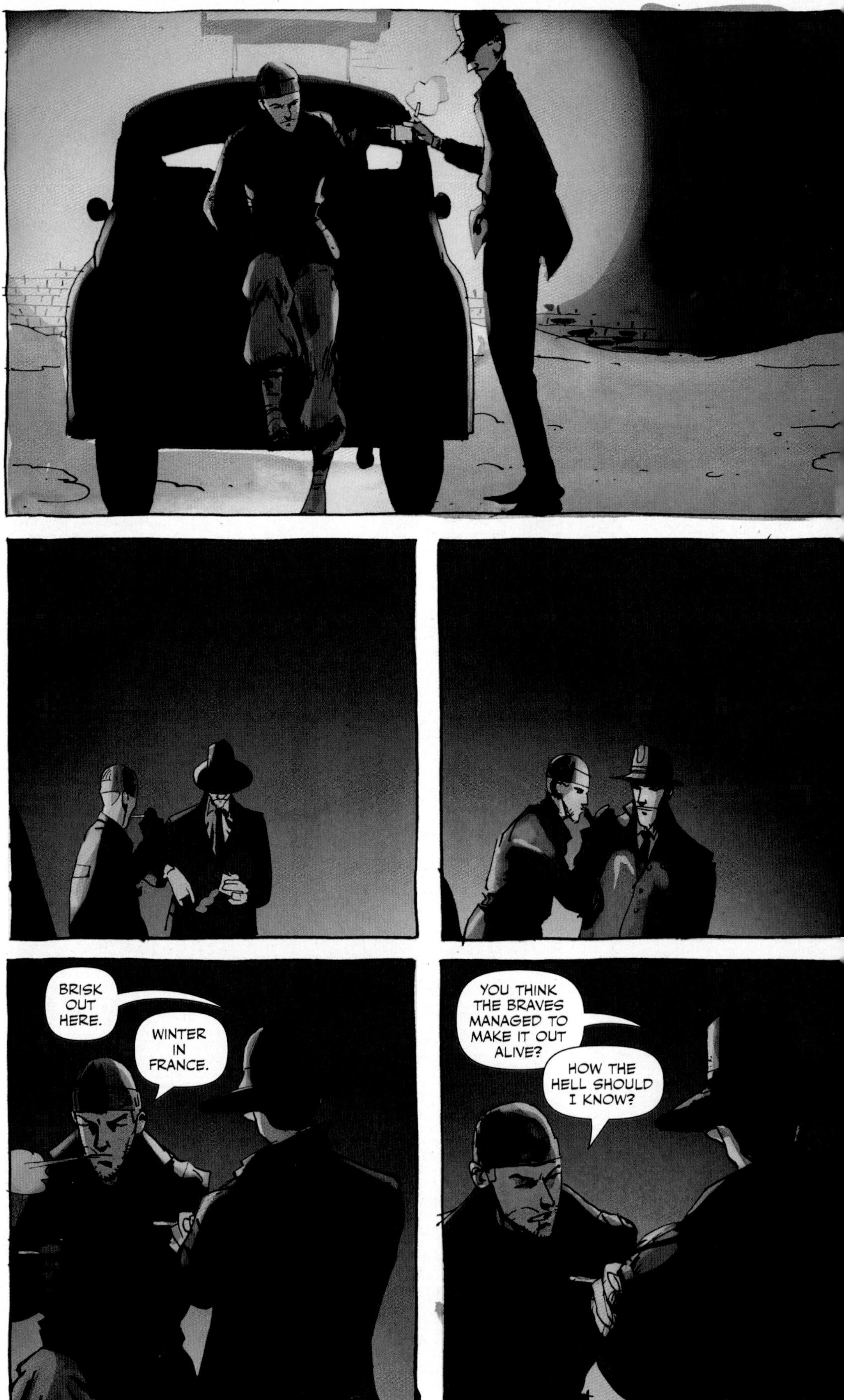
BRISK OUT HERE.
WINTER IN FRANCE.
YOU THINK THE BRAVES MANAGED TO MAKE IT OUT ALIVE?
HOW THE HELL SHOULD I KNOW?

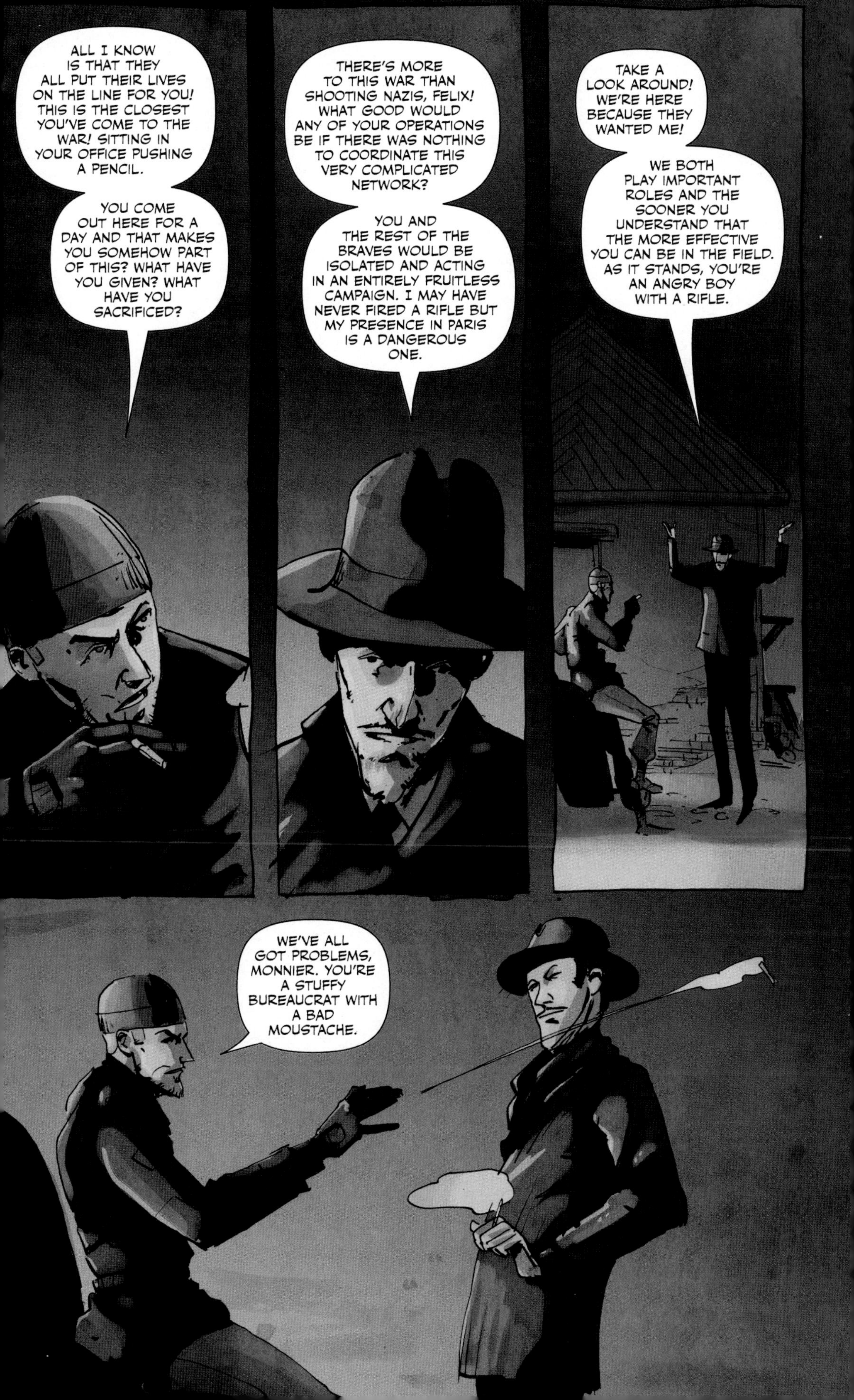

ALL I KNOW IS THAT THEY ALL PUT THEIR LIVES ON THE LINE FOR YOU! THIS IS THE CLOSEST YOU'VE COME TO THE WAR! SITTING IN YOUR OFFICE PUSHING A PENCIL.
YOU COME OUT HERE FOR A DAY AND THAT MAKES YOU SOMEHOW PART OF THIS? WHAT HAVE YOU GIVEN? WHAT HAVE YOU SACRIFICED?
THERE'S MORE TO THIS WAR THAN SHOOTING NAZIS, FELIX! WHAT GOOD WOULD ANY OF YOUR OPERATIONS BE IF THERE WAS NOTHING TO COORDINATE THIS VERY COMPLICATED NETWORK?
YOU AND THE REST OF THE BRAVES WOULD BE ISOLATED AND ACTING IN AN ENTIRELY FRUITLESS CAMPAIGN. I MAY HAVE NEVER FIRED A RIFLE BUT MY PRESENCE IN PARIS IS A DANGEROUS ONE.
TAKE A LOOK AROUND! WE'RE HERE BECAUSE THEY WANTED ME!
WE BOTH PLAY IMPORTANT ROLES AND THE SOONER YOU UNDERSTAND THAT THE MORE EFFECTIVE YOU CAN BE IN THE FIELD. AS IT STANDS, YOU'RE AN ANGRY BOY WITH A RIFLE.
WE'VE ALL GOT PROBLEMS, MONNIER. YOU'RE A STUFFY BUREAUCRAT WITH A BAD MOUSTACHE.

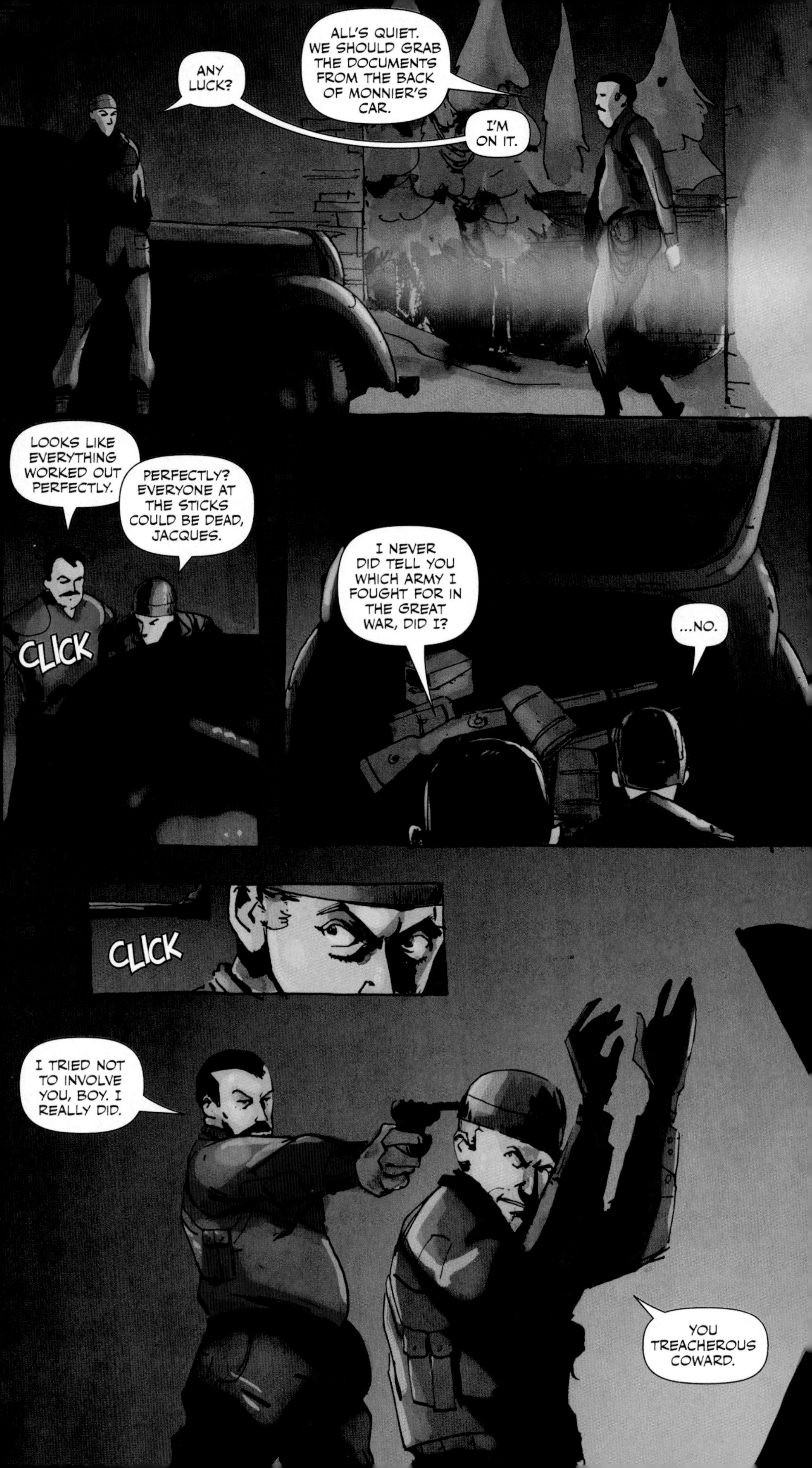
ANY LUCK?
ALL'S QUIET. WE SHOULD GRAB THE DOCUMENTS FROM THE BACK OF MONNIER'S CAR.
I'M ON IT.
LOOKS LIKE EVERYTHING WORKED OUT PERFECTLY.
PERFECTLY? EVERYONE AT THE STICKS COULD BE DEAD, JACQUES.
CLICK
I NEVER DID TELL YOU WHICH ARMY I FOUGHT FOR IN THE GREAT WAR, DID I?
...NO.
CLICK
I TRIED NOT TO INVOLVE YOU, BOY. I REALLY DID.
YOU TREACHEROUS COWARD.

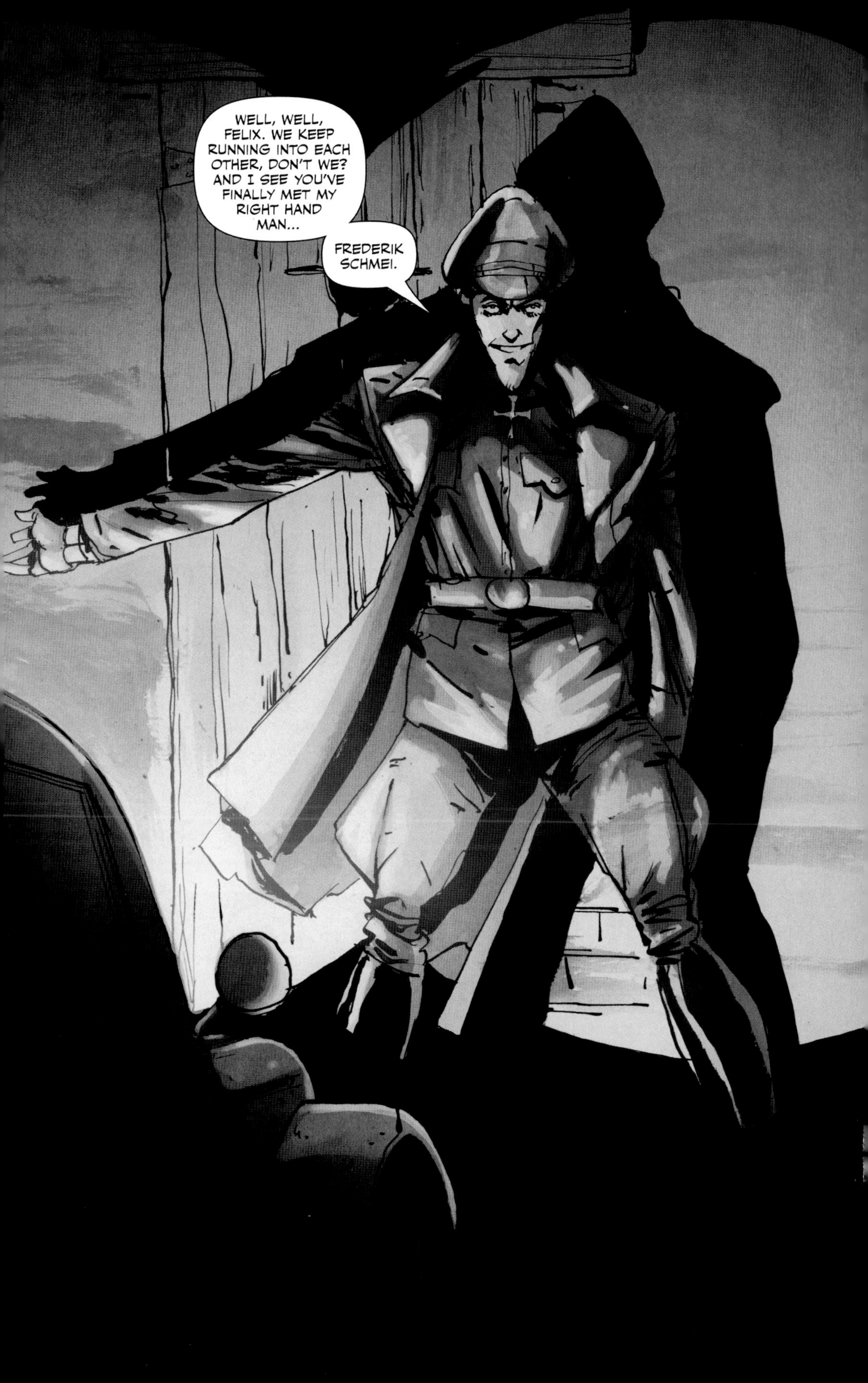
WELL, WELL, FELIX. WE KEEP RUNNING INTO EACH OTHER, DON'T WE? AND I SEE YOU'VE FINALLY MET MY RIGHT HAND MAN...
FREDERIK SCHMEI.

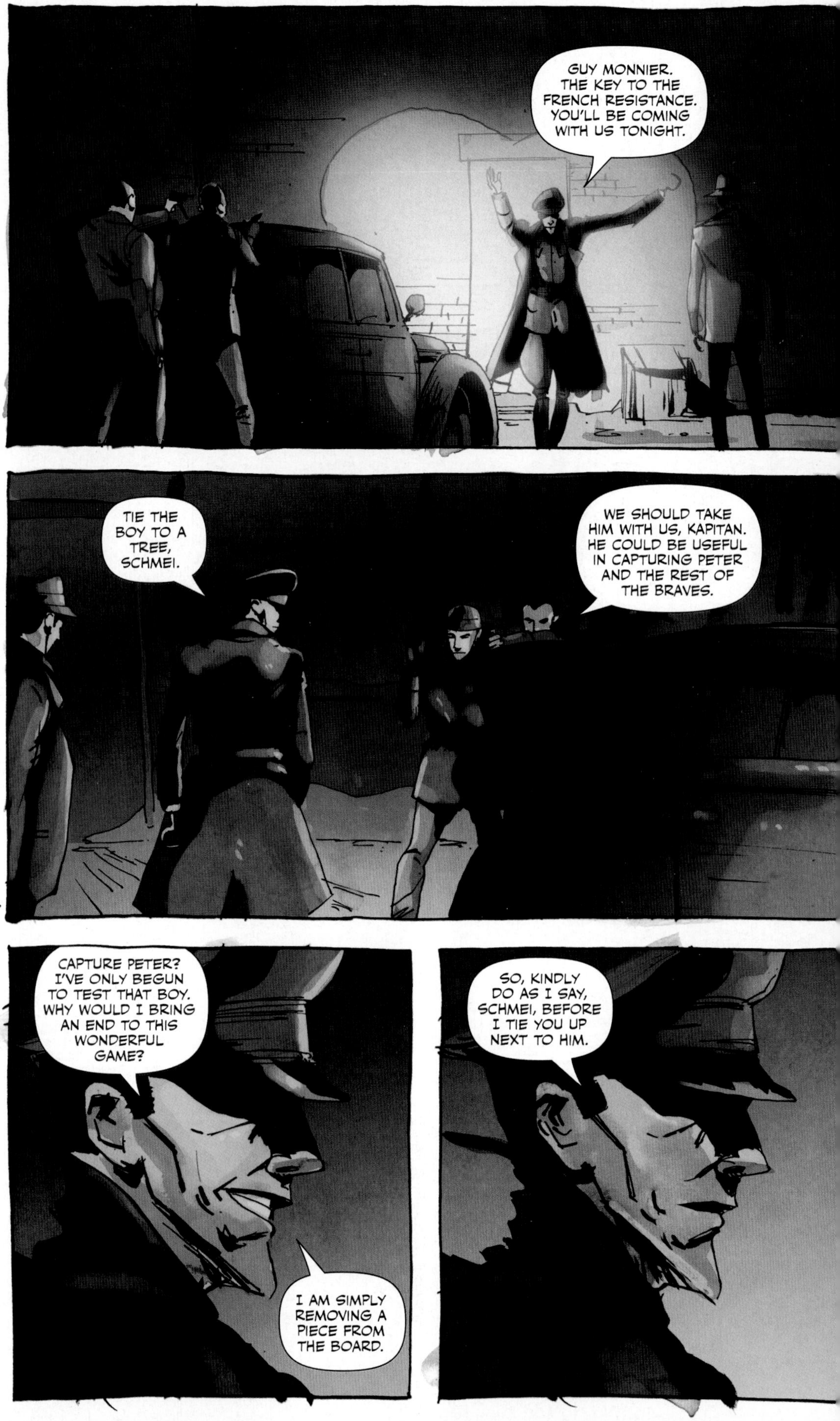
GUY MONNIER. THE KEY TO THE FRENCH RESISTANCE. YOU'LL BE COMING WITH US TONIGHT.
TIE THE BOY TO A TREE, SCHMEI.
WE SHOULD TAKE HIM WITH US, KAPITAN. HE COULD BE USEFUL IN CAPTURING PETER AND THE REST OF THE BRAVES.
CAPTURE PETER? I'VE ONLY BEGUN TO TEST THAT BOY. WHY WOULD I BRING AN END TO THIS WONDERFUL GAME?
I AM SIMPLY REMOVING A PIECE FROM THE BOARD.
SO, KINDLY DO AS I SAY, SCHMEI, BEFORE I TIE YOU UP NEXT TO HIM.

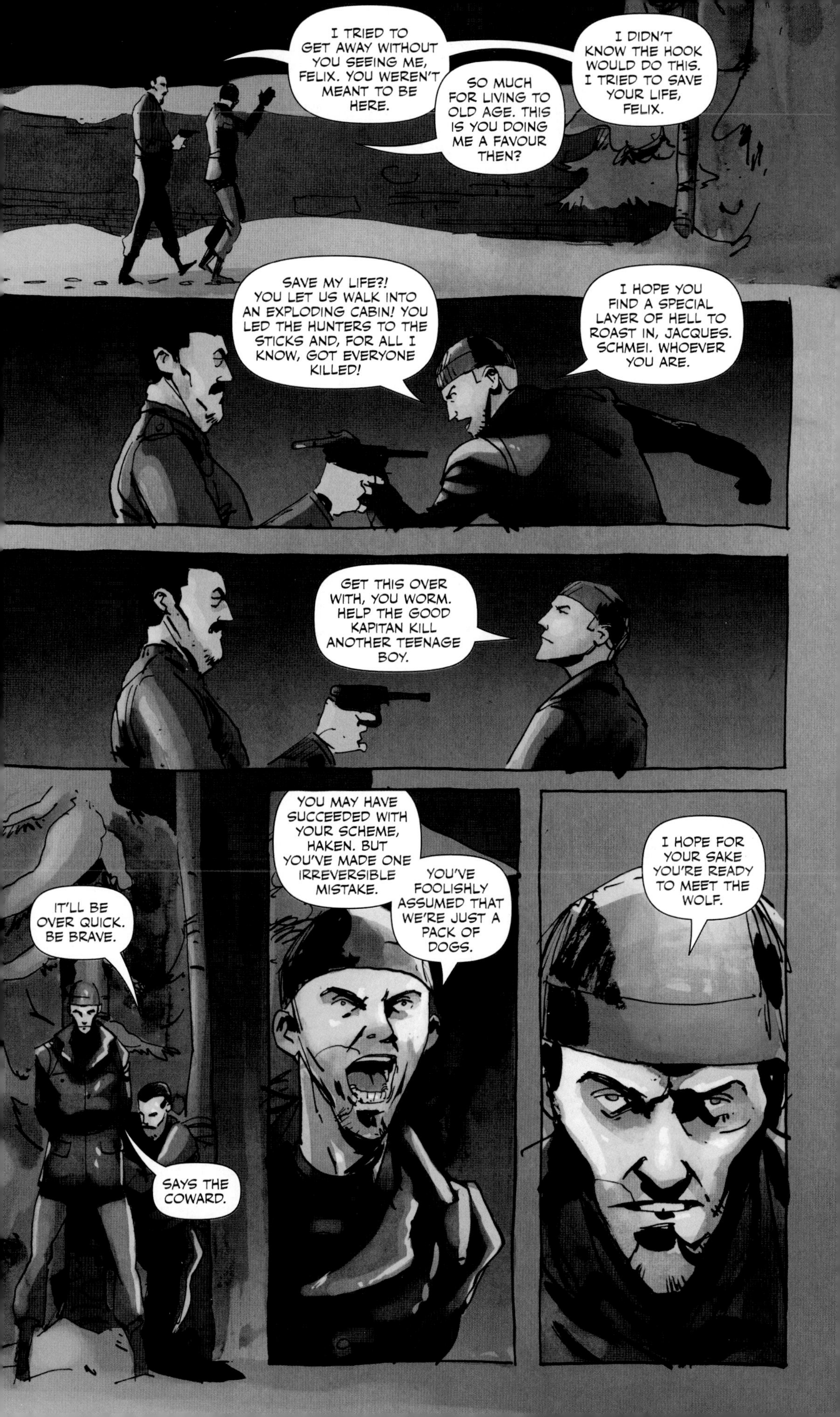
I TRIED TO GET AWAY WITHOUT YOU SEEING ME, FELIX. YOU WEREN'T MEANT TO BE HERE.
SO MUCH FOR LIVING TO OLD AGE. THIS IS YOU DOING ME A FAVOUR THEN?
I DIDN'T KNOW THE HOOK WOULD DO THIS. I TRIED TO SAVE YOUR LIFE, FELIX.
SAVE MY LIFE?! YOU LET US WALK INTO AN EXPLODING CABIN! YOU LED THE HUNTERS TO THE STICKS AND, FOR ALL I KNOW, GOT EVERYONE KILLED!
I HOPE YOU FIND A SPECIAL LAYER OF HELL TO ROAST IN, JACQUES. SCHMEI. WHOEVER YOU ARE.
GET THIS OVER WITH, YOU WORM. HELP THE GOOD KAPITAN KILL ANOTHER TEENAGE BOY.
IT'LL BE OVER QUICK. BE BRAVE.
SAYS THE COWARD.
YOU MAY HAVE SUCCEEDED WITH YOUR SCHEME, HAKEN. BUT YOU'VE MADE ONE IRREVERSIBLE MISTAKE.
YOU'VE FOOLISHLY ASSUMED THAT WE'RE JUST A PACK OF DOGS.
I HOPE FOR YOUR SAKE YOU'RE READY TO MEET THE WOLF.

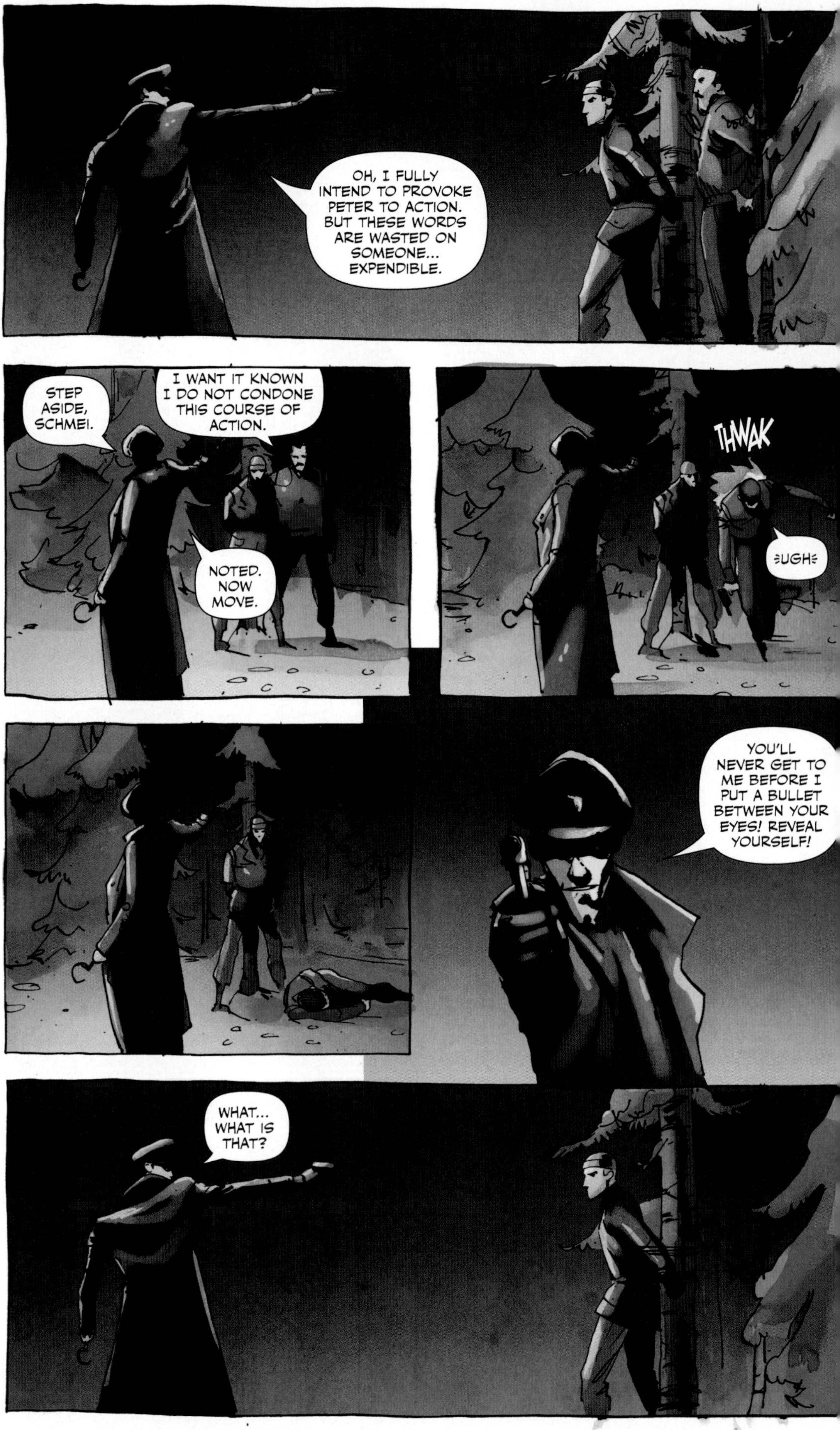
OH, I FULLY INTEND TO PROVOKE PETER TO ACTION. BUT THESE WORDS ARE WASTED ON SOMEONE... EXPENDIBLE.
STEP ASIDE, SCHMEI.
I WANT IT KNOWN I DO NOT CONDONE THIS COURSE OF ACTION.
NOTED. NOW MOVE.
THWAK
UGH
YOU'LL NEVER GET TO ME BEFORE I PUT A BULLET BETWEEN YOUR EYES! REVEAL YOURSELF!
WHAT... WHAT IS THAT?

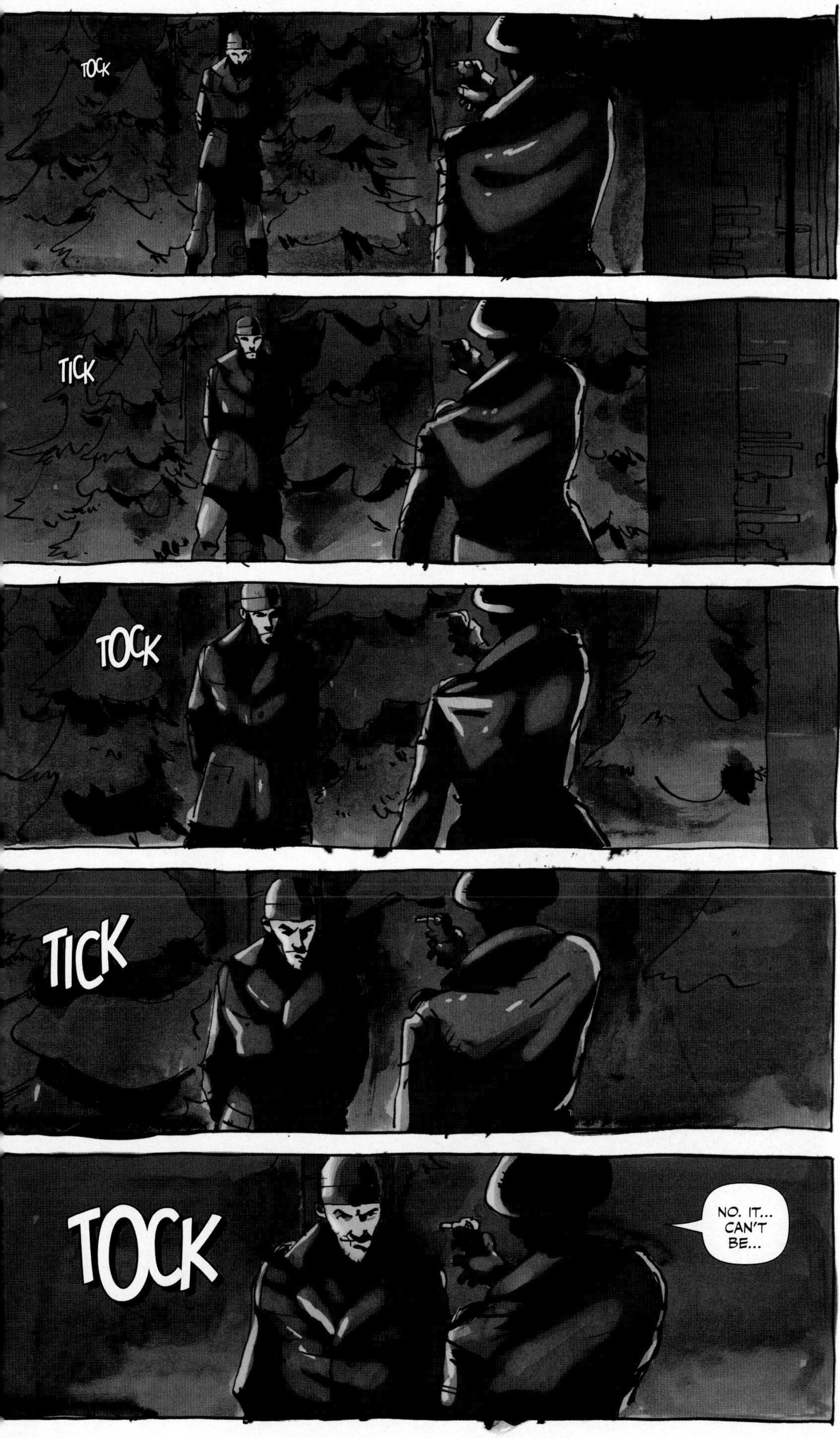
TOCK
TICK
TOCK
TICK
TOCK
NO. IT... CAN'T BE...

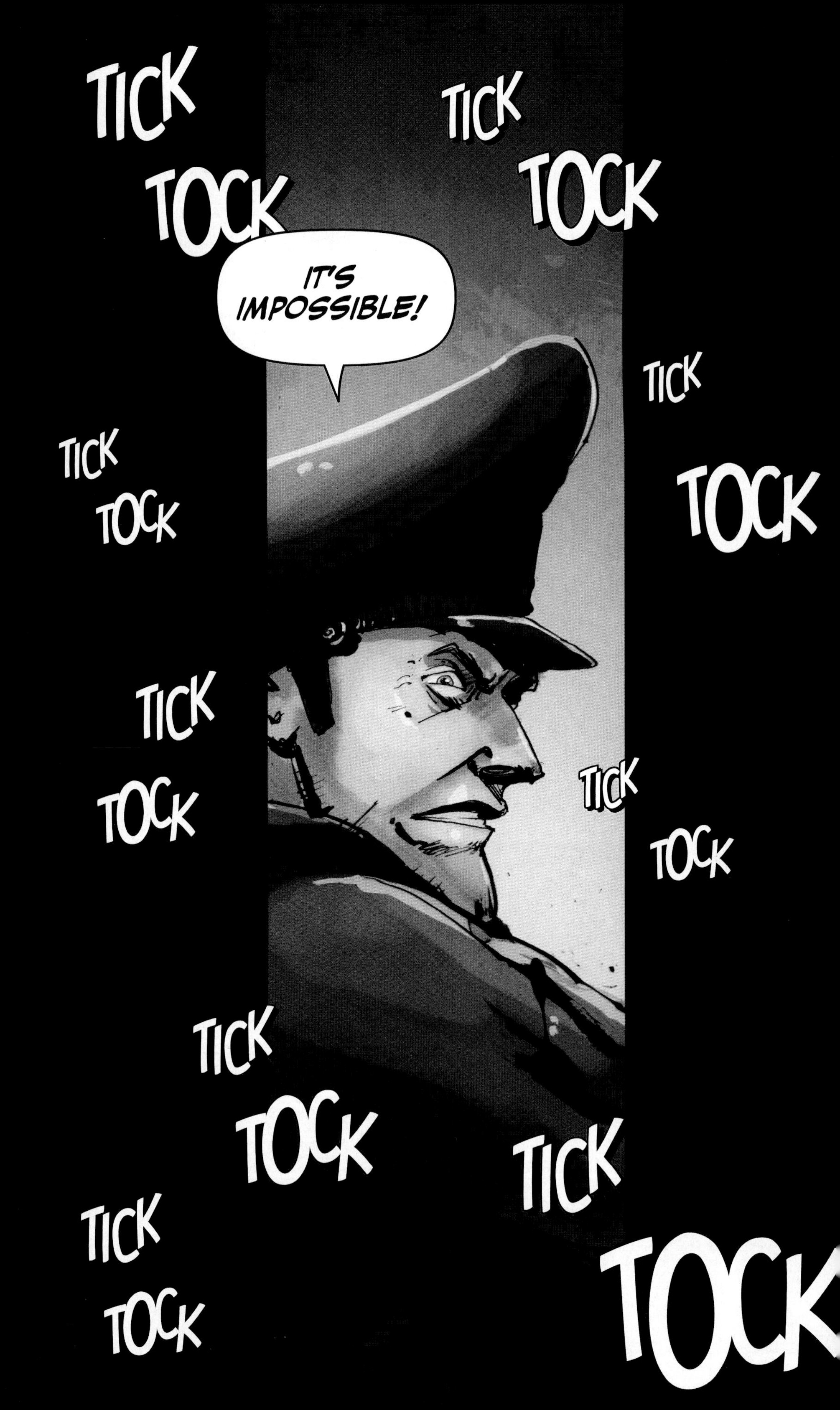
TICK
TOCK
TICK
TOCK
IT'S IMPOSSIBLE!
TICK
TICK
TOCK
TOCK
TICK
TOCK
TICK
TOCK
TICK
TOCK
TICK
TICK
TOCK
TOCK

CHAPTER FIFTEEN

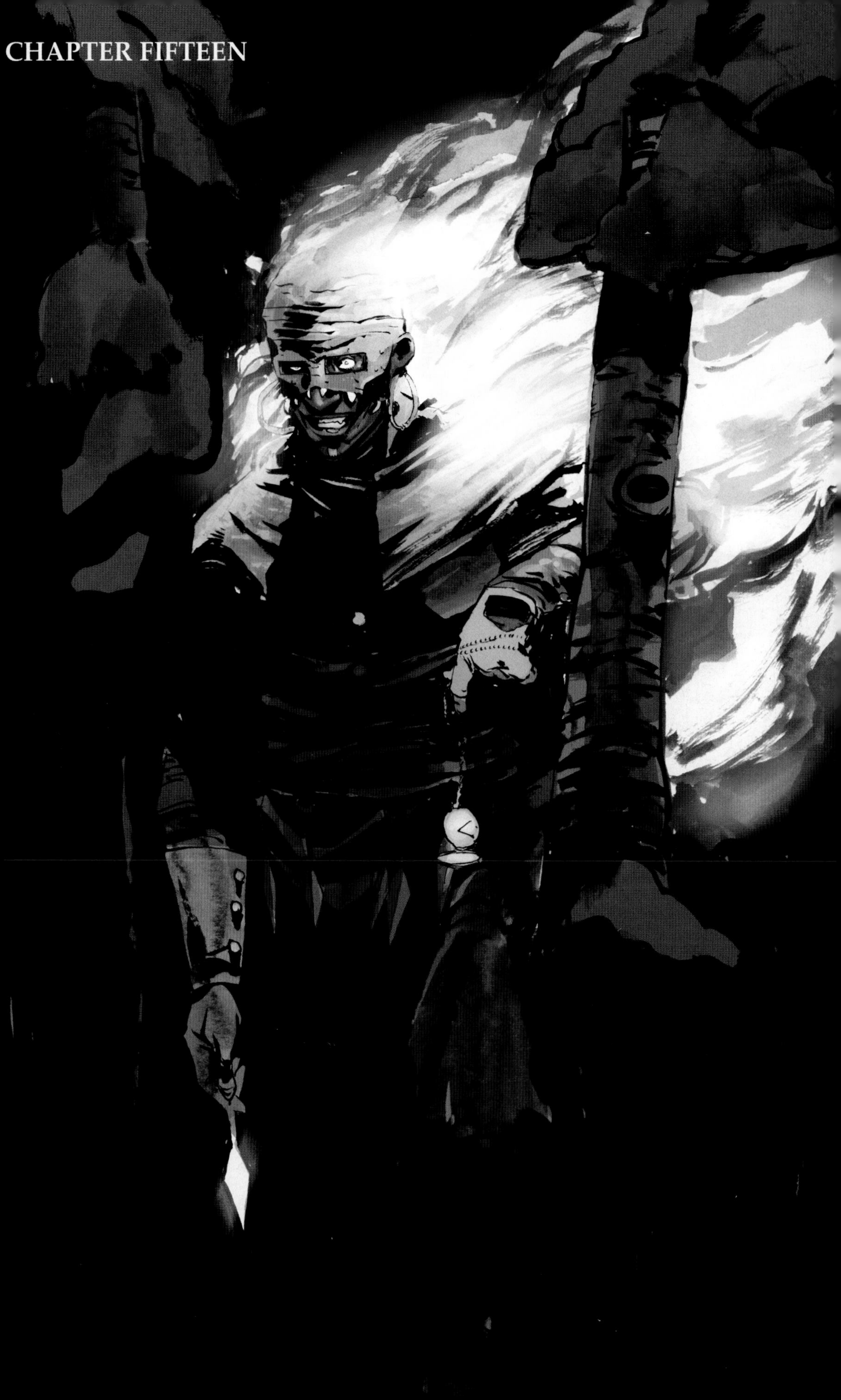

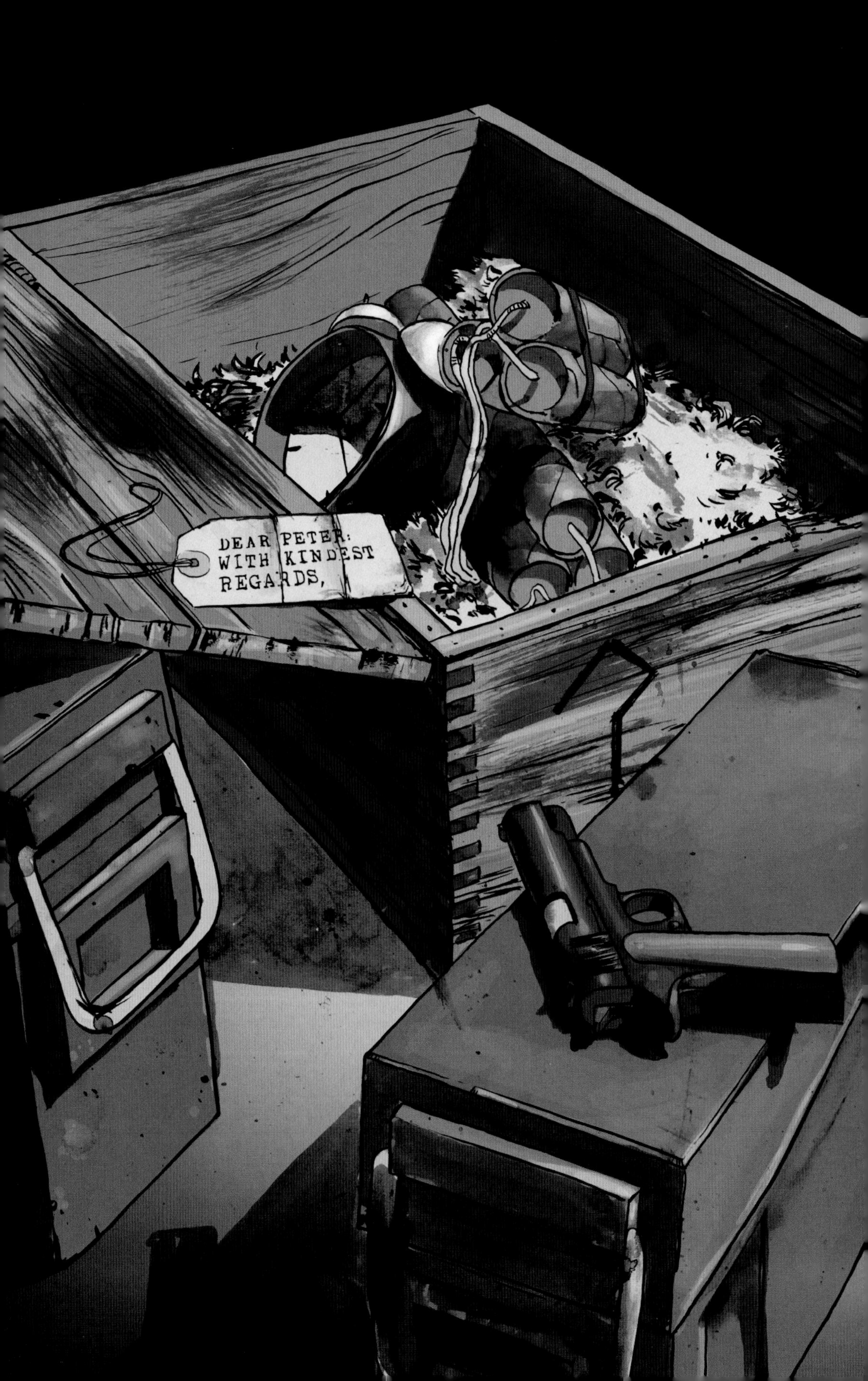
DEAR PETER:
WITH KINDEST
REGARDS,

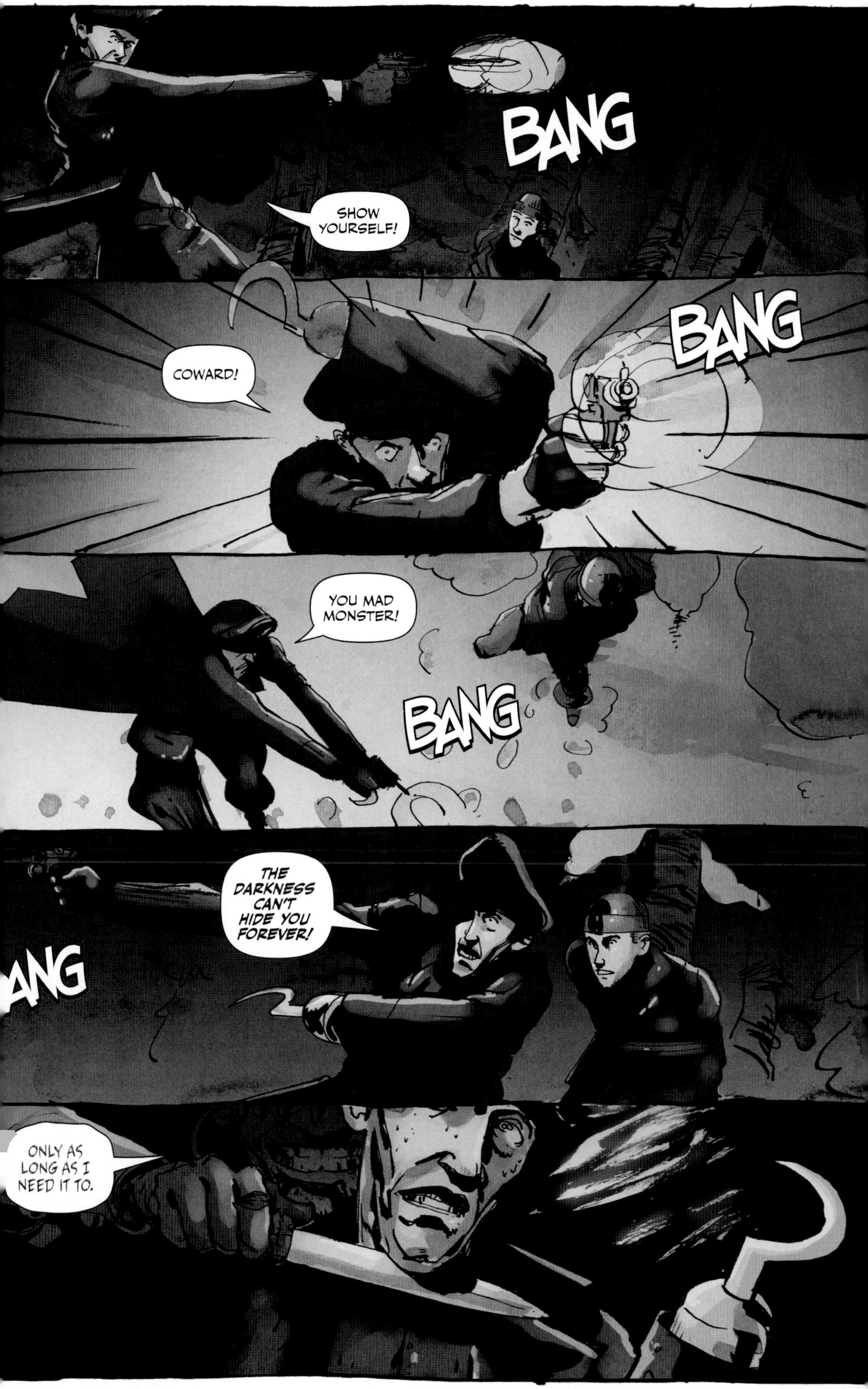
BANG
SHOW YOURSELF!
BANG
COWARD!
YOU MAD MONSTER!
BANG
THE DARKNESS CAN'T HIDE YOU FOREVER!
ANG
ONLY AS LONG AS I NEED IT TO.

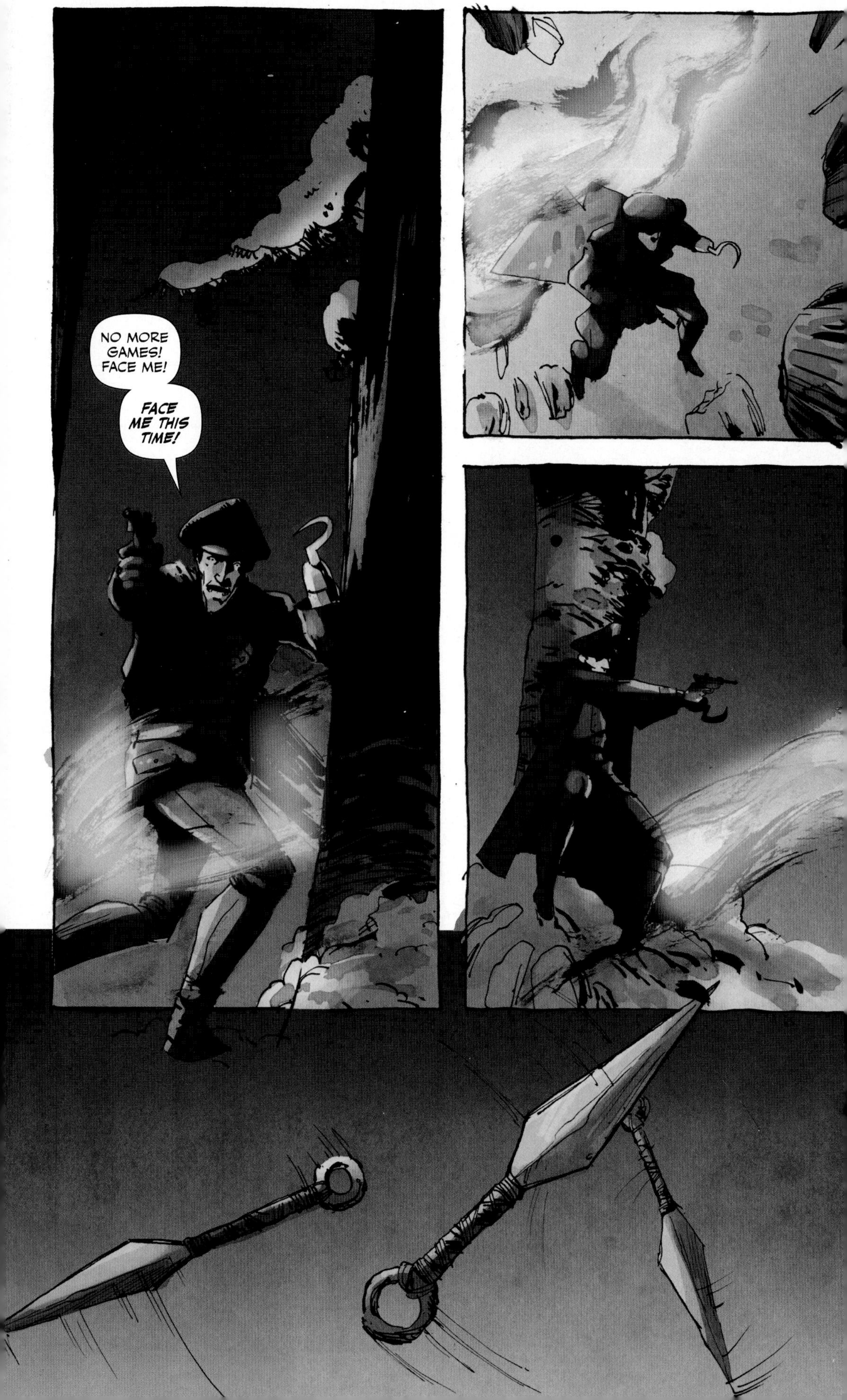
NO MORE GAMES! FACE ME!
FACE ME THIS TIME!

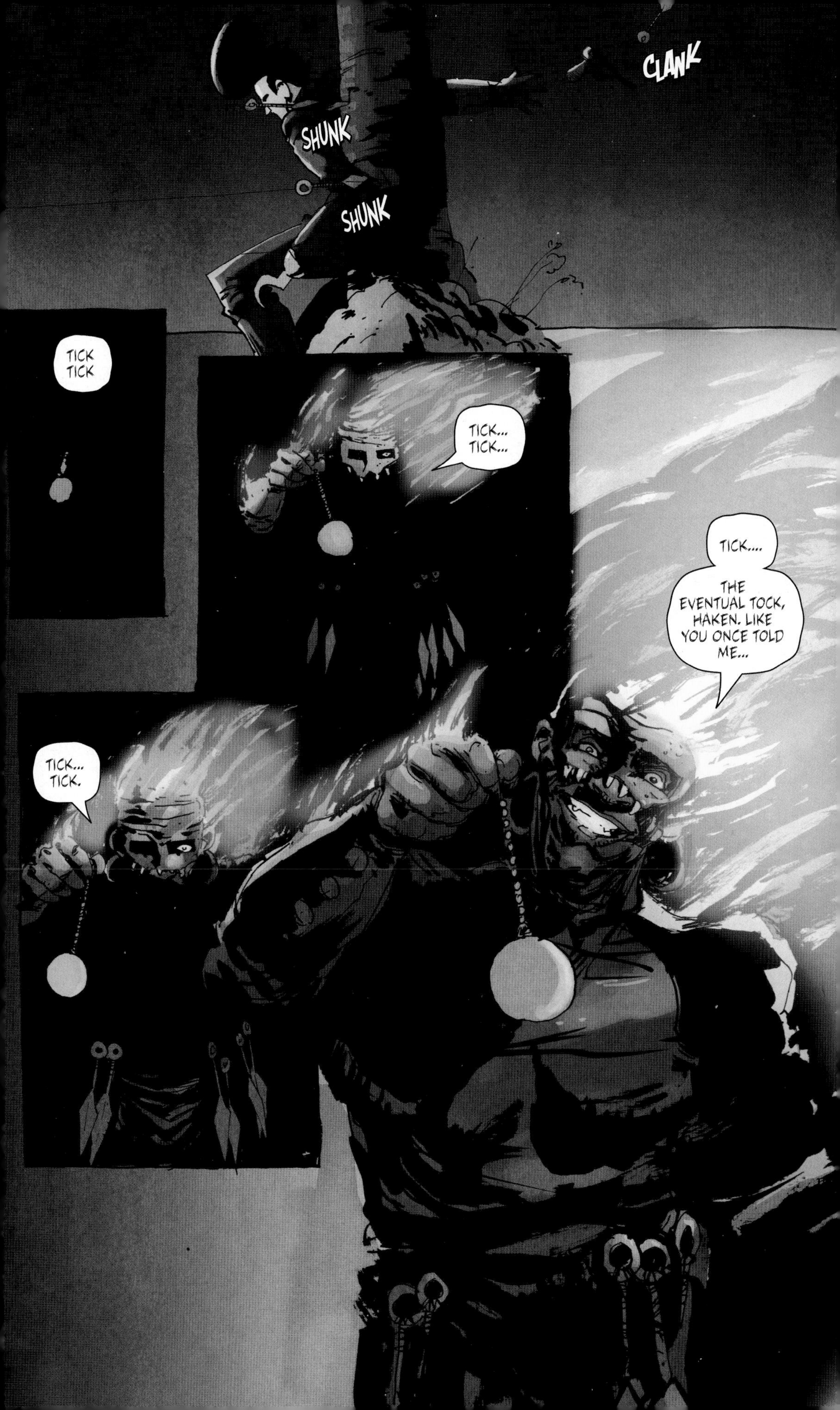
CLANK
SHUNK
SHUNK
TICK TICK
TICK... TICK...
TICK....
THE EVENTUAL TOCK, HAKEN. LIKE YOU ONCE TOLD ME...
TICK... TICK.

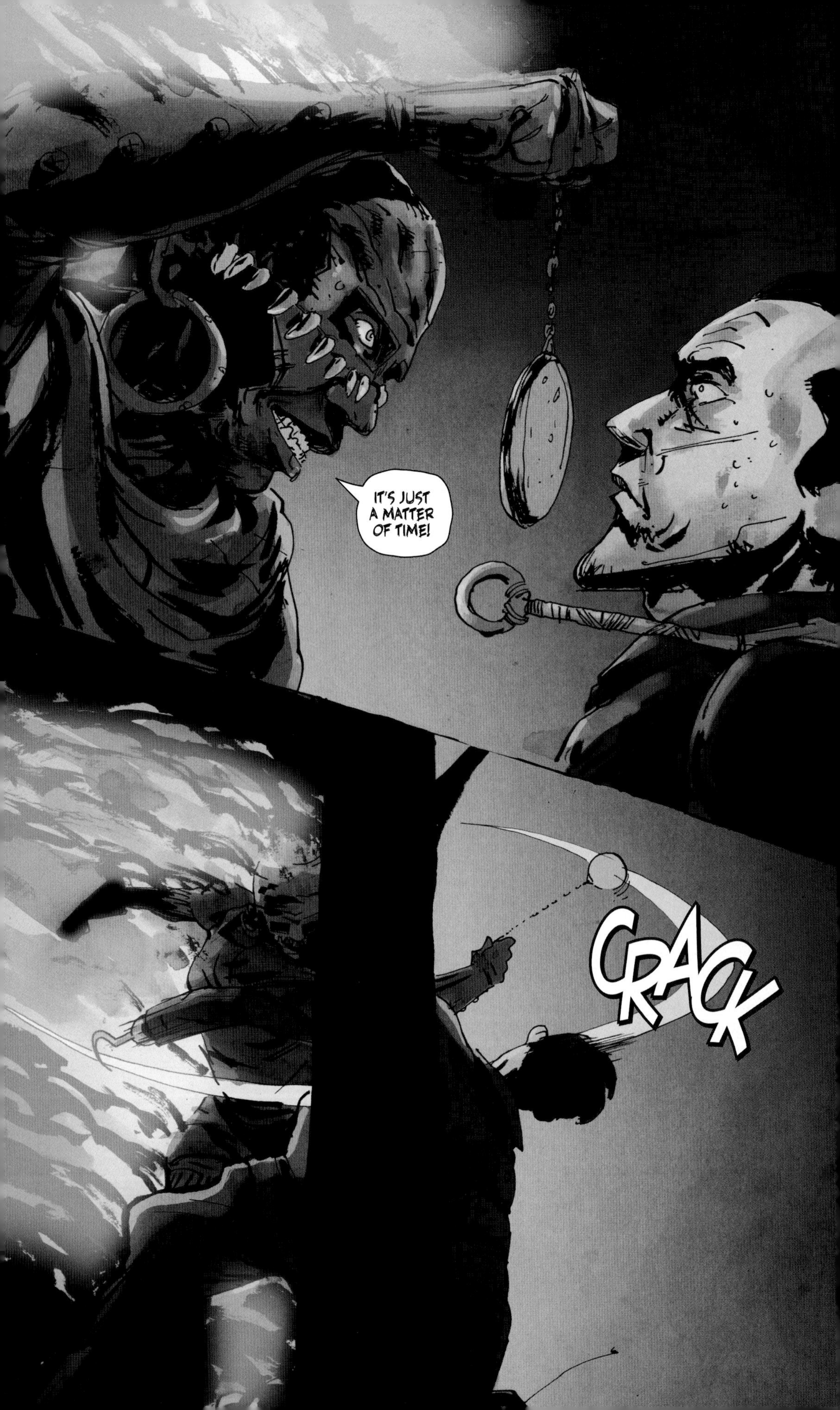
IT'S JUST
A MATTER
OF TIME!
CRACK

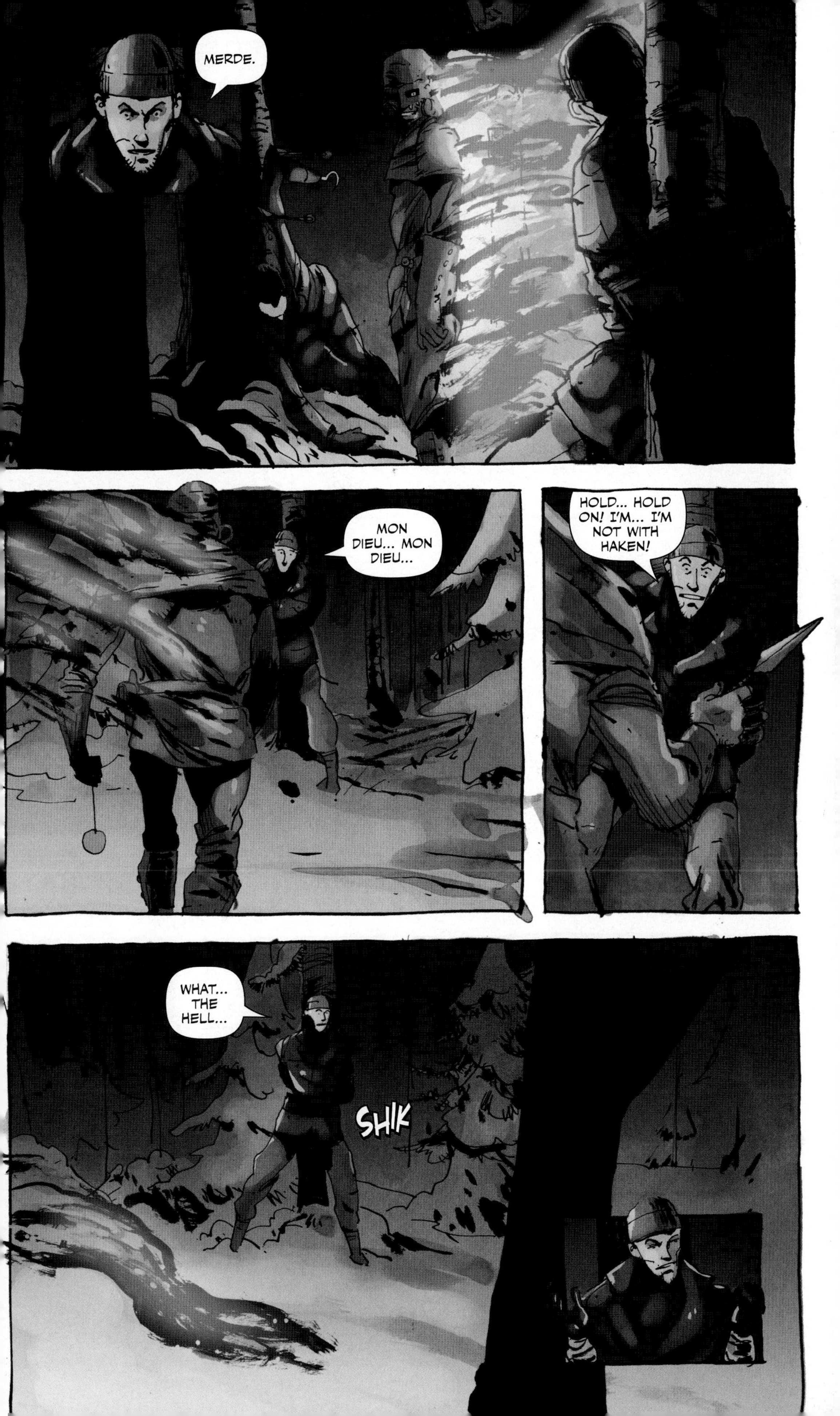
MERDE.
MON DIEU... MON DIEU...
HOLD... HOLD ON! I'M... I'M NOT WITH HAKEN!
WHAT... THE HELL...
SHIK

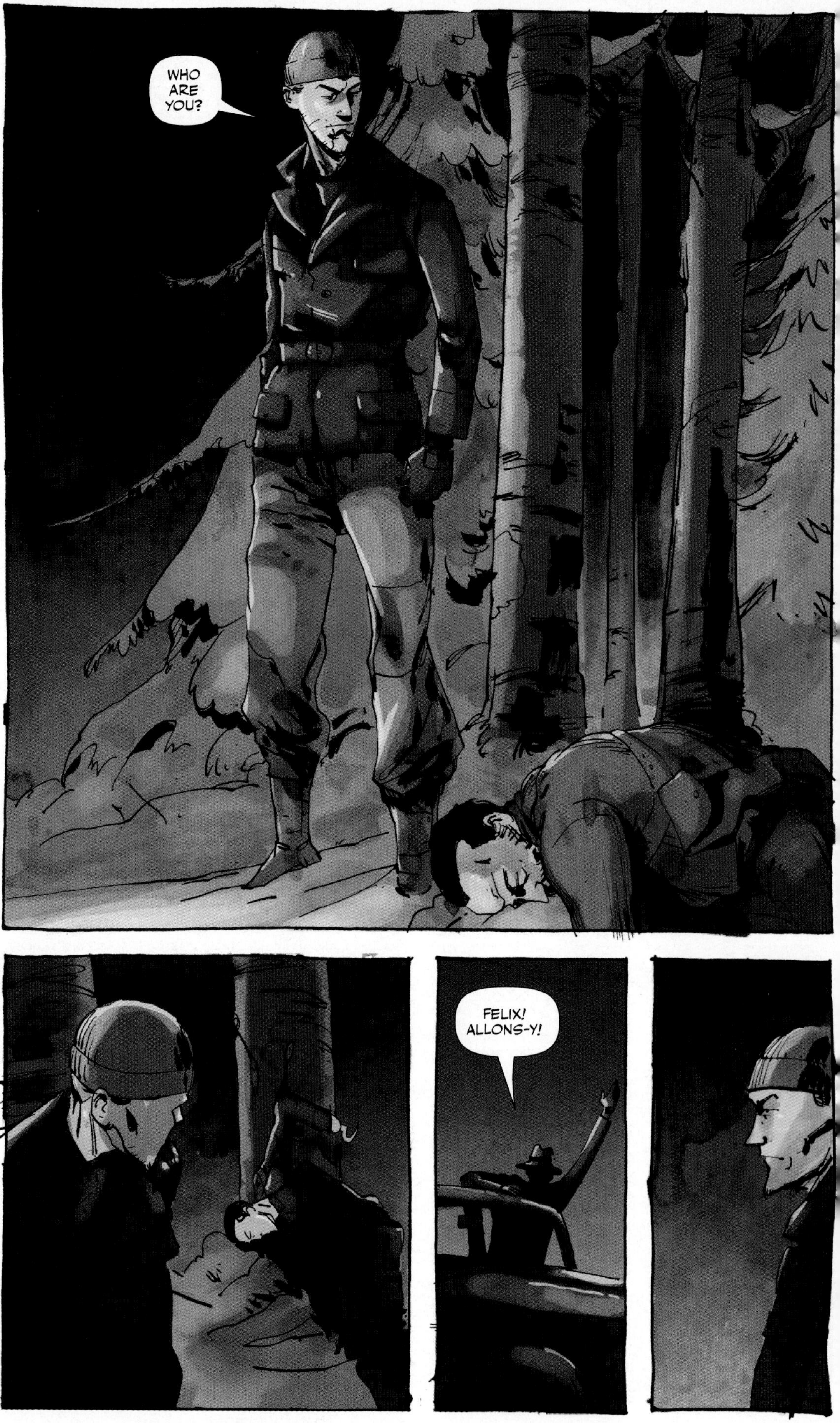
WHO ARE YOU?
FELIX! ALLONS-Y!

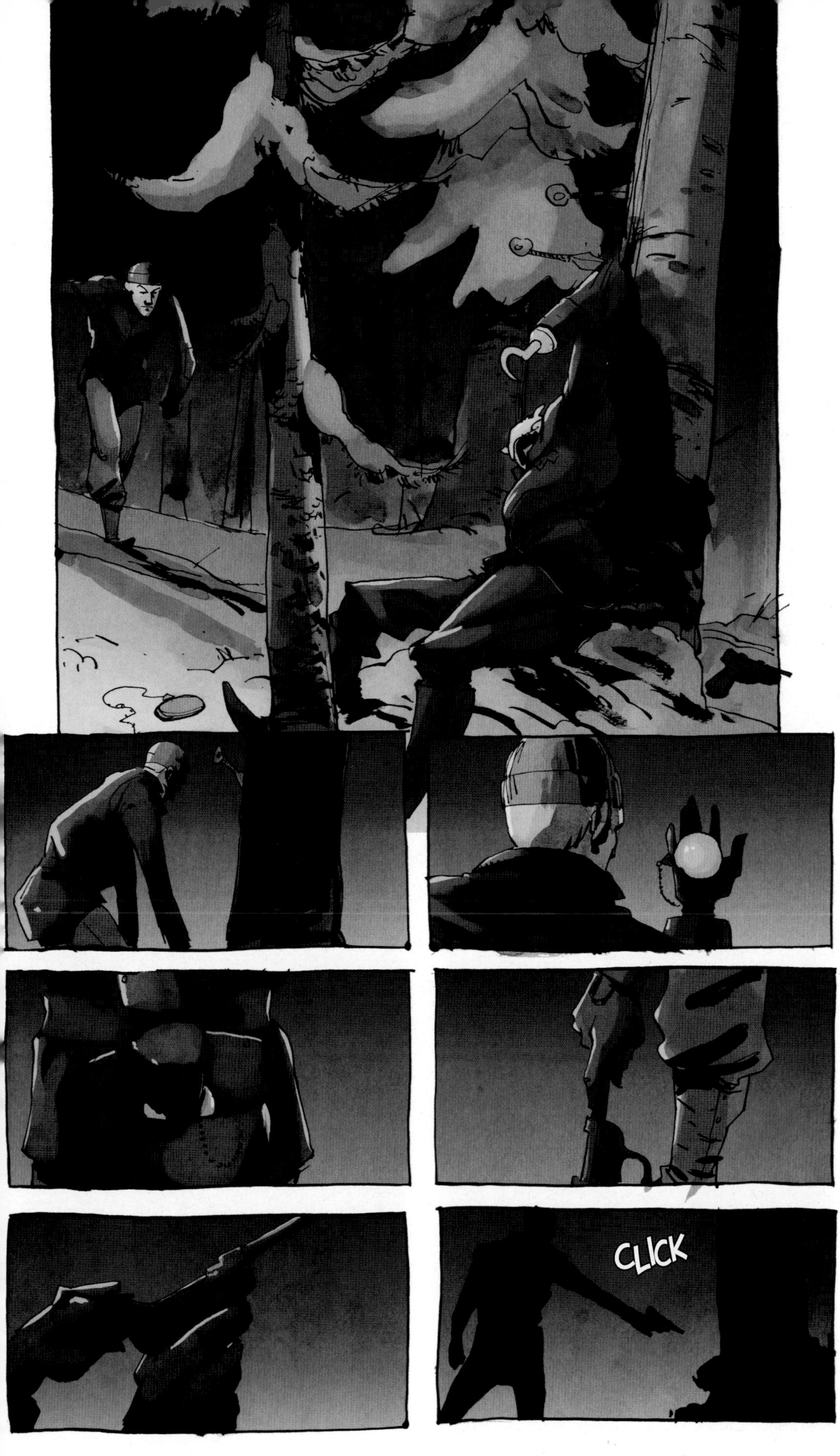
CLICK

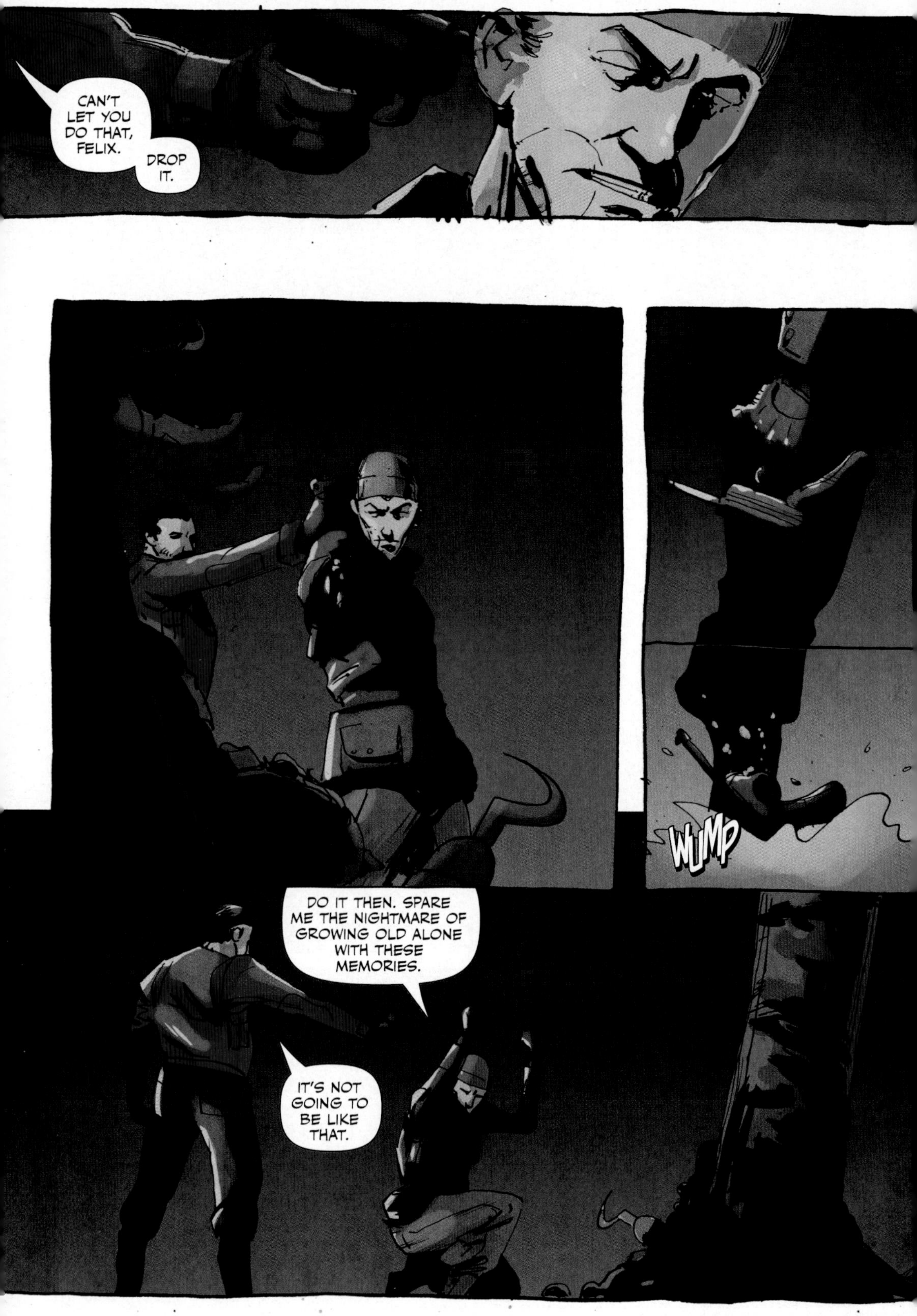
CAN'T LET YOU DO THAT, FELIX.
DROP IT.
WUMP
DO IT THEN. SPARE ME THE NIGHTMARE OF GROWING OLD ALONE WITH THESE MEMORIES.
IT'S NOT GOING TO BE LIKE THAT.

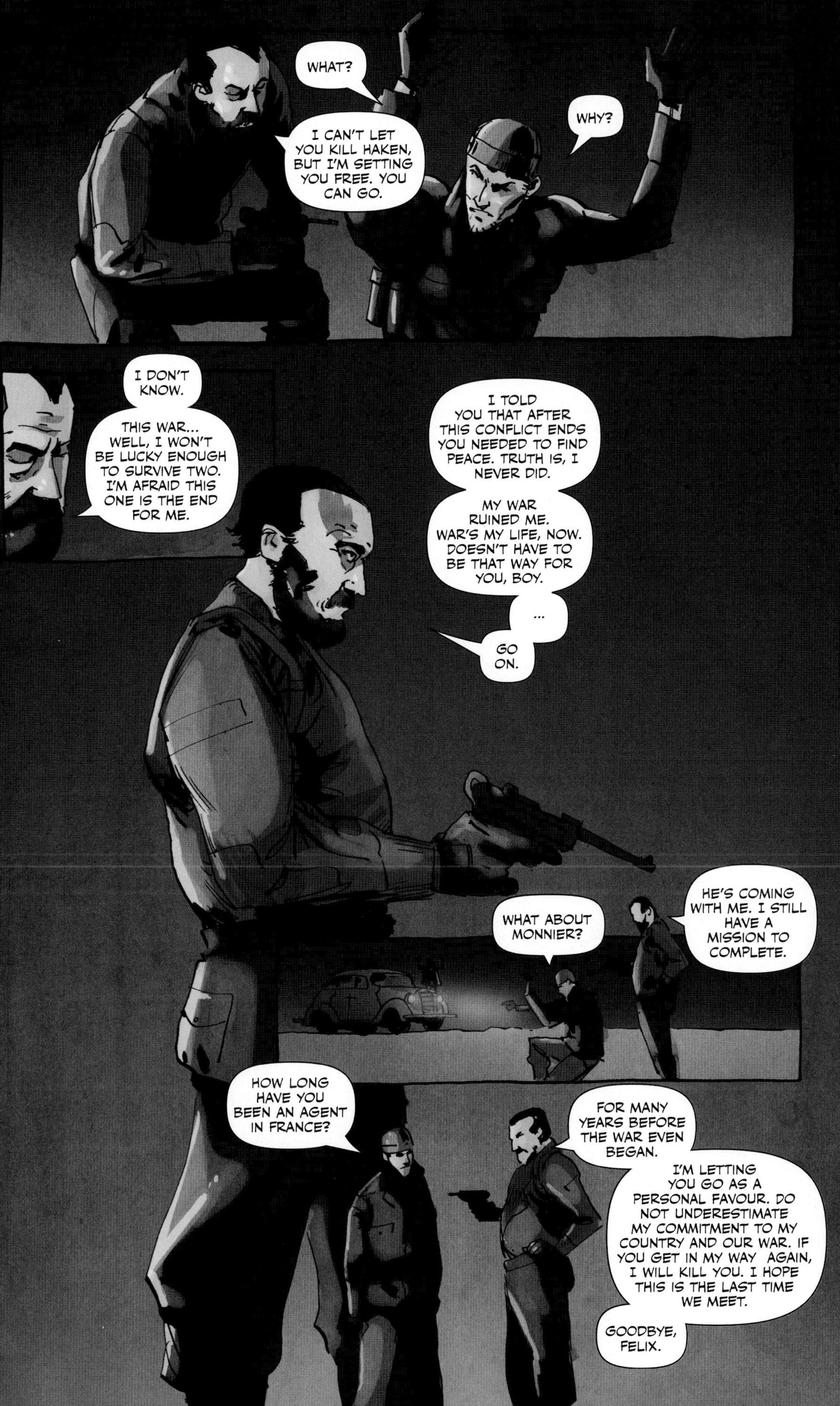
WHAT?
I CAN'T LET YOU KILL HAKEN, BUT I'M SETTING YOU FREE. YOU CAN GO.
WHY?
I DON'T KNOW.
THIS WAR... WELL, I WON'T BE LUCKY ENOUGH TO SURVIVE TWO. I'M AFRAID THIS ONE IS THE END FOR ME.
I TOLD YOU THAT AFTER THIS CONFLICT ENDS YOU NEEDED TO FIND PEACE. TRUTH IS, I NEVER DID.
MY WAR RUINED ME. WAR'S MY LIFE, NOW. DOESN'T HAVE TO BE THAT WAY FOR YOU, BOY.
...
GO ON.
WHAT ABOUT MONNIER?
HE'S COMING WITH ME. I STILL HAVE A MISSION TO COMPLETE.
HOW LONG HAVE YOU BEEN AN AGENT IN FRANCE?
FOR MANY YEARS BEFORE THE WAR EVEN BEGAN.
I'M LETTING YOU GO AS A PERSONAL FAVOUR. DO NOT UNDERESTIMATE MY COMMITMENT TO MY COUNTRY AND OUR WAR. IF YOU GET IN MY WAY AGAIN, I WILL KILL YOU. I HOPE THIS IS THE LAST TIME WE MEET.
GOODBYE, FELIX.

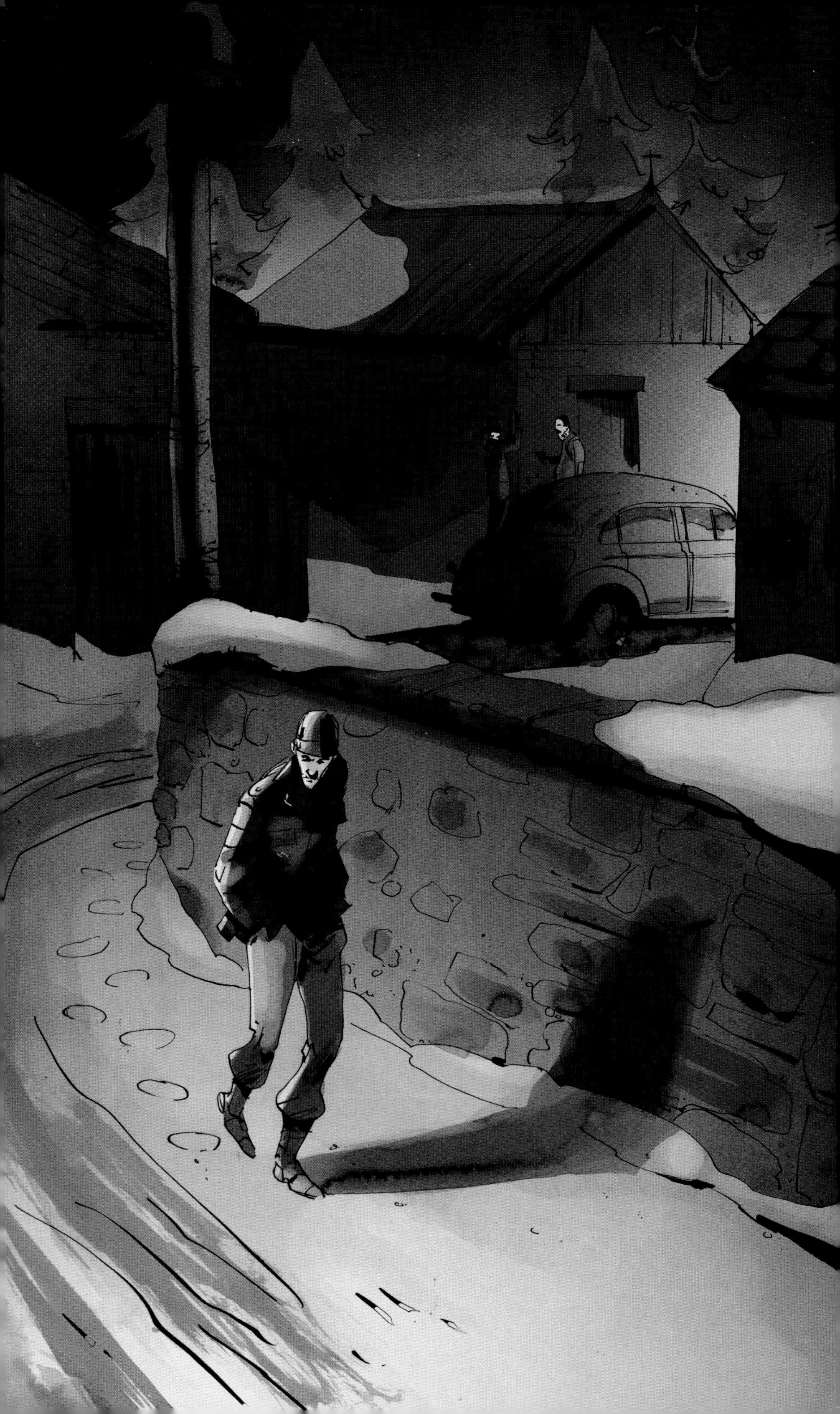

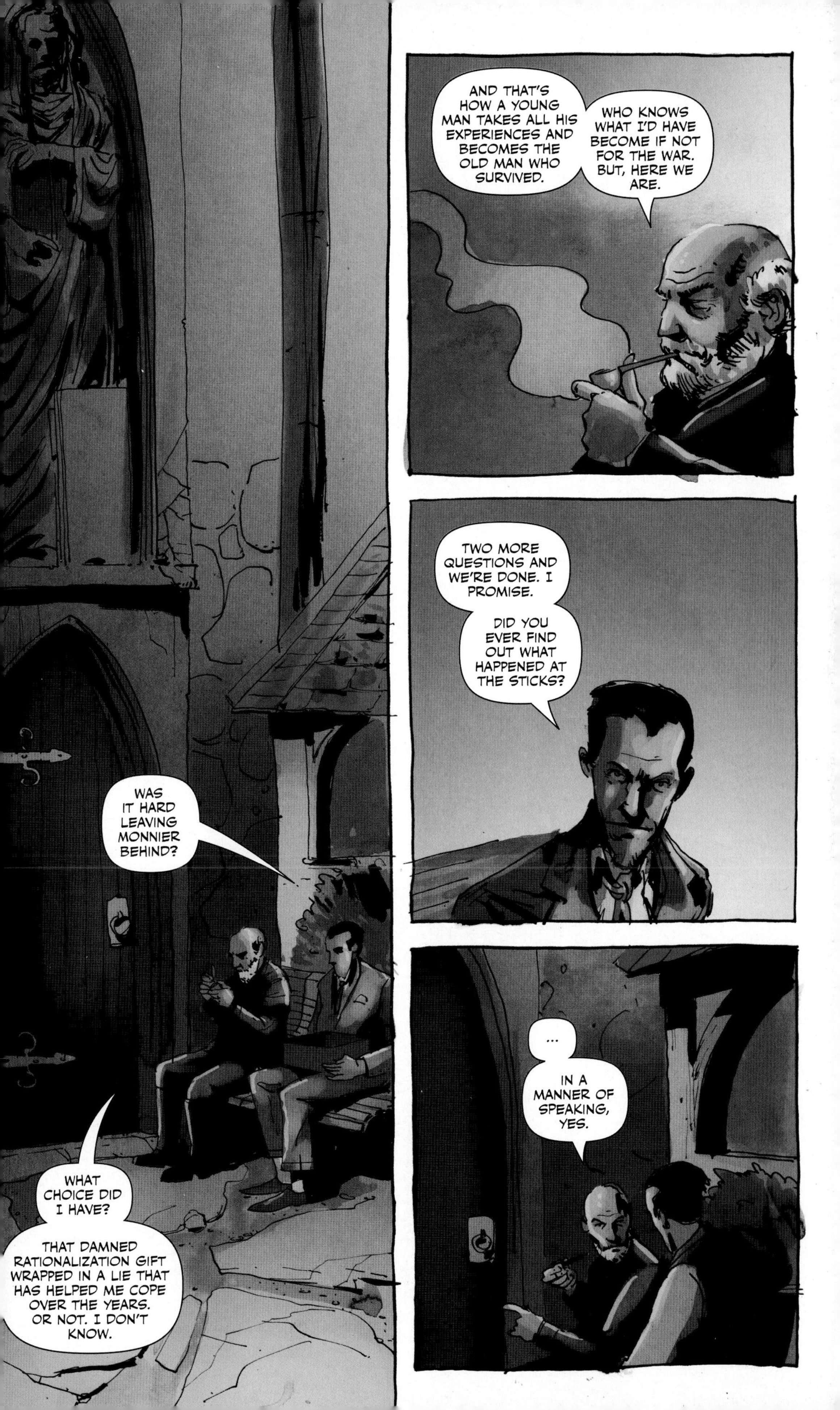
WAS IT HARD LEAVING MONNIER BEHIND?
WHAT CHOICE DID I HAVE?
THAT DAMNED RATIONALIZATION GIFT WRAPPED IN A LIE THAT HAS HELPED ME COPE OVER THE YEARS. OR NOT. I DON'T KNOW.
AND THAT'S HOW A YOUNG MAN TAKES ALL HIS EXPERIENCES AND BECOMES THE OLD MAN WHO SURVIVED.
WHO KNOWS WHAT I'D HAVE BECOME IF NOT FOR THE WAR. BUT, HERE WE ARE.
TWO MORE QUESTIONS AND WE'RE DONE. I PROMISE.
DID YOU EVER FIND OUT WHAT HAPPENED AT THE STICKS?
...
IN A MANNER OF SPEAKING, YES.

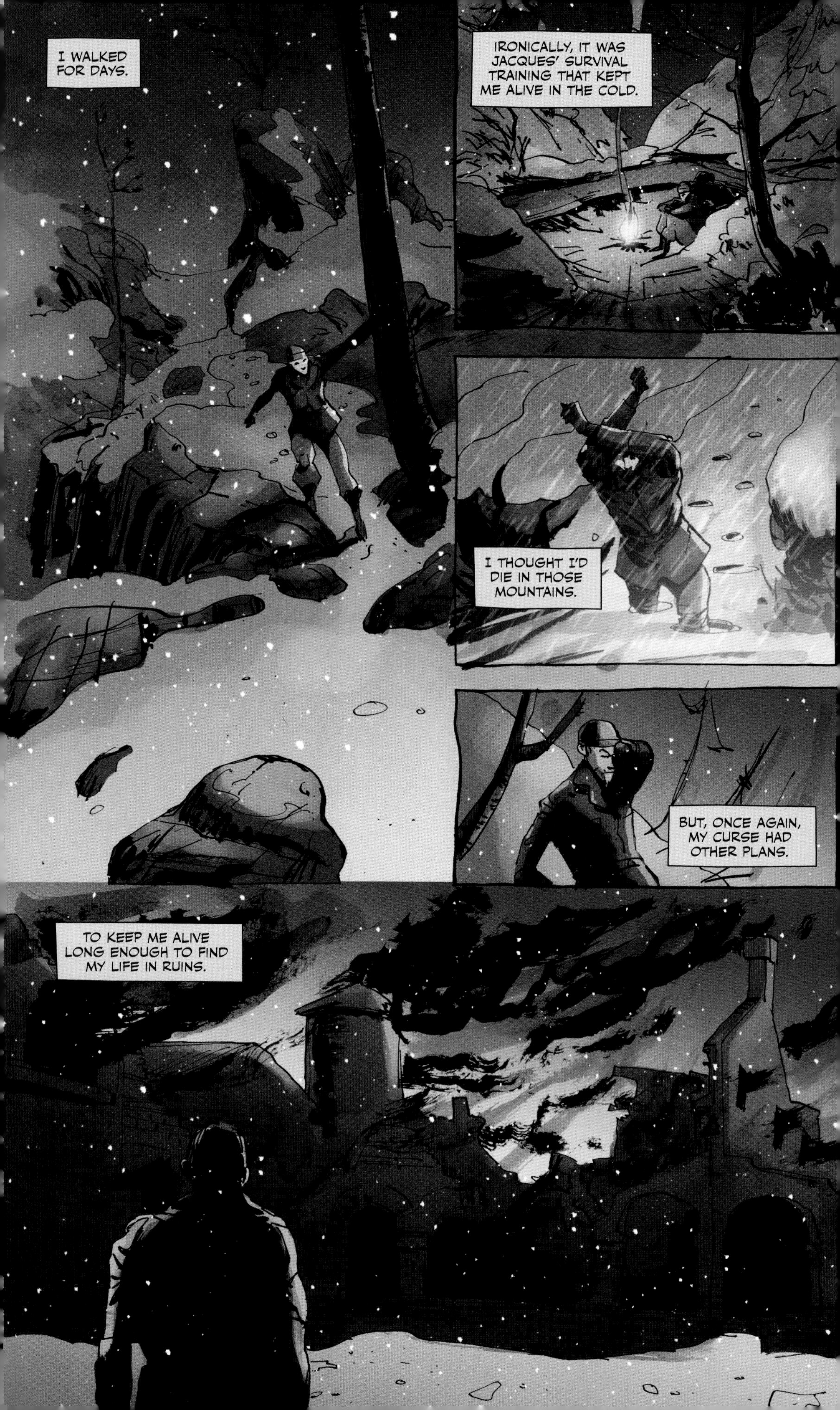
I WALKED FOR DAYS.
IRONICALLY, IT WAS JACQUES' SURVIVAL TRAINING THAT KEPT ME ALIVE IN THE COLD.
I THOUGHT I'D DIE IN THOSE MOUNTAINS.
BUT, ONCE AGAIN, MY CURSE HAD OTHER PLANS.
TO KEEP ME ALIVE LONG ENOUGH TO FIND MY LIFE IN RUINS.

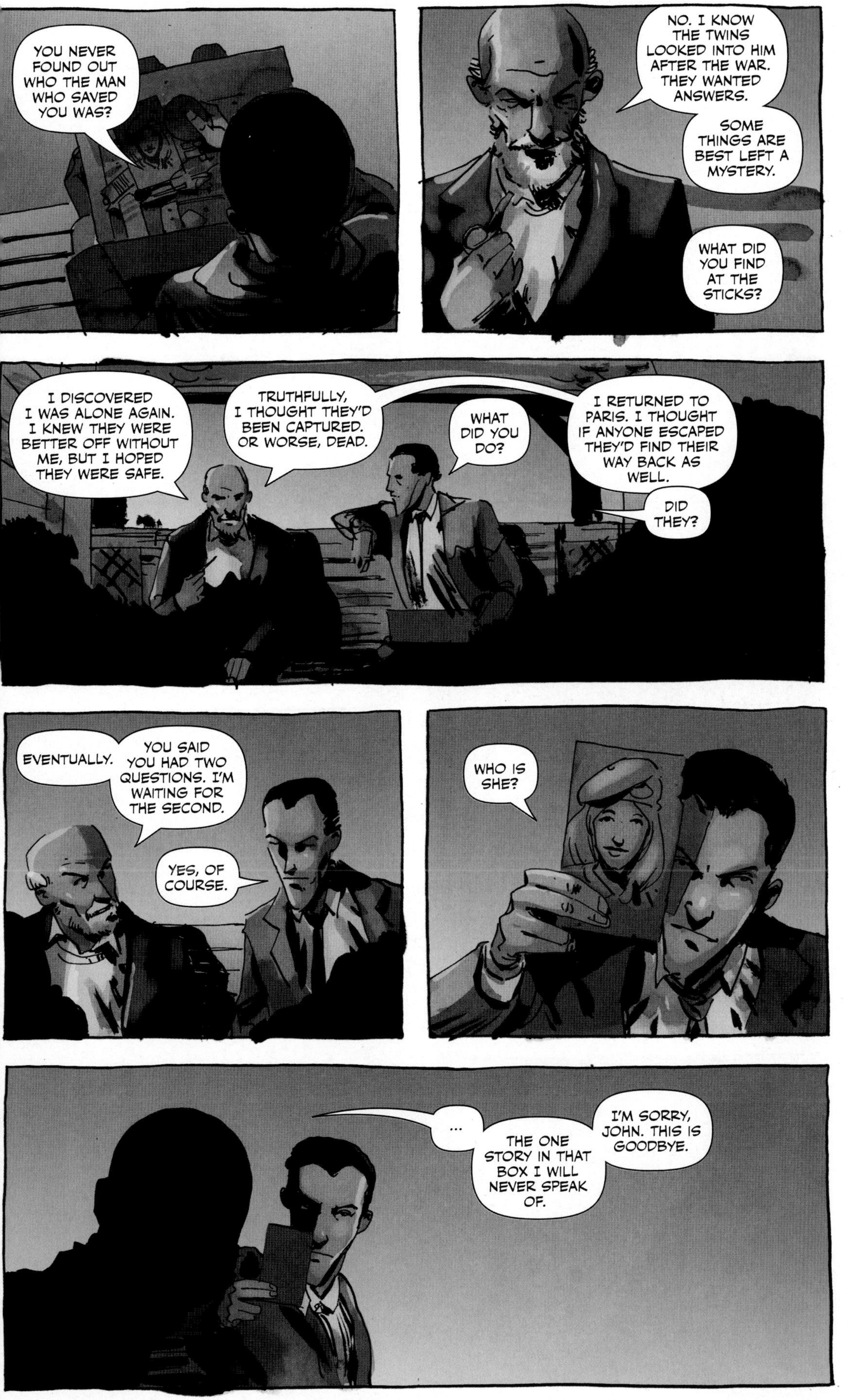
YOU NEVER FOUND OUT WHO THE MAN WHO SAVED YOU WAS?
NO. I KNOW THE TWINS LOOKED INTO HIM AFTER THE WAR. THEY WANTED ANSWERS.
SOME THINGS ARE BEST LEFT A MYSTERY.
WHAT DID YOU FIND AT THE STICKS?
I DISCOVERED I WAS ALONE AGAIN. I KNEW THEY WERE BETTER OFF WITHOUT ME, BUT I HOPED THEY WERE SAFE.
TRUTHFULLY, I THOUGHT THEY'D BEEN CAPTURED. OR WORSE, DEAD.
WHAT DID YOU DO?
I RETURNED TO PARIS. I THOUGHT IF ANYONE ESCAPED THEY'D FIND THEIR WAY BACK AS WELL.
DID THEY?
EVENTUALLY.
YOU SAID YOU HAD TWO QUESTIONS. I'M WAITING FOR THE SECOND.
YES, OF COURSE.
WHO IS SHE?
...
THE ONE STORY IN THAT BOX I WILL NEVER SPEAK OF.
I'M SORRY, JOHN. THIS IS GOODBYE.

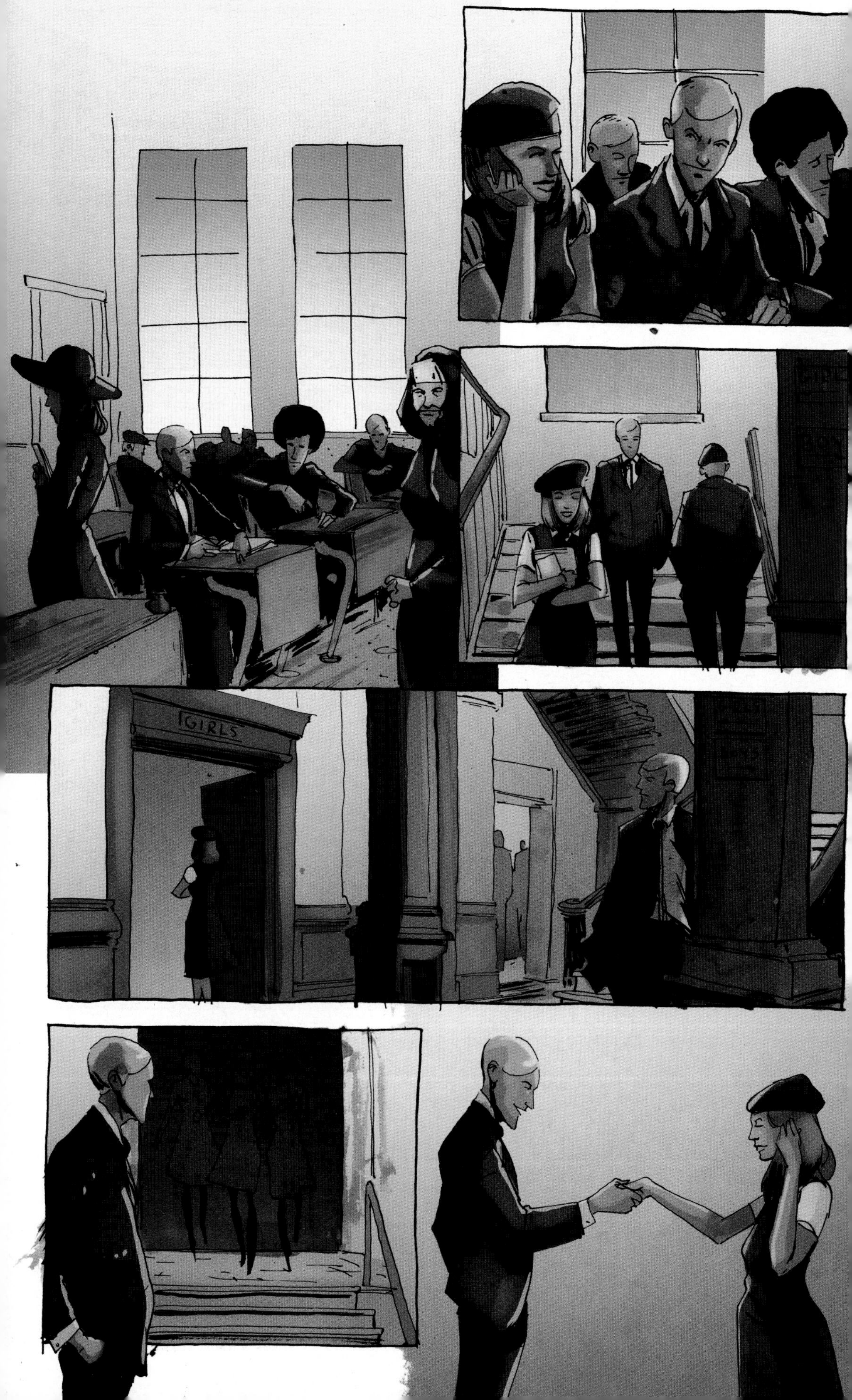
GIRLS

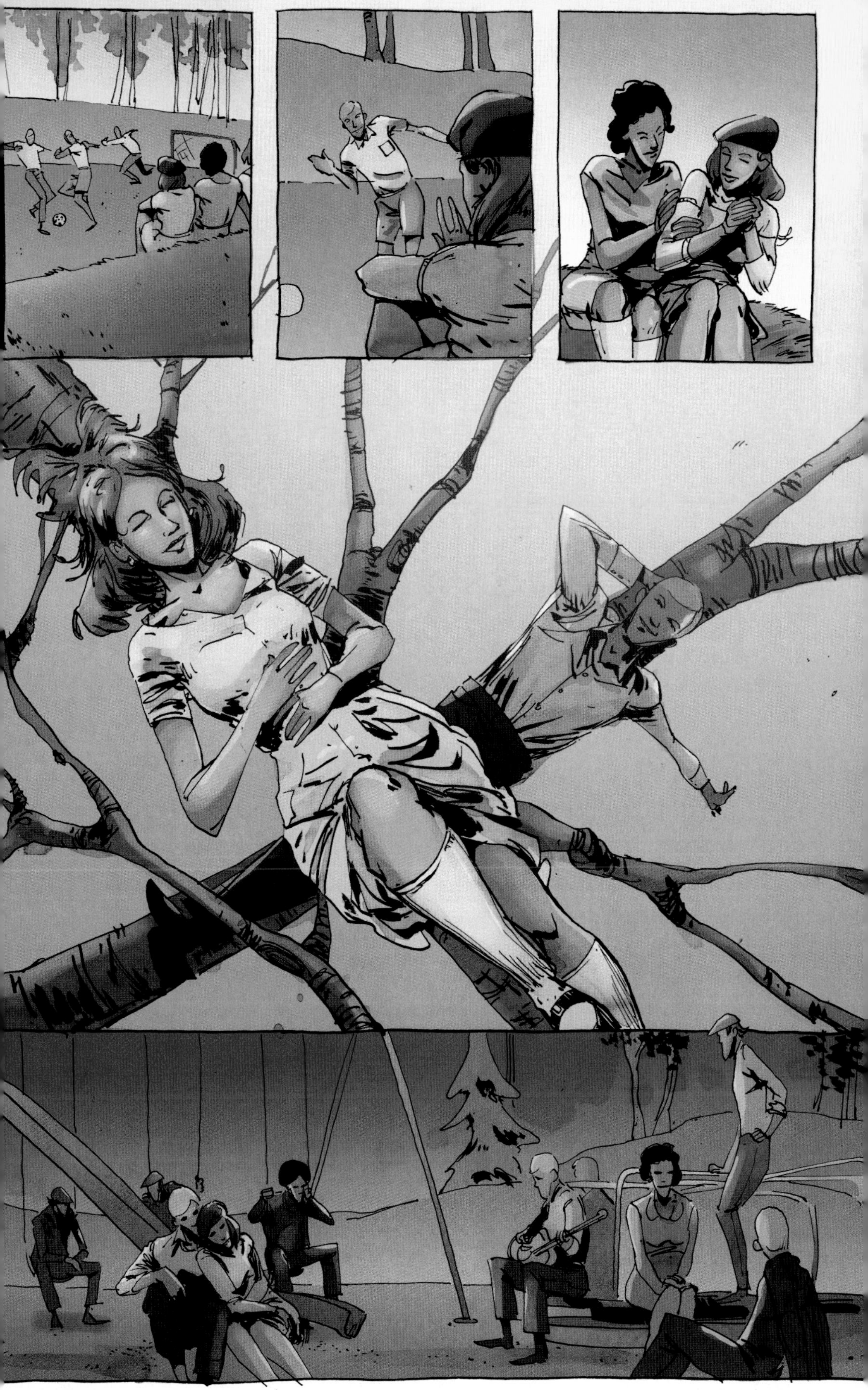

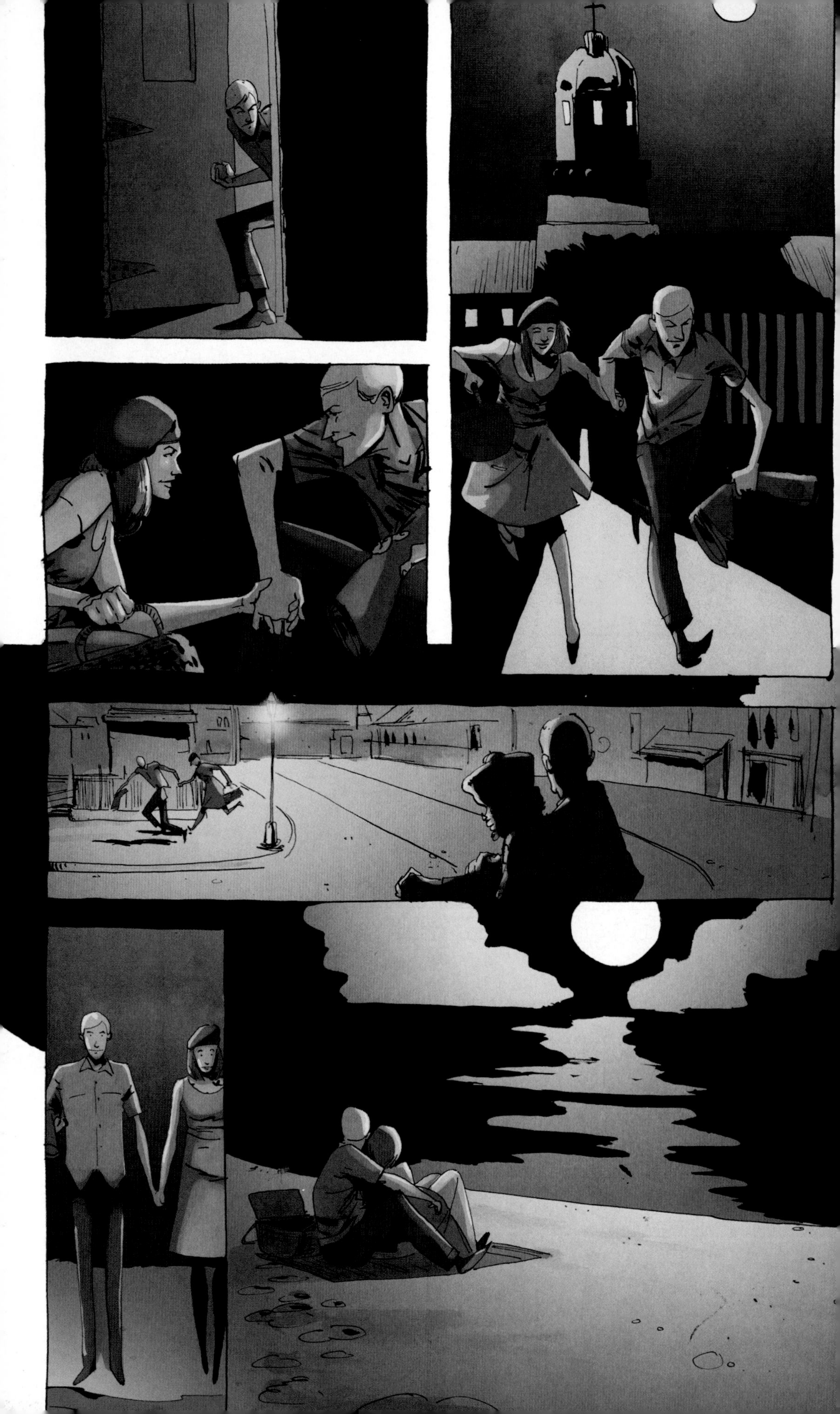

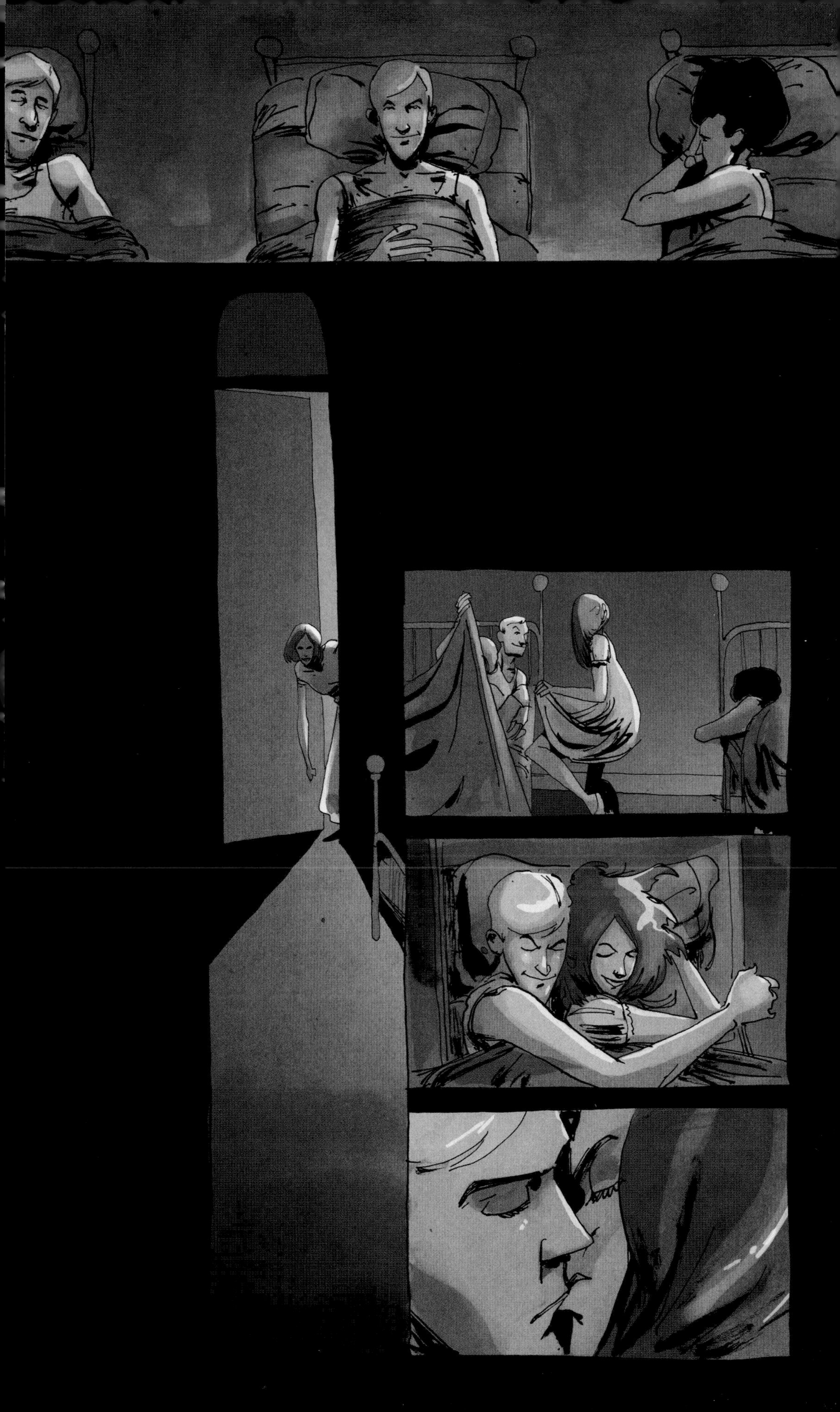

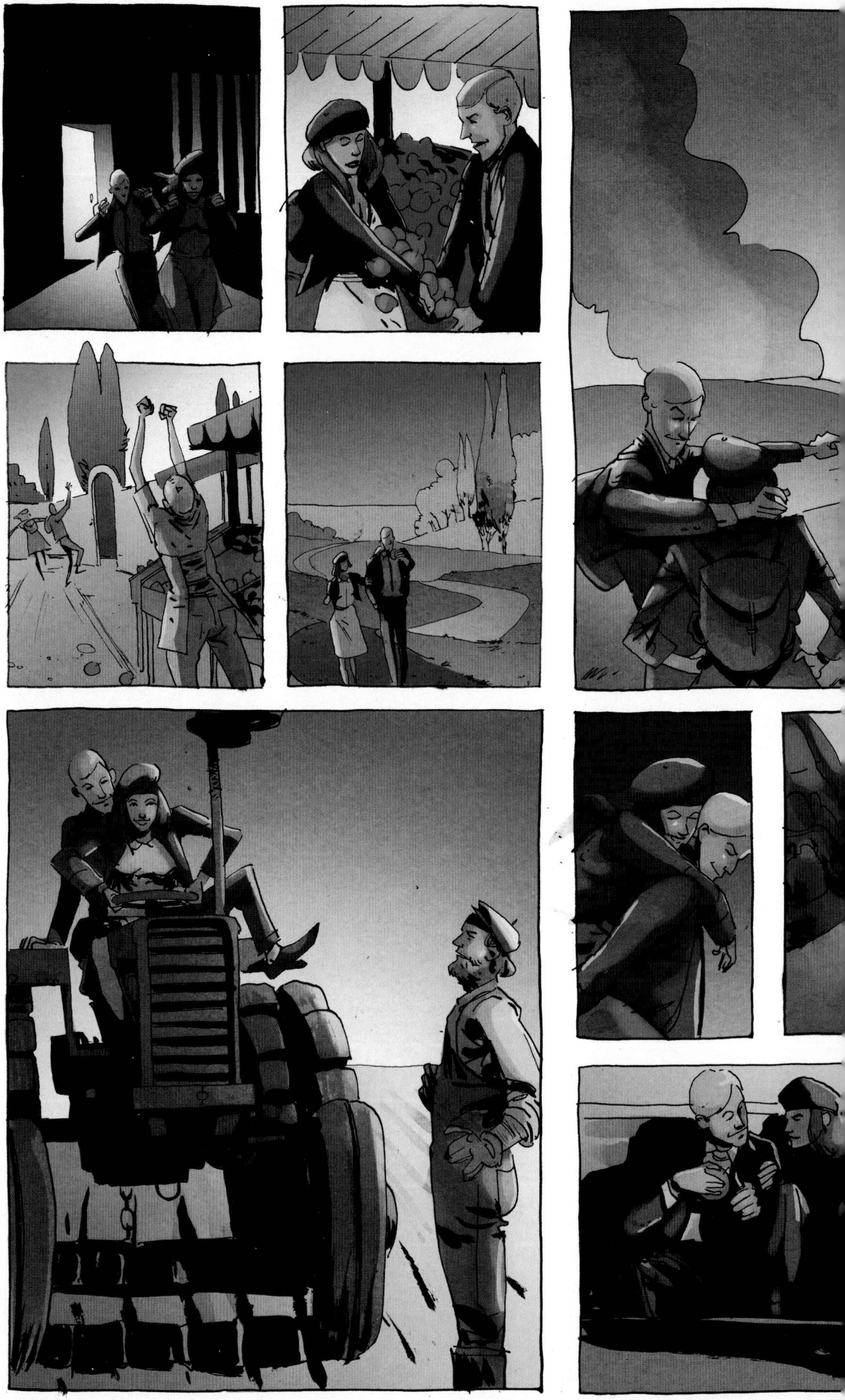

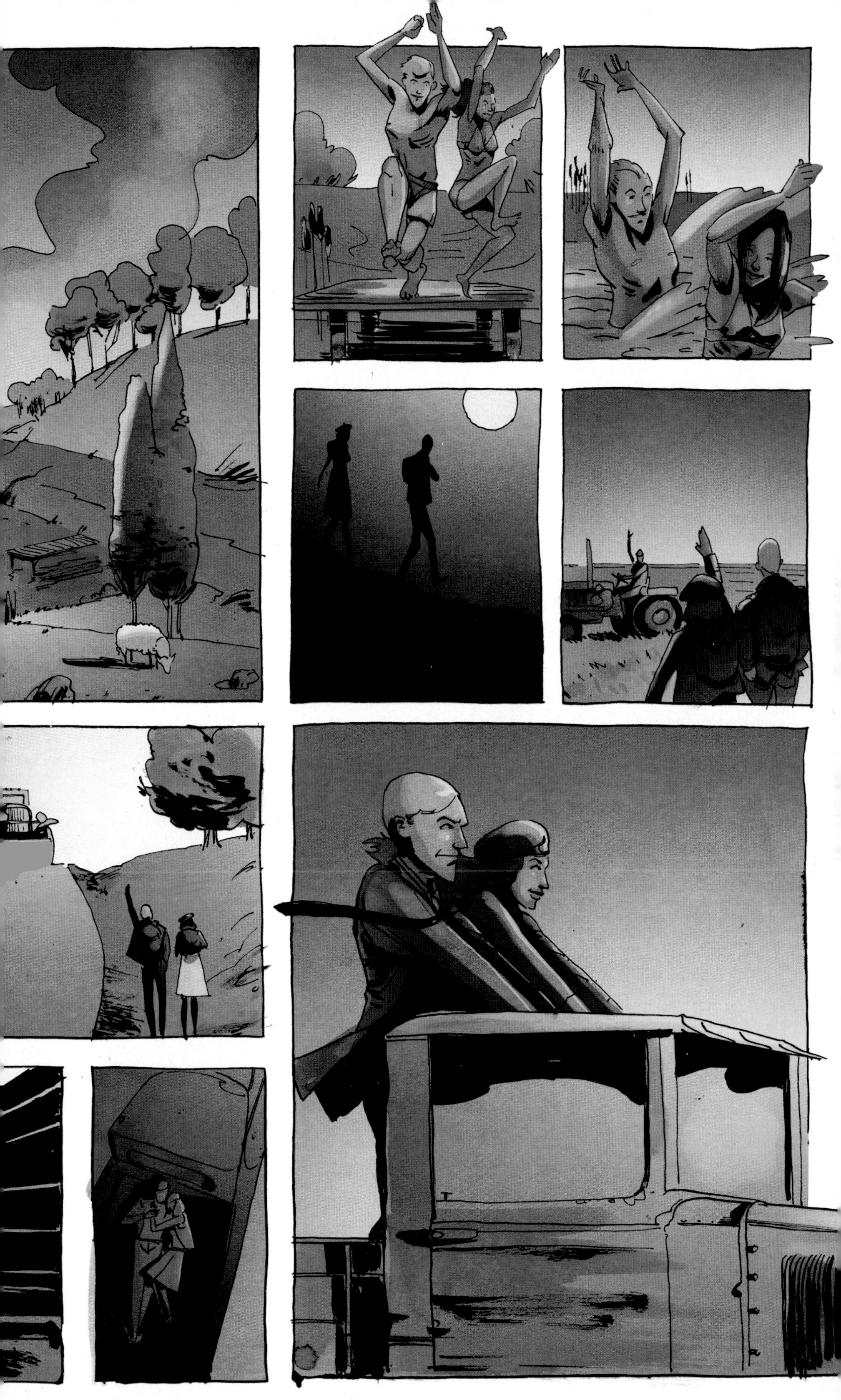

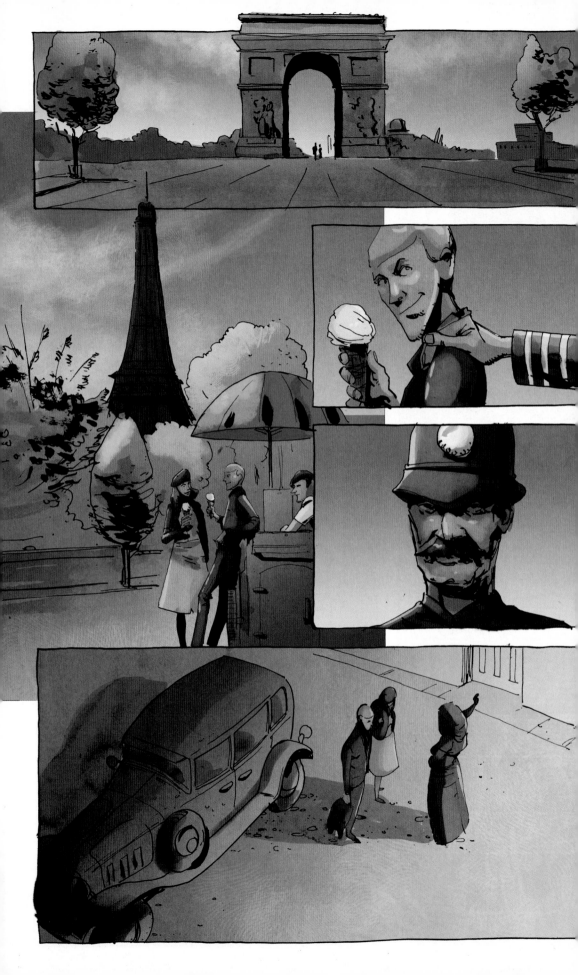

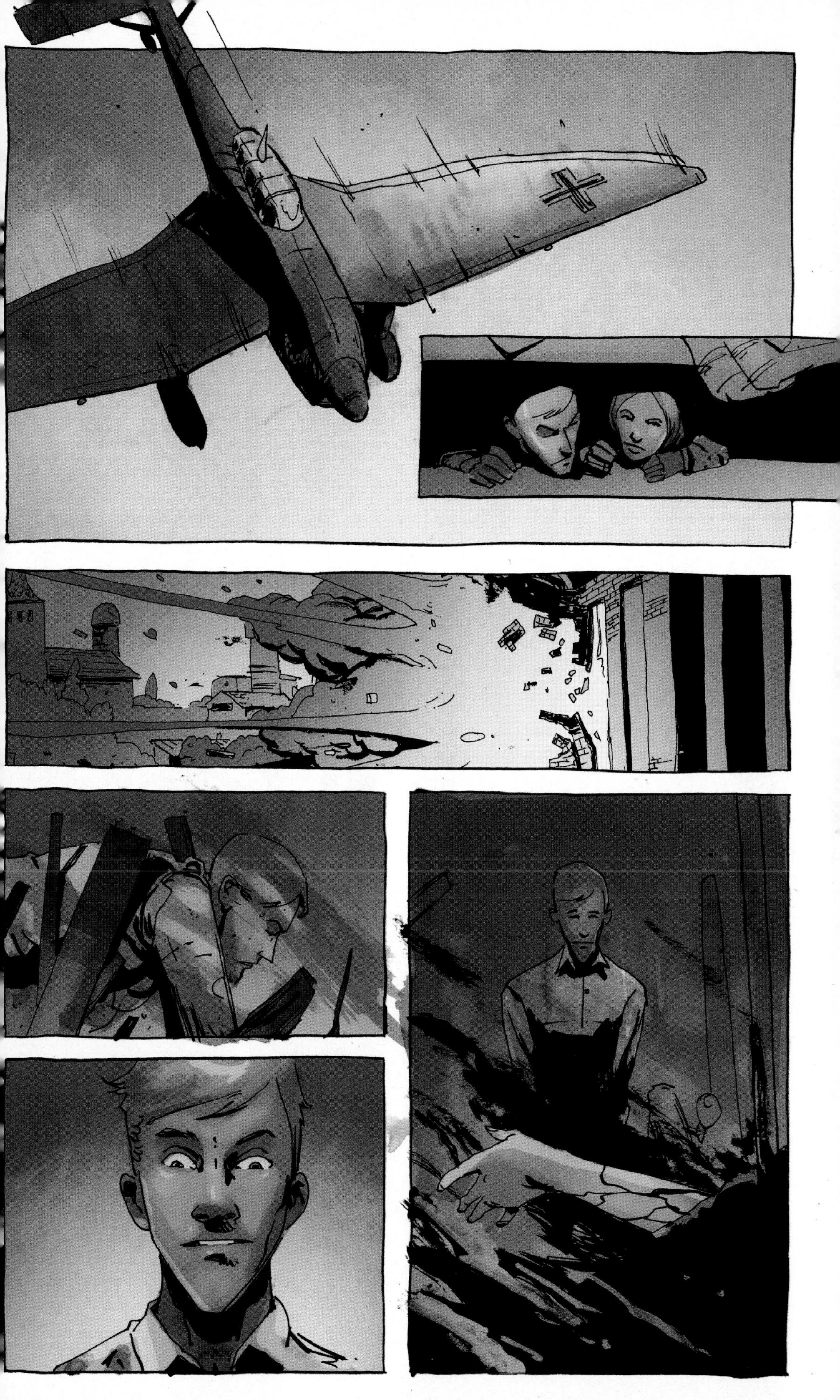

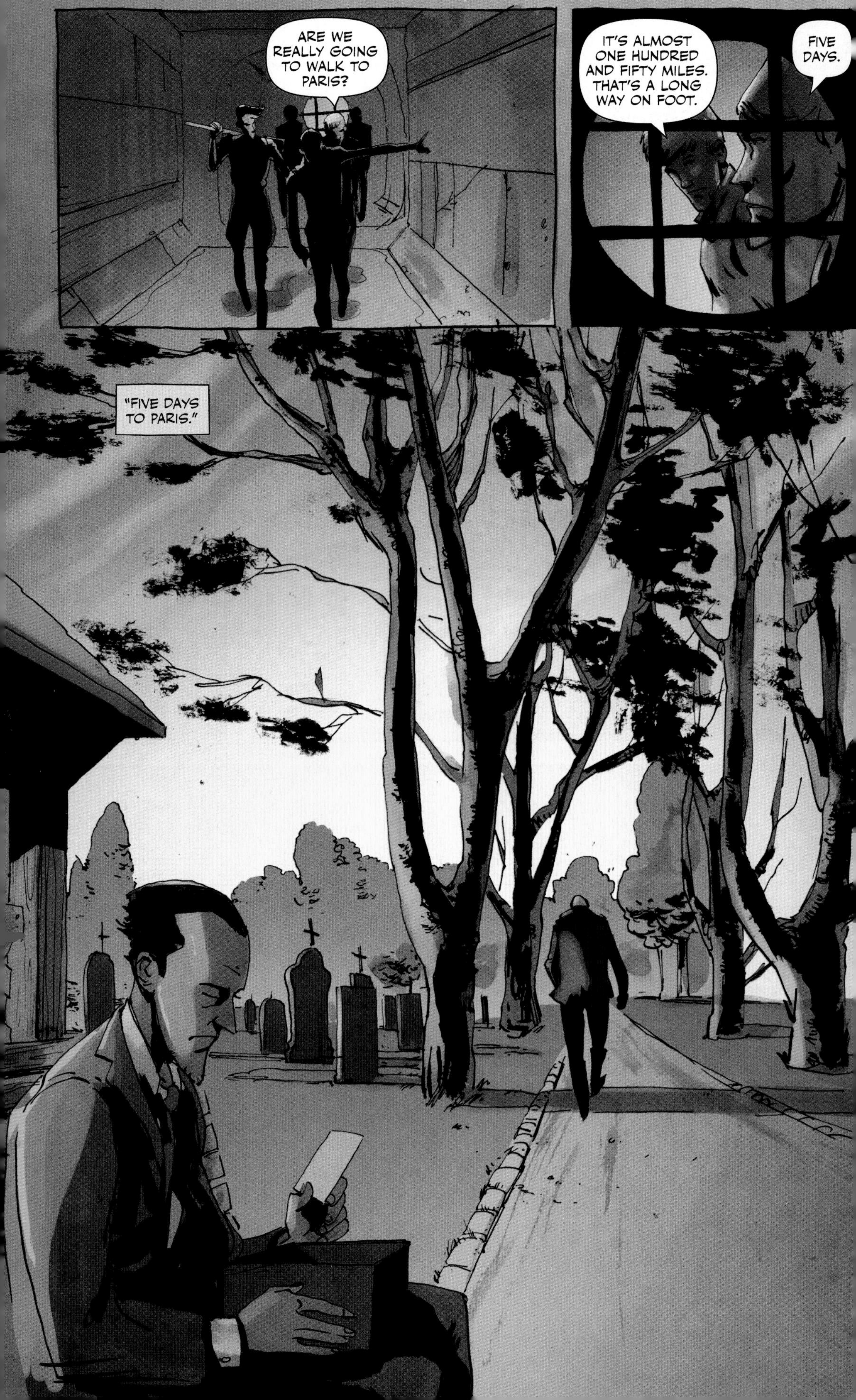
ARE WE REALLY GOING TO WALK TO PARIS?
IT'S ALMOST ONE HUNDRED AND FIFTY MILES. THAT'S A LONG WAY ON FOOT.
FIVE DAYS.
"FIVE DAYS TO PARIS."

GEOF DARROW'S GHOST VARIANT COVER

Thomas Gaul of CornerStoreComics in Anaheim, CA and his group approached us about his commissioning a "Ghost Variant" cover for Peter Panzerfaust #15. "Ghost Variant" covers, for those who may not know, are unannounced and unsolicited limited edition covers (hence the clever name!) sold on the secondary market by select comic stores, such as Thomas'.

Thomas enlisted the services of one of our all-time favorite artists, the amazing Geof Darrow who, along with award-winning colorist supreme, Dave Stewart, created the wonderful wrap-around cover that opens this volume and that can be seen in all its glory on the pages following.

We reprint it here by kind permission of Thomas, Geof and Dave.

www.cornerstorecomics.com ghostvariant.tumblr.com facebook.com/GhostVariant

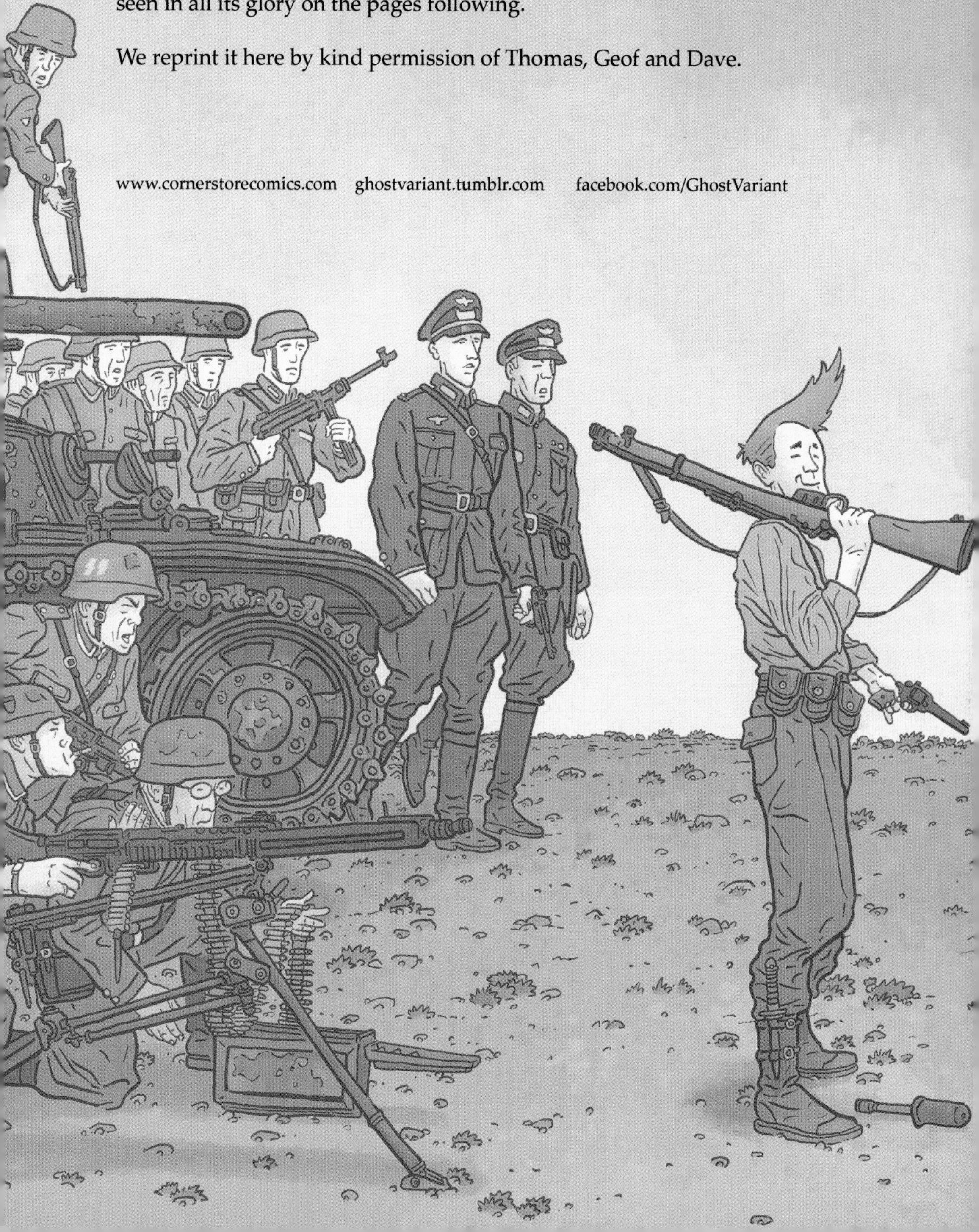

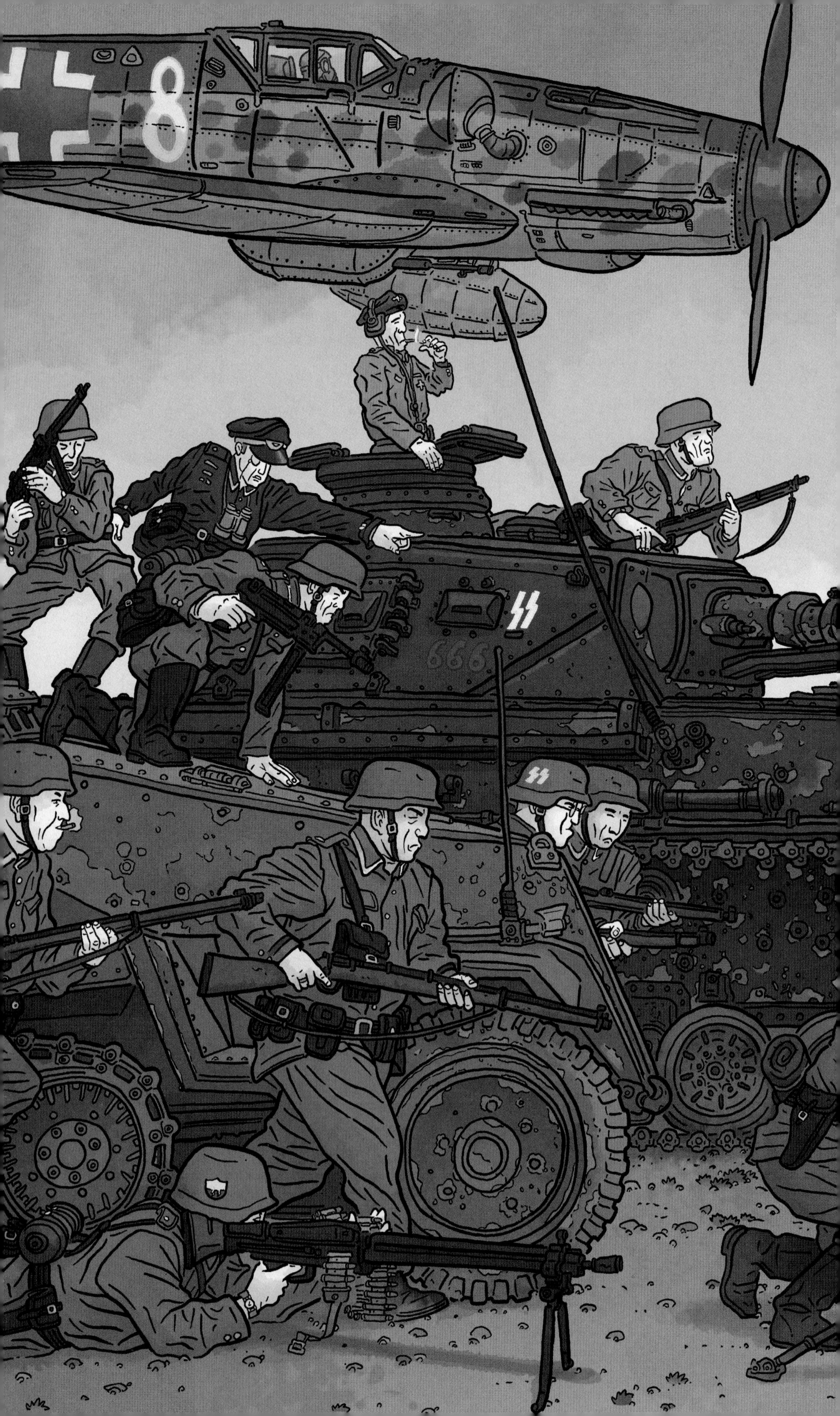
8
666